Catholic Social Teaching and Theologies of Peace in Northern Ireland

GW00758932

This book investigates the response of the Catholic Church in Northern Ireland to the conflict in the region during the late twentieth century. It does so through the prism of the writings of Cardinal Cahal B Daly (1917–2009), the only member of the hierarchy to serve as a bishop throughout the entire conflict.

This book uses the prolific writings of Cardinal Daly to create a vision of the 'Peaceable Kingdom' and demonstrate how Catholic social teaching has been used to promote peace, justice, and nonviolence. It also explores the public role of the Catholic Church in situations of violence and conflict, as well as the importance for national churches in developing a voice in the public square.

Finally, the book offers a reflection on the role of Catholic social teaching in contemporary society and the ways in which the lessons of Northern Ireland can be utilised in a world where structural violence, as evidenced by austerity, and reactions to Brexit in the United Kingdom, is now the norm.

This work challenges and changes the nature of the debate surrounding the role of the Catholic Church in the conflict in Northern Ireland. It will, therefore, be a key resource for scholars of religious studies, Catholic theology, religion and violence, peace studies, and twentieth-century history.

Maria Power is a Fellow of Blackfriars Hall, University of Oxford, where she is the Director of the Human Dignity Project at the Las Casas Institute for Social Justice.

Routledge New Critical Thinking in Religion, Theology and Biblical Studies

The *Routledge New Critical Thinking in Religion, Theology and Biblical Studies* series brings high-quality research monograph publishing back into focus for authors, international libraries, and student, academic, and research readers. This open-ended monograph series presents cutting-edge research from both established and new authors in the field. With a specialist focus yet clear contextual presentation of contemporary research, books in the series take research into important new directions and open the field to new critical debate within the discipline, in areas of related study, and in key areas for contemporary society.

Racism and the Weakness of Christian Identity
Religious Autoimmunity
David Kline

Past and Present Political Theology
Expanding the Canon
Edited by Dennis Vanden Auweele and Miklos Vassányi

Schleiermacher's Theology of Sin and Nature
Agency, Value, and Modern Theology
Daniel J. Pedersen

Investigating the Resurrection of Jesus Christ
A New Transdisciplinary Approach
Andrew Loke

Catholic Social Teaching and Theologies of Peace in Northern Ireland
Cardinal Cahal Daly and the Pursuit of the Peaceable Kingdom
Maria Power

For more information about this series, please visit: www.routledge.com/religion/series/RCRITREL

Catholic Social Teaching and Theologies of Peace in Northern Ireland

Cardinal Cahal Daly and the Pursuit of the Peaceable Kingdom

Maria Power

Routledge
Taylor & Francis Group

LONDON AND NEW YORK

First published 2021
by Routledge
2 Park Square, Milton Park, Abingdon, Oxon OX14 4RN

and by Routledge
605 Third Avenue, New York, NY 10017

First issued in paperback 2022

Routledge is an imprint of the Taylor & Francis Group, an informa business

British Library Cataloguing-in-Publication Data
A catalogue record for this book is available from the British Library

Library of Congress Cataloging-in-Publication Data
A catalog record for this book has been requested

ISBN 13: 978-0-367-53699-2 (pbk)
ISBN 13: 978-0-367-45916-1 (hbk)
ISBN 13: 978-1-003-02609-9 (ebk)

DOI: 10.4324/9781003026099

Typeset in Sabon
by Apex CoVantage, LLC

For Gabriel James Power

Contents

Acknowledgements

No book is a solo endeavour and there have been many people who have helped me in my work. My first thanks go to the librarians and staff of the Northern Ireland Political Collection at the Linen Hall Library who assisted me as I gathered the material for this study of Cardinal Cahal Daly. Second to my colleagues and friends at the Las Casas Institute for Social Justice, Blackfriars Hall, University of Oxford, who have provided me with invaluable support and friendship. Rev. Dr Richard Finn, Professor John Loughlin, Kinga Róna-Gabnai, and Edward Hadas in particular have always been willing to discuss ideas with me and console me when the inevitable writer's block hit. Third, many thanks to my editor at Routledge, Joshua Wells, for answering all of my questions with such patience and guiding me through this process.

Other colleagues and friends have also been an immense source of guidance and encouragement: Professor Christopher Baker, Goldsmiths, University of London; Professor Elaine Graham, University of Chester; Dr Clare Downham, University of Liverpool; Dr Carmen Mangion, Birkbeck, University of London; Professor Stephen Bullivant, St Mary's University, London; Rev. Dr Helen Paynter, Bristol Baptist College; and Professor Timothy White, Xavier University. Special thanks are due to you all for helping me to see the importance and relevance of this project and especially to Chris for providing so much laughter and fun along the way, and for reading initial drafts for me, and to Carmen for all of the tea and cake!

To my friends: Lucie Follett Maitland, Felma Barbo, Jennifer Cruz, Dr Sandra Buchanan, Professor Rosemary Mitchell, Sr Margaret Atkins, Sheila Isaac, Dr David Shaw, Hamida and Khadija Choudhury, Fr Nigel Woollen, Virginia Hedge, and Gemma, Luiz and Kobi Veiga. Thank you for always being there for me and for putting up with the inevitable absences that are part of a project like this.

To my family, I could not have written this book without your love and belief in me. To my mother, Alice, for acting as my research assistant on our trips to Belfast; to my father, Eric, for his calm counsel; to my brother, Claude, and sister-in-law, Andrea, for their unfailing support; and finally to my nephew, Gabriel, I dedicate this book to you in the hope that you will one day see the emergence of the Peaceable Kingdom.

Introduction

The conflict in Northern Ireland, the most violent phase of which lasted from 1968–1996, presented the Catholic Church there with a new challenge which historians, sociologists, and political scientists studying the period have yet to fully comprehend. The nature of this challenge was primarily ecclesiological rather than political, as the conflict coincided with the new spirit of *aggiornamento*[1] – a task proposed by John XXIII (r. 1958–1963) when he called the Second Vatican Council (1962–1965) in 1962. This process redefined the nature and mission of the Catholic Church. Gone was the idea that the Church's mission was primarily to save souls by converting people and then demanding that they remain in a version of Plato's Cave: a place where the flickers on the wall were provided by the national hierarchies and the Holy See who viewed themselves as political actors defending the faithful and the institution from a corrupt and sinful world. In its place, the Church rediscovered its mission in the Gospels and the example set by the early Christian communities. Inspired by prayer and sacramental devotion, all of its members were asked to enter into a dialogue with the modern world – actions which would ultimately result in the creation of societies founded upon the twin ideals of justice and peace. In short, the Catholic Church sought the creation of what Stanley Hauerwas called the Peaceable Kingdom[2] inspired by the prophet Isaiah,[3] and given a form by Jesus in the Beatitudes.[4]

Such a change raises important questions for our understandings of the Catholic Church in Ireland as a whole, and Northern Ireland in particular. In both parts of the island before the 1960s, the Catholic hierarchy had enthusiastically embraced the fortress church mentality. In the south, this enabled the Church to influence social and educational policy in the newly formed state. In the north, it led to the creation of conditions in which the needs of the Catholic community, both spiritually and materially (until the advent of the Welfare State at least) were provided for by the Church. In the late 1960s in Northern Ireland, the Church was faced with a significant challenge when, at a time of institutional change prompted by the Second Vatican Council, a conflict based upon ethno-national aspirations and socio-economic inequality erupted.[5] During a period when sociologists argued that religion in the rest of the Global North was privatising and society was secularising,[6] Northern Ireland remained resolutely religious (in name if not deed). The conflict forced the Catholic Church there to undertake a public role for which it was not properly prepared and for which its behaviour since the formation of the Northern Irish state in 1921 made it very difficult to act as a primarily ecclesiastical institution focused upon justice and peace. Church leaders had been firmly opposed to the partition of Ireland, a feeling which was shared by the laity. Consequently, 'after partition northern Catholic society turned in on itself and like the Protestant minority in the South, developed a parallel universe to the majority.'[7] In what Fulton has called 'a spirit of pillarization',[8] the Church created a state within a state for its community, providing institutions and leadership, thereby minimising their interaction with the Northern Irish state. Consequently, when the conflict began, the Church, through its bishops, was expected to act as a spokesperson for the Catholic community. Initially, the bishops also became de facto community leaders in the absence of political representation within the nationalist community, eventually becoming interlocutors between the British government and the community in the early years of the Troubles.[9] The subsequent failure of the Northern Catholic bishops to create a unified voice combined with its ineffectual denunciations of the violence created a picture of an impotent institution able to do little to stem the tide of militant republicanism emerging in its midst.[10]

Given the religious gloss put on the Troubles as a result of religious labels being used to define the ethno-national communities in conflict with one another, it is not difficult to understand why academic studies of the Catholic Church have characterised and defined its role as being motivated by political rather than religious aspirations in Northern Ireland.[11] However, if the Catholic Church in Northern Ireland is defined as an ecclesial institution, the nature and mission of which is the establishment of the Kingdom of God as proclaimed in the Gospels, then a different picture emerges. The picture is one in which *aggiornamento* based upon the specific needs of Northern Irish society and influenced by global trends within Catholicism, shaped the Church's response there. Whilst a study of the effect of *aggiornamento* on the Catholic Church in the Republic of Ireland is much needed, the focus of this book is on the Northern Church, and in particular the contribution of Cardinal Cahal B Daly. In his role as bishop-theologian and later leader of Ireland's Catholics Daly reacted to the conflict by using an ecclesiological framework to answer the political questions being posed and in doing so created a response to the violence and injustice by developing a vision for the Peaceable Kingdom which was a roadmap for change.

Cahal Daly: pastor and prophet

Cardinal Cahal Brendan Daly (1917–2009) was the only member of the hierarchy to hold office from the start of the conflict in 1968 until the ceasefires in 1996.[12] A philosopher by training,[13] Daly was appointed to the bishopric of Ardagh and Clonmacnois in 1967, translated to Down and Connor (encompassing Belfast) in 1982, and Armagh in 1990. He was made a cardinal in June 1991, serving until his retirement in 1996. He was the only Northern Irish bishop to have served in this role throughout the Troubles as well as a peritus at Vatican II, having witnessed and contributed to the discussions leading to the reforms of the Council. Daly was well known for his pronouncements on the causes of conflict in Northern Ireland and his views on the best means for its amelioration, and whilst he was certainly not alone in voicing his opinion, his was the voice to which the Vatican listened.[14] Daly was seen as a divisive figure, praised for his calm assessments of the Northern Irish situation in Britain, and vilified for the same pronouncements in Northern Ireland. Indeed, he was so disliked, even amongst his own clergy, that in her book on Northern Irish Catholics, Fionnuala O'Connor commented that 'His was the name that switched off the tape recorder'[15] and republican-minded parishioners in Belfast would leave when he came to the altar to celebrate Mass.[16] However, such criticisms did not detract from what he defined, through his vast catalogue of sermons, publications, and broadcasts, as his mission within the Church and within Northern Irish society: the creation of the Peaceable Kingdom. Thus, throughout his bishopric, he undertook the role of both pastor and prophet, or as the Second Vatican Council termed it, 'a servant of all the sheep.'[17] Through this he used the moral imagination, the space where alternative possible futures arise from the creative tension between consciousness raising and the vivid envisioning of a non-existent (but entirely possible) society based upon justice and peace.

In 2001, five years after he retired as Archbishop of Armagh, Daly donated eight volumes of his sermons, public addresses, and newspaper articles, all of which were concerned with peace and social justice in Northern Ireland, to the Northern Ireland Political Collection at the Linen Hall Library in Belfast. This, when combined with Daly's prolific output as a writer of tracts and author in the field of peace and social justice, allows us to build a strong understanding of the vision that Daly had for Northern Ireland as well as the methods that he felt would be most conducive to the development of more harmonious community relations there. This moral imagination was primarily ecclesial rather than political as it was centred upon the teachings of Christ, and in particular the Sermon on the Mount, and Catholic social teaching,[18] and was inspired by Vatican II. Once the groundwork had been laid, the laity were then expected to take these ideas which by this point represented a blend of spiritual, and political and communal praxis, such as development schemes in West Belfast, and enact them in the public sphere. Herein lies one of the problems with Daly's method: it can be seen as pure rhetoric and the methodological deficiencies of contemporary history mean that we have no way of measuring how impactful these ideas were within the ranks of the Catholic laity. This does not mean, however, that Daly's ideas are not worthy of study; instead as the work of a prominent ecclesiastical leader, they are, as Daniel Levine has argued in the context of Latin America, to be seen as a new starting point in our understandings of the role of the Catholic Church in Northern Ireland and, equally importantly, in the development of the universal Church's teachings on peace and its use of the moral imagination as a method of evangelisation.

The structure of the Catholic Church makes a study of Daly's works feasible. At a global or universal level, each bishop is completely autonomous within his own diocese, as Vallier puts it, 'the bishop is in the broadest sense of the term, a local religious king';[19] a situation that became more pronounced during the pontificate of John Paul II, and which was espoused by Daly himself in his approach to episcopal matters. At a local level, the Catholic Bishops' Conference did not produce a coherent or unified response to the conflict.[20] As Brian Lennon SJ argued in *After the Ceasefires*, 'there was little in the type of the faith practiced [by the bishops and clergy] that could help them [the laity] to develop a more appropriate political stance . . . it did not help them to bring their faith to bear on politics. And it did not help them to link justice with reconciliation.'[21] Thus, the individualised nature of leadership in the Catholic Church, especially in Ireland, means that in order to understand its response to the conflict and why it behaved as it did, the work and attitudes of individual bishops need to be explored. They are significant because as Levine argues: 'Much of the impact of religious institutions depends on their leaders – on the problems they see, the roles they assume, their characteristic styles of action, and the constraints and imperatives that they shape their action to fit.'[22] It is therefore intended that this study, by exploring the ecclesiological meaning behind the behaviour of one of the most senior Catholic clerics in Ireland, will enable us to understand how changes in Church teachings and structures affected his stance on issues relating to the conflict in Northern Ireland and create a more nuanced account of the Church's behaviour, based upon a wider frame of reference than has hitherto been employed. In short, the Catholic Church, despite appearances to the contrary, is an ecclesial rather than political institution, and should be anaylsed as such.

In dialogue with the modern world?

Using Church teachings on mission, lived Christianity, church and state, political participation, violence, peace, and social justice as a starting point, this book thus explores Daly's responses to the conflict primarily in relation to Catholic structures and teachings. It was these, rather than his nationalism, which motivated his work, and which led him into conflict with those who expected him (and indeed all Catholic clergy) to be an advocate for the nationalist cause. He was a *Roman* Catholic[23] first, and his Irish nationalism came a very distant second to this.[24] In doing so, this work seeks to explain how the Catholic Church's teachings influenced and shaped Daly's reasoning, and how this allowed him to respond to the violence and conflict in Northern Ireland. It argues that Daly's reaction to the conflict was rooted in a vision of the Kingdom and was binary in its approach: he wanted to enact the Kingdom on earth whilst preparing individuals spiritually for the afterlife. It shows how Church teachings were contextualised for the situation in Northern Ireland as the Council Fathers had taught. As a consequence, it argues that Daly's response was based upon invitation and persuasion,[25] meaning that theoretically the Church no longer acted in its own self-interest but for the interests of the whole of humanity. The Church was now missionary: serving society rather than seeking to dominate it. The moral imagination was crucial to such an endeavour and defined the social mission of the Church as constructed by Daly in the period between 1968 and 1998. In the context of Northern Ireland, this social mission should be defined as articulating a coherent vision of justice and peace that would heal the divisions that were one of the primary causes of the conflict amongst the communities there.

Chapter 1 outlines the methods used by Cardinal Cahal Daly to create his vision of the Peaceable Kingdom. Daly developed his moral imagination to build and promote this vision using three elements: the Gospel, empirical analysis, and dialogue. When taken together, these create a holistic picture of the society in which the Church is operating and provide a vision of an alternative, but entirely possible, society. For Daly, the creation of the Peaceable Kingdom was about creating both the internal and external conditions necessary for each person to flourish and to reach their full potential. Before working for change in wider society, the Catholic Church had to ensure that it reflected the values of the Peaceable Kingdom. Chapter 2 explores how the Church, by acting as a contrast community, can become more visible in society by engaging in ecumenical and cross-community dialogue. Such practices embody the essence of Catholic social teaching by enabling participants to see everyone as their neighbour and to work for justice for the good of all and not merely their 'own community'. Chapter 3 explores the issues of social and economic justice. This chapter demonstrates how Daly combined his twin goals of spiritual and communal salvation to create an alternative possible future for the people of Northern Ireland. This was to be achieved by members of the laity building upon the prayer and interaction outlined in Chapter 2, to develop a social spirituality in which love of neighbour permeated every aspect of their lives. Much of Daly's thinking in this regard focused upon the economy, and he taught that it was incumbent upon those with material goods to provide for the needs of those who found themselves without enough to meet their basic needs. However, this was not to be achieved through charity but through a commitment to justice and payments towards the social mortgage that is held on all material goods. Political structures have played a key role in stabilising Northern Ireland since 1998, and Daly used Catholic concepts of democracy and statecraft to explore alternative possible futures for Northern Ireland. Chapter 4 shows how much of his discourse on the nature of the state centred upon the nature of political justice, and in particular the steps that the British and Irish states needed to take in order to create the Peaceable Kingdom. He sought to hold the British and Irish governments to account. He sometimes quite forcefully reminded them of the need to take responsibility in the search for an equitable solution to the conflict rather than relying upon the suppression of violence as a means of conflict management. Chapter 5 deals with the issue of direct violence in the region. It demonstrates that his teachings were intended to interrupt the cycle of both governmental and paramilitary oppression. This, Daly hoped, would leave people open to creating and working towards the alternative possible future in Northern Ireland based upon Christ's Peaceable Kingdom as described in the Gospels.

This book shows how Daly sought to create such a moral vision, and not always successfully the ethical roadmap for Northern Ireland which can be defined as the Peaceable Kingdom. It argues that rather than taking political conceptions as a starting point, it was based upon his conception of the church's mission or role in society, and that this understanding was founded upon the teachings of the Gospels, and Catholic social teaching. Through the creation of such a vision, Daly shaped a Catholic ecclesial response to the conflict in Northern Ireland, and in doing so contributed to Catholic conceptions of just peace, helping to strengthen it and providing an out-working of it for a specific context in which violence rather than peace was the main means of political communication.

Notes

1 This term literally means bringing an institution or organisation up to date and is best summed up by John XXIII's oft-quoted adage: 'I want to throw open the windows of the Church so that we can see out and the people can see in.' A thorough search has yielded no citations for this quotation so it may be apocryphal.
2 This is a phrase borrowed from Stanley Hauerwas's seminal work *The Peaceable Kingdom: A Primer in Christian Ethics* (South Bend, IN: University of Notre Dame Press, 1983).
3 Isaiah describes the future House of God thus: 'He shall judge between the nations, and shall arbitrate for many peoples; they shall beat their swords into ploughshares, and their spears into pruning hooks; nation shall not lift sword against nation, neither shall they learn war any more.' Isa 2:4.
4 Mt 5:3–10, and Lk 6:20–22.
5 For an understanding of the causes and scale of this conflict, see Feargal Cochrane, *Northern Ireland: The Reluctant Peace* (New Haven, CT: Yale University Press, 2013).
6 See for example: Callum G Brown, *The Death of Christian Britain: Understanding Secularisation 1800–2000* (Abingdon: Routledge, 2009); Steve Bruce (ed.), *Religion and Modernisation: Sociologists and Historians Debate the Secularisation Thesis* (Oxford: Clarendon Press, 1992); Sharon Hanson, 'The Secularisation Thesis: Talking at Cross Purposes', *Journal of Contemporary Religion*, 1992, vol. 12, no. 2, pp. 159–179; David Martin and Rebecca Catto, 'The Religious and The Secular', in Linda Woodhead and Rebecca Catto (eds.), *Religion and Change in Modern Britain* (Abingdon: Routledge, 2012), pp. 373–390.

7   Marianne Elliott, *When God Took Sides: Religion and Identity in Ireland –
    Unfinished History* (Oxford: Oxford University Press, 2009), p. 241.
8   John Fulton, *The Tragedy of Belief: Division, Politics and Religion in Ireland*
    (Oxford: Clarendon, 1991), p. 99.
9   Marianne Elliott, *The Catholics of Ulster, a History* (London: Penguin, 2000),
    p. 466.
10 Elliott, *The Catholics of Ulster*, pp. 472–473.
11 The literature in this field is not vast, but it shares a common focus on the politi-
    cal rather than ecclesial elements of Catholicism in Northern Ireland. See Gerald
    McElroy, *The Church and the Northern Irish Crisis, 1968–86* (Dublin: Gill and
    Macmillan, 1994); Oliver P Rafferty SJ, *Catholicism in Ulster, 1603–1983, an
    Interpretive History* (London: C Hurst and Co, 1994); Oliver P Rafferty SJ,
    Violence, Politics and Catholicism in Ireland (Dublin: Four Courts Press, 2016);
    Margaret M Scull, *The Catholic Church and the Northern Ireland Troubles,
    1968–1998* (Oxford: Oxford University Press, 2019); Nukhet Sandal, *Religious
    Leaders and Conflict Transformation: Northern Ireland and Beyond* (Cam-
    bridge: Cambridge University Press, 2017).
12 For more biographical information see Maria Power, 'Cahal Brendan Daly
    (1917–2009)', *Oxford Dictionary of National Biography* (Oxford University
    Press, January 2013), https://ezproxy-prd.bodleian.ox.ac.uk:2095/10.1093/
    ref:odnb/101596 (accessed 27 January 2020).
13 Daly completed his PhD on Tertullian in 1944. It was subsequently published
    as *Tertullian the Puritan and His Influence* (Dublin: Four Courts Press, 1993).
    According to Lisa Sowle Cahill, 'Tertullian defines Jesus as a peacemaker whose
    power consists in the pursuit of peace (citing Is. 2:3–4) . . . . A pacifist but not
    a separatist, Tertullian is concerned most of all with obedience to God in every
    facet of life.' *Blessed Are the Peacemakers: Pacifism, Just War and Peacebuilding*
    (Minneapolis, MN: Fortress Press, 2019), pp. 81–82.
14 'It was Cahal Daly's advice and views on the conflict in Northern Ireland which
    were sought by the Vatican.' Dara O'Hagan, 'Allies or Antagonists? Irish Cathol-
    icism and Irish Republicanism during the 1980s', Unpublished PhD, Queen's
    University, Belfast, 1998.
15 Fionnuala O'Connor, *In Search of a State: Catholics in Northern Ireland* (Bel-
    fast: Blackstaff, 1995), p. 286.
16 For an exemplar of the tone and form of this criticism see Columbanus Mac-
    nee, 'An Open Letter to Bishop Cahal Daly', *Fortnight*, March 1984, pp. 2–3;
    O'Hagan, 'Allies or Antagonists?' p. 30.
17 Second Vatican Council, *Christus Dominus*, 30 October 1965, §30, www.
    vatican.va/archive/hist_councils/ii_vatican_council/documents/vat-ii_
    decree_19651028_christus-dominus_en.html (accessed 13 August 2019).
18 Catholic social teaching is also known as Catholic social thought, or sometimes
    as Catholic Social Thought and Practice. I use the term 'Catholic social teaching'
    as it represents to me a more iterative process which allows for an interactive
    process of dialogue and praxis to develop, thus creating a unified whole rather
    than two separate elements as the former terms suggest.
19 Ivan Vallier, *Catholicism, Social Control, and Modernization in Latin America*
    (Englewood Cliffs: Prentice Hall, 1970), p. 86.
20 Maria Power, 'Providing a Prophetic Voice? Church Leaders and Faith-Based
    Peacebuilding in Northern Ireland', in Maria Power (ed.), *Building Peace in
    Northern Ireland* (Liverpool: Liverpool University Press, 2011), pp. 73–92.
21 Brian Lennon, *After the Ceasefires: Catholics and the Future of Northern Ireland*
    (Dublin: Columba, 1995), p. 26.
22 Daniel H Levine, *Religion and Politics in Latin America: The Catholic Church
    in Venezuela and Columbia* (Princeton: Princeton University Press, 1981), p. 99.

23 The word 'Roman' is italicised to highlight the idea that Daly's identity, both religious and political, was shaped by his Roman Catholicism rather than his Irishness.

24 'Reconciliation' Down and Connor Diocesan Pilgrimage to Knock, 9 June 1990 in Northern Ireland Political Collection, Linen Hall Library, Belfast, *Addresses on Peace in Northern Ireland, 1989–1990*, vol. 5, P13582.

25 John W O'Malley, *What Happened at Vatican II* (Cambridge, MA: Harvard University Press, 2008), p. 11.

1 Defining the Peaceable Kingdom

The conflict in Northern Ireland began during a time of evolution in the Catholic Church. The Second Vatican Council brought many changes which sought to return the Church to its early Christian roots of evangelisation through witness. At the most visible level, the liturgy was restyled; with the priest turning to face the people during the celebration of the Mass which was now in the vernacular, church architecture became plainer and more focused upon the inclusion of the congregation, and women religious adopted simpler modes of attire. Despite such headline-grabbing adjustments, it was in the areas of structure and responsibility that the most dramatic transformations were to be found, and it was through these that the values and practices of early Christianity could be most clearly restored and enacted. In theory, if not in practice, Catholicism now became an egalitarian religion with each section of the Church, clergy, religious, and laity having distinct roles or areas of responsibility that were equal in importance to one another. The Church thus sought to become a pastoral and prophetic voice within society, stepping back from its previous understanding of itself as a nation-state, instead seeking to promote human flourishing and adopting a missionary rather than political stance to facilitate this. 'The council fathers were calling for a more adult form of participation [by the laity] in the life of the church. It was the laity who were to take the lead in applying the Gospel to the most pressing concerns of the modern age,'[1] with the clergy 'proclaiming a moral vision' which would assist the laity in their process of discernment.

Local churches therefore needed to discern the most pressing concerns within their own areas. For the English and Welsh Church in the 1980s, for example, it was the damage being wrought by Thatcherism on already-deprived communities through its policy of deindustrialisation. But within Northern Ireland, there was only one issue: the need to bring an end to the violence and conflict that ravaged the region and destroyed the potential of everyone who lived there. To achieve this, Daly used his moral imagination to influence the development of the social order, guiding it towards the creation of the Peaceable Kingdom on earth whilst ensuring that Catholics were prepared for the afterlife. This process of moral imagination involved two elements: understanding the world as it is and envisaging it as it could be. Thus, the inequalities that triggered and sustained violence and conflict were highlighted, whilst the benefits of an alternative possible future in which inequality did not exist were expounded. *All* members of the Church were expected to play a role in this reordering of society, with the clergy and laity using their distinct areas of expertise to ensure that this moral reflection mirrored the teachings of Christ as shown in the New Testament and subsequently developed through the Magisterium. Daly's reasoning in adopting such a method to overcome the violence and conflict in the region was characteristically clear: 'Peace is a state of mind and of conviction before it is a state of society. It is an ideal and hope for communities, it is a vision of what human existence could be and should be, before it is a fact.'[2] This short chapter, therefore, explains the meaning of the 'moral imagination' and places the methods used by Daly to achieve this within a wider context.

War and peace through a Catholic lens

This alteration can be seen in the Church's changing attitudes towards the issues of war and peace. Before Vatican II, the Church's stance regarding these matters was traditionally aligned with the teaching of Just War, the purpose of which 'was not to rationalise violence, but to limit its scope and methods in a world where force was a tragic but necessary instrument of the political process.'[3] Although Pius XII (r. 1939–1958) had reduced the legitimate causes of war from three (defence, avenging evil, and restoring violated rights) to one, self-defence of one's own nation or of others being unjustly attacked,[4] it was John XXIII who through his 1963 encyclical, *Pacem in Terris*,[5] began to broaden the Magisterium's understandings of war and peace. This task was continued in Vatican II's *Gaudium et Spes* and the Papal World Day for Peace Messages inaugurated by Paul VI (r. 1963–1978) on 1 January 1968. This allowed teachings on war and peace to be evaluated with 'an entirely new attitude'[6] and remain in a constant state of review and development for the rest of the twentieth century. Thus, through the teachings of John XXIII, an authentic pluralism in Catholic attitudes to war and peace emerged: just war and pacifism[7] (and along with it the right to adopt a stance of conscientious objection)[8] were from 1965 onwards both taught as legitimate Catholic responses to war and conflict.[9]

But what brought about this paradigm shift? The twentieth century witnessed a change in the nature and scale of warfare. War became increasingly mechanised and technologised and by the 1940s genocide was being enacted on an industrial scale.[10] As James W Douglass argued in 1968:

> The techniques of modern war, automatic and usually controlled at some point remote from the human victims, have made it possible for men to execute massive slaughters without feeling any of the normal pain or anguish implied in a single act of killing. Divorced from the

living consequences of their actions, the technicians of military power have had no difficulty in justifying human carnage on their charts and boards, although few would wish to pour napalm personally over a child.[11]

The end of the Second World War also heralded the commencement of the nuclear age that brought with it the threat of the total annihilation of humanity, leading Popes to 'sound increasingly clearer notes of caution and reserve about embarking on military solutions to political problems, or even defense against aggression.'[12] Daly clearly understood the implications of such changes, writing in 1976:

> When, however, the state of technology and the breakdown of the Christian moral consensus combine to make these efforts at restriction more and more unrealistic and irrelevant, then the time has come to ask whether there are in fact any situations of war or revolution in which the conditions for a just war or a just revolution could be verified. I believe that the theology of the just war is still valid in principle; but I see it as more and more difficult to verify its conditions in modern practice of either war or revolution.[13]

War and peace could therefore no longer be justified or evaluated on the same terms as before.

The Church's definition of peace provided an acknowledgement of this new paradigm. Within the Catholic tradition, peace was not the mere absence of war or violence. Indeed, such a state of affairs was not considered to be peace at all. As Pius XI (r. 1922–1939) argued in 1922: 'The nations today live in a state of armed peace which is scarcely better than war itself, a condition that tends to exhaust national finances, to waste the flower of youth, to muddy and poison the very fountainheads of life, physical, intellectual, religious and moral.'[14] Catholic conceptions of peace therefore were somewhat different to those of other actors which prioritised security and focused upon often very short timelines.[15] This resulted in the development of the state of affairs described by Pius XI. Its definition instead was built upon a desire to make peace, rather than violence and war, the social norm. Until 2003, the Catholic Church retained the idea that the sinful nature of human beings meant that 'the danger of war hangs over them and will hang over them till the coming of Christ.'[16] This did not mean that Christians were powerless to prevent it. Instead, from this viewpoint, peace was not a static state: rather, the understanding of the term employed by the Church offered a vision of society towards which all were expected to work. As Kenneth R Himes, put it, 'Peace in the political realm was not simply a blessing from God but a task that was to be undertaken by human beings. Peace could be actualised as people of goodwill worked to create a more just social order.'[17] This was the Peaceable Kingdom, a state which encompassed justice, the dignity of the human person, the common good, development, solidarity, and dialogue and accommodation with other ideologies, denominations, and religions. It was a collective endeavour undertaken by both God and humanity[18] aimed at challenging and changing the social and political structures of society as well as the attitudes of individuals because as Daniel Levine argues, 'individual acts of kindness and charity are negated by unjust structures of society.'[19] All of the Popes since John XXIII have taught that peace could only exist when justice prevails. The most famous statement on this issue came from Paul VI in his 1972 World Day for Peace Message which taught that 'if you want peace, work for justice.'[20] The only way to achieve peace was through an ongoing collective praxis[21] focused upon securing social justice which included amongst other things solidarity between peoples, both within communities and internationally, dialogue with the other, and development. Through this a positive conception of peace, such as that expounded by Johan Galtung, would emerge.[22] Via the use of such a definition, the Catholic Church moved the conversation and action from a focus on security and the international order to an emphasis upon social justice at the heart of which was human dignity and community.

Seeking the Peaceable Kingdom: creating a moral vision

From a Catholic perspective, peace was a task which required social and political transformation. Through working for peace, Catholics could effect the creation of the Peaceable Kingdom in the temporal realm as well as prepare themselves spiritually for the afterlife. But, one could not be achieved without the other.[23] Peace was therefore both personal and political, the perfect example of the 'already but not yet,'[24] the meaning of which is perfectly summed up by Gustavo Gutiérrez: 'the Kingdom is the final meaning in history; its total fulfilment takes place beyond history, and at the same time is present from this moment on.'[25] This binary was to be a fundamental element of Daly's response to the conflict in Northern Ireland.

But how does the Catholic Church as an institution view its role in this metamorphosis? As Ronald H Bainton and Ernst-Troeltsch have shown, the Christian moral response to war and peace has always been related to an ecclesiological analysis of the Church's role in society.[26] The Second Vatican Council had led to a reconsideration of what it meant to be church. The Church now began to see itself as a servant of society. In his opening address to the second session of the Council, Paul VI expressed this, stating, 'May the world know with certainty that the Church looks lovingly upon it, that she nurtures a sincere admiration for it, and that she is moved by the frank desire not to dominate it but to serve it, not to look down on it but to promote its dignity, not to condemn it but to offer it consolation and salvation.'[27] The Church's mission was henceforth to proclaim the reign of God: 'the Church seeks but a solitary goal: to carry forward the work of Christ himself.'[28] This was not proselytisation but evangelisation (the Council

Fathers had accepted religious freedom and the papacy would go on to promote interreligious dialogue as a means of peacebuilding).[29] Conversion was replaced with the desire for peace and social justice, and evangelisation was to be achieved through witness because 'above all the gospel must be proclaimed by witness.'[30] Each person had a role to play in this redefined church which was, as a result of *Gaudium et Spes*, firmly situated within the world. Thus, the moral vision of the Gospel had to be taken and integrated into everyday life. The Church could no longer concentrate upon the eschatological with its promise of a better life after death and resultant isolation of ordinary Catholics from society with any social engagement being closely monitored by the clergy. Instead, it had to engage with the lived realities of its members working with them both spiritually *and* socially. Additionally, John XXIII had focused the nature of the Church's mission on justice and peace, an undertaking which conformed with Christ's message of the historical reality of the Peaceable Kingdom. According to John Fullenbach:

> The Kingdom is not only the central theme of Jesus' preaching, the reference point of most of his parables, and the subject of a large number of his sayings, it is also the content of his symbolic actions. A large part of his ministry consists of such activities as his table fellowship with tax-collectors and sinners as well as his healings and exorcisms. In his communion with the outcast Jesus lives out the Kingdom, demonstrating in action God's unconditional love for undeserving sinners.[31]

The Gospel therefore provided a summons to work for justice and peace by challenging structural injustice in addition to offering charity. From the 1960s onwards, the Church served society pastorally by attending to the social as well as spiritual conditions of those in need, and prophetically by providing a vision of the Kingdom on earth based upon the teachings of Christ. Through such an understanding of its mission, it attended to both the personal and social requirements of its members. It did so by enabling them to transform themselves spiritually through service to society.[32] The needs of society were met by applying Catholic ethics to political and social matters, thereby combatting injustice. Consequently, Catholics were focused on creating a more equal and perfect society which concentrated upon the love of one's neighbour, because as Simone Weil argued, 'the Gospel makes no distinction between the love of our neighbour and justice.'[33]

To achieve this, however, the Church, both globally and locally, had to employ its moral imagination through which its vision of the Kingdom on earth could be articulated. Andrew Greeley, in his study of the Catholic imagination, describes this as 'the way that Catholics picture the world and God's relationship to it.'[34] This when combined with John Paul Lederach's understanding of it as 'the capacity to imagine something rooted in the challenges of the real world yet capable of giving birth to that which does not yet exist'[35] provides a strong definition of the method needed to create such a

vision. This, based upon a reading of the Gospels, the Magisterium, and crucially 'the signs of the times',[36] will provide the prophetic and pastoral nourishment needed for the laity to bring about constructive social change based
upon the need for justice. In societies affected by deep-rooted conflict such
as Northern Ireland, this moral imagination was inevitably turned towards
building the positive conception of peace taught by the Catholic Church.
Papal teaching on peace through the World Day for Peace Messages, has,
since 1967, been based upon the provision of such a vision, 'the restoration
of which can link theory and practice in a transformative manner'.[37] Liberation theologian, Leonardo Boff, in *Virtues For Another Possible World*,[38]
has also used this technique through which he:

> Argues for the importance of imagining 'alternality' for shifting an
> unjust status quo. In this light, his vision offers an ethical map to move
> a greater mass of humanity toward contributing to a more substantively
> peaceful world by placing the virtues of hospitality, co-living, respect,
> tolerance, and communality simultaneously at the centre and on the
> horizon of the moral community. For Boff, this is at the heart of a pos-
> sible and necessary world.[39]

This trope has also been commonly used by peace builders from a Protestant
tradition, such as the Quaker, Elise Boulding, in *Cultures of Peace* where
she argues that 'Peace cultures thrive on and are nourished by visions of
how things might be, in a world where sharing and caring are part of the
accepted lifeways for everyone. The very ability to imagine something different and better than what currently exists is critical for the possibility of
social change.'[40] This would then lead to a dialogue between church and
society, during which the vision expressed by the Church would enter into
social consciousness, eventually effecting the change needed to create a more
peaceful and just community.

Catholics, both clergy and lay, tend to emphasise the presence rather than
absence of God in the world, with a focus upon anthropomorphic conceptions of Christ.[41] This attitude is rooted in the idea that the Peaceable
Kingdom is a historical reality, something that Christians can work to bring
about, as well as an eschatological offer of hope to believers. The Catholic
Church in its role as servant to society therefore had to offer a vision of what
the reality of the Peaceable Kingdom would look like. It is only through this
that the translation from imagination to collective praxis, which is after all
a necessary expression of faith, would be able to occur. Such a vision was
always to be based upon the historical circumstances in which the local
church found itself as Paul VI had taught in *Ecclesiam Suam*, 'the Church
must always adapt to the situations in which it finds itself.'[42] It was also to
be centred upon the teachings of Christ in the Gospels, documents that were
written with a very particular audience in mind who would understand the
nuances of many of the cultural references used by Jesus in his parables.[43]

This presents each generation of Christians with a challenge to understand the historical reality of the Gospel within their own particular context. Through this they are given an opportunity to be engaged in both social and spiritual transformation by becoming part of the communal creation of the Peaceable Kingdom in the temporal realm, whilst preparing themselves spiritually for heaven through a focus upon the needs of others. Christians are thus expected to reinterpret the stories of the Gospels and create peace and justice based upon the particular needs of their local communities and the wider society in which these communities are located. However, to achieve this, the moral imagination of the Catholic Church must be deployed both to create a vision of another possible world and a method for accomplishing this. One of the main functions of a bishop is to assist the community in carrying out this task, taking the role of teacher by developing such a vision and supporting the laity as they use their expertise to translate this into the temporal realm.[44]

But once consciences had been alerted to the issue of injustice, Christians had a moral obligation to act, and it was the role of the church, defined as all of its members, 'to develop new models and strategies for meeting modern forms of poverty and need.'[45] Indeed, the establishment of the Peaceable Kingdom on earth based upon the twin pillars of peace and justice was, according to Daly, the fundamental reason for a Christian's existence[46]; for example, in 1993 he argued that 'if we wish peace, we must seek justice.'[47] The relationship of social justice to the establishment of the Peaceable Kingdom was clear: one could not exist without the other. Speaking in 1978, and echoing the teachings of *Populorum Progressio*,[48] Daly furthered his case for a nonviolent approach to creating the Peaceable Kingdom in Northern Ireland:

> To assume that security successes amount to a solution of the Northern Ireland problem would be to confuse the symptom with the disease. Violence in the North of Ireland is a symptom of a complex of underlying problems and until these are resolutely and radically tackled, Northern Ireland will remain a chronically violence prone society.[49]

In arguing for a nonviolent approach to the security situation, Daly was starting to create a bridge between consciousness building and the task of describing an alternative possible future – a bridge that he would cross many times throughout his ministry and which illustrates the role that the Catholic Church through its teachings created for itself in sites of conflict as one of vision and action created in a continuous dialogue amongst *all* (clergy and laity) its members. Thus, dealing with the social injustice, which Daly argued was the underlying cause of violence, and the subsequent establishment of a just society, was not only the 'authentic Christian response'[50] to the issues in society but was the path to both personal and communal salvation as 'the politics of justice is the only politics worthy of the Christian man [sic.]. . . . It is the politics by which, in the end, we shall all of us be judged, voters as well as politicians.'[51]

Envisaging an 'alternative possible future'

However, the form of this praxis is entirely dependent upon the local milieu. Whilst the Catholic Church offers guidance on the phenomena that should trigger action,[52] it does not offer a programme for such action. Furthermore, although these guidelines or moral principles come from the Magisterium's engagement with society, they require further refinement in the light of indigenous circumstances. In terms of Catholic hermeneutics, the praxis of social justice is directed by a process known as 'reading the signs of the times'.[53] Whilst it could be argued that such a phrase has eschatological significance,[54] the Council Fathers make it clear that it is to be a worldly engagement based upon the social, political, and economic elements of society.[55] The starting point of any such encounter must be with the world as it stands, allowing for the local church (through its bishop) to undertake a critical and ethical reflection upon the realities faced by those living in his diocese, or in the case of Daly during his tenure as primate of Ireland, his country. Such a method has the twin focus of consciousness raising (both in the bishop himself, and through his subsequent teaching, others) and of fuelling the moral imagination, allowing alternative possible futures to be envisioned and articulated.[56] Taken together, these elements allow for the creation of 'social dynamism'[57] which allow the conditions for the Kingdom of God on earth to be realised. The reading of the signs of the times takes place at the crossroads of the Gospel and life or to paraphrase Reinhart Koselleck at the intersection of the space of experience and a horizon of expectation.[58] Such analysis therefore leads to the development of a moral vision created by both elements which can be used to reform society. As I argue elsewhere, within Catholicism this moral vision is born from the combination of three elements: the Gospel and Magisterium, empirical analysis, and most crucially, dialogue.[59] Such a combination is crucial because as Johan Verstvaeten points out:

> Judgements on the world cannot be made merely on the basis of faith propositions. Without social and economic analysis, the faith perspective loses touch with reality or leads to the construction of a world of pious ideas, which risks being an expression of social alienation rather than a solution to it.[60]

Through the use of such a method, the 'already but not yet' emerges for each particular context, enabling the binary goals of the Catholic Church for individuals of personal and communal salvation, or the individual attainment of a place in the heavenly kingdom combined with a contribution to the creation of the earthly peaceable kingdom, to be achieved.

The starting point for the creation of a moral vision using these three elements centres on the supposition that 'the world should not be the way that it is.'[61] This was one of the reasons for the incarnation of Christ and therefore the justification for the use of the Gospel and teachings of the Magisterium in the development of a moral vision that will lead to the Peaceable Kingdom. The position taken by Jesus in the Gospels towards the poor means that there is little room for impartiality in the moral imagination: so when, for example, a crucifixion analogy (the most powerful in the Christian faith) is used by writers to describe the plight of those who find themselves poor, marginalised, and deprived, it is easy to comprehend the stance of the Church.[62] Without the Gospel and tradition, the connection between faith and action so crucial to the creation of a just society cannot be made as the experience of the poor, marginalised, and deprived cannot be understood. This is not only because of Christ's preference for the poor as recipients of the Good News but also because 'the mystery of poverty springs from the kenosis of Christ, Christ's emptying of himself.'[63] In terms of the Magisterium, this attitude has been expressed as the preferential option for the poor and vulnerable, or as I express it, in terms of the Northern Irish conflict: the preferential option for the poor, marginalised, and deprived.[64] This expression is based upon the fact that poverty, marginalisation, and deprivation are not inevitable but rather caused by the unjust structures of society which must be reformed to allow for a substantive peace to emerge. Or as Daly so succinctly put it in 1989: 'The poor do not deserve to be poor. Neither do they just happen to be poor.'[65] Such changes cannot be based upon charitable giving but rather a change in society which allows every person to flourish, a point made potently by St. Ambrose: 'You are not making a gift of what is yours to the poor man, but you are giving him back what is his. You have been appropriating things that are meant to be for the common use of everyone. The earth belongs to everyone, not to the rich.'[66] Thus, as Gutiérrez argues, 'The poverty of the poor is not a call to generous relief action, but a demand that we go and build a different social order. . . . It means taking sides with the dispossessed. It means entering into the world of the exploited social class. . . . It means entering into solidarity with its interests and its struggles.'[67] As we will see in his denunciations of paramilitary activity, government security policy, and promotion of nonviolence, although Daly never directly articulated the phrase 'option for the poor', in his work creating an alternative future for Northern Ireland which would take the form of the Peaceable Kingdom, a manifestation of this concept primarily based upon his readings of the Gospels was at the heart of his thinking. The Gospels taught that poverty was an affront to all believers and therefore prevented a just society from being established, and this was potently reflected in his work.

However, as Verstvaeten points out, to base a vision of the Peaceable Kingdom entirely upon the Gospels and subsequent teachings of the Church would be sheer folly. Therefore, in order to develop a moral vision which will empower people to become agents for change within society whilst forming them spiritually, 'there has to be . . . an insertion into reality and a reflection on reality. This double function enables us to know and act on reality, which in turn then acts on us.'[68] This allows any tensions between conscientisation and the creation of alternative possible futures to be resolved by creating a vision which provides the information and empathy needed for Christians to develop solidarity with the poor, enabling them to act to challenge injustice, thereby creating the conditions for the Peaceable Kingdom to emerge. This is achieved through empirical analysis and dialogue, which when combined with the Gospels and the Magisterium provide the material necessary for the process of ethical reflection leading to a moral vision of society that creates the Peaceable Kingdom.

A reflection upon reality that forms the heart of empirical analysis is important for two reasons. First, although statistical data has the power to depersonalise the experiences of the poor, marginalised, and deprived, reducing them to an amorphous mass, an issue that Daly was very aware of, it can be deployed 'to open the minds of all but the most hardened.'[69] In doing so, it alerts consciences to injustice. Second, such empirical analysis alerts people to where injustice lies and thus helps to create a plan for action. This was a crucial part of the mission of the Church and central to Daly's teaching role as a bishop as 'the Church [through the clergy was] given the responsibility of inspiring a rational approach to issues of justice.'[70] Exactly how this vision was to be achieved, however, was, in the spirit of Vatican II, entrusted to the expertise of the laity, and Daly's contribution generally remained conceptual, providing a vision of what peace should look like rather than a plan for action.[71] As Daly pointed out in 1975, the clergy (including bishops) were not believed to be competent in such matters:

> Proclaiming the Gospel message is primarily the task of the clergy. Interpreting its social and political implications in terms of concrete political decisions and legislative programmes is the task of the laity. The two roles cannot be confused. It is no part of the competence of the cleric to compose or to stand on political platforms or to give political directives.[72]

Social and political matters were the responsibility of the laity, and members of the Church were now taught that

> Christians who take an active part in present-day socio-economic development and fight for justice and charity should be convinced that they can make a great contribution to the prosperity of mankind and to the peace of the world. In these activities let them, either as individuals or as members of groups, give a shining example. Having acquired the absolutely necessary skill and experience, they should observe the right

order in their earthly activities in faithfulness to Christ and His Gospel. Thus their whole life, both individual and social, will be permeated with the spirit of the beatitudes, notably with a spirit of poverty.[73]

Daly put this more succinctly when he argued that 'It is their vocation as laymen to transmit the message of the Gospel into the temporal and social and political order.'[74] For the laity then, life and faith were to be integrated, and Christians were expected to work towards a society that realised the Gospel's teachings.

If social analysis is a reflection upon reality, then dialogue must, in the absence of opportunities to live amongst the poor and oppressed in the manner of some orders such as the Jesuits, Redemptorists, Franciscans, and Dominicans, provide bishops such as Daly with an insertion into the reality of poverty. 'Those who read (and write) books like this already have education, contacts, and resources that preclude full identification with the poor, but we must make as empathetic an attempt as we can to see and hear the people and voices'[75] out of which the alternative possible future leading to the Peaceable Kingdom will emerge. This will in some ways allow those involved to 'enter the world of the other – of the insignificant person, the excluded.'[76] It is the encounter with the suffering face of Christ which allows for the spiritual and communal development so important to Daly's teaching. Such dialogue needs to take place across all parts of society, between clergy and laity, the poor and the rich, politicians and voters, thus engaging the peacebuilding pyramid[77] developed by John Paul Lederach to facilitate meaningful change. The creation of a just society which is a prerequisite for the creation of the Peaceable Kingdom is something that must emerge in partnership, solidarity with the poor must be combined with subsidiarity so that Christians are working with the poor, marginalised, and deprived rather than enacting a form of *noblesse oblige* which serves merely to disempower all of those involved. Dialogue is therefore the nexus between Gospel and the Magisterium, and empirical analysis, allowing them to interact meaningfully with one another to allow for the creation of a vision for challenging injustice based upon lived experience of the poor, marginalised, and deprived in a given milieu. It helps people 'to ensure that they have a voice' rather than allowing the privileged (clergy and bishops included) to become the 'voice of the voiceless'.[78] Although, as Lederach's pyramid indicates and the experience of Daly so effectively illustrates, there are times when church leaders need to act as 'the voice of the voiceless' to ensure that the views of the underprivileged are heard by the sectors of society, such as politicians and investors, who are more likely to listen to those in privileged positions. This effectively removes any notions of charity, which whilst important for resolving short-term issues, does not lead to long-term transformation in society, the ideas for which have to come from those most affected. This is best illustrated by the experiences of one Dominican community worker in

West Belfast who commented when reflecting upon the establishment of an ecumenical community that:

> We knew that we could not come in here and start doing what we thought the area needed that would have been unhealthy, what we needed to do was to come in here and be part of the community around here, talk to them, and dialogue with them because we wanted to be part of the area as well and through that we would learn what would emerge.[79]

Such an approach strongly resonates with the consensus model of social change advocated by Paul VI in *Populorum Progressio*,[80] which focuses upon the importance of dialogue and collaboration[81] as a means of challenging social injustices, and facilitating the transformation of unjust structures into those needed for the Peaceable Kingdom to be realised.

Conclusion

Daly's bishopric was defined by a duality of purpose: to ensure salvation for individuals (both Catholic *and* Protestant) whilst working towards and assisting the people of Northern Ireland in their efforts to reorder society along the lines of the Kingdom. In doing so, Daly was answering the most fundamental question challenging Northern Ireland's Christians in the late twentieth century: what does it mean to be a Christian in the context of violence and injustice? His answer, discerned from the exacting challenge of the Second Vatican Council to 'scrutinize the signs of the times and interpret them in the light of the gospel',[82] was the creation of the Peaceable Kingdom. Daly was very clear that Christ and the Gospels should be at the centre of any 'solutions' to the problems in Northern Ireland:

> Since my appointment and at my arrival [as Bishop of Down and Connor], some have been asking: "What solutions do you have to offer?". To such questions the only reply I can give or want to give is this: "I have no solutions – except Jesus Christ". "I have nothing to offer – except Jesus Christ and His Gospel".[83]

The main source of inspiration for this pronouncement was the Sermon on the Mount, and in particular the Beatitudes.[84] Daly argued that Christ had brought the new law of love: 'I give you a new commandment: love one another; you must love one another just as I have loved you.'[85] The foundation of his vision for society can therefore be found in a lived Christianity defined by love, humility, and service, which 'ought to find its expression in deeds more than in words.'[86] For Daly, 'to believe in the gospel is above all to believe in love – where love is not a warm glow of individualist sentiment but is also the fulfilment of the law of justice and must therefore be embodied in just laws and just social structures.'[87] In the next chapter, we see how he sought to bring these ideals into the Catholic Church itself.

Notes

1 Richard R Gaillardetz and Catherine E Clifford, *Keys to the Council: Unlocking the Teaching of Vatican II* (Collegeville: Liturgical Press, 2012), pp. 98–99.
2 'Address for World Peace Day', St Mel's Cathedral, 1 January 1974 Northern Ireland Political Collection, Linen Hall Library, Belfast, *Addresses on Peace in Northern Ireland, 1968–1975*, vol. 1, P13578.
3 J Bryan Hehir, 'The Just-War Ethic and Catholic Theology: Dynamics of Change and Continuity', in Thomas A Shannon (ed.), *War or Peace? The Search for New Answers* (New York: Orbis, 1980), pp. 15–39, 16.
4 See for example Pius XII, *Radio Message Given to the World*, 23 December 1948, https://archive.org/details/1948christmasmespius (accessed 12 August 2019).
5 John XXIII, *Pacem in Terris*, 11 April 1963, §167, http://w2.vatican.va/content/john-xxiii/en/encyclicals/documents/hf_j-xxiii_enc_11041963_pacem.html (accessed 27 January 2020).
6 Second Vatican Council, *Gaudium et Spes*, 7 December 1965, www.vatican.va/archive/hist_councils/ii_vatican_council/documents/vat-ii_const_19651207_gaudium-et-spes_en.html (accessed 12 August 2019).
7 'This understanding of pacifism in the Catholic tradition means that it is committed not only to the abolition of war but to the establishment of an authentic peace. Pacifism is not an expression of sectarian withdrawal by Christians who do not value the social order, nor may pacifism be founded on a dismissal of the state's right to self-defence.' Kenneth R Himes, *Christianity and the Political Order: Conflict, Cooptation, and Cooperation* (New York: Orbis, 2013), p. 330.
8 *Gaudium et Spes*, §§ 78 and 79.
9 The issue of whether the Catholic Church has adopted a completely pacifist stance has been the subject of much debate, see: Maria Power and Christopher Hrynkow, 'Qualified Advocacy for JustPeace: The Popes' World Day of Peace Messages (1968–2020) in Historical and Ethical Perspective', *Peace and Change: A Journal of Peace History*, 2020, vol. 45, no. 3; Lisa Sowle Cahill, *Love Your Enemies: Discipleship, Pacifism, and Just War Theory* (Minneapolis, Fortress Press, 1994), pp. 205–213; Lisa Sowle Cahill, 'Just War, Pacifism, Just Peace and Peacebuilding', *Theological Studies*, 2019, vol. 80, no. 1, pp. 169–185; Hehir, 'The Just-War Ethic and Catholic Theology: Dynamics of Change and Continuity'; Maryann Cusimano Love, 'Just Peace and Just War', *Expositions*, 2018, vol. 12, no. 1, pp. 60–71; and Gerard Powers, 'From an Ethics of War to an Ethics of Peacebuilding', in Heinz Gehard Justenhoven and William A Barbieri (eds.), *From Just War to Modern Peace Ethics* (Berlin: De Gruyter Press, 2012), pp. 275–312, 286. For a full account of modern Catholic social teaching on just war and pacifism, see Kenneth R Himes, 'Pacifism and the Just War Tradition in Roman Catholic Social Teaching', in John A Coleman (ed.), *One Hundred Years of Catholic Social Thought: Celebration and Challenge* (New York: Orbis, 1991), pp. 329–344.
10 One only has to visit Auschwitz-Birkenau in Poland to understand the sheer scale of industrialised murder in the mid-twentieth century.
11 James W Douglass, *The Non-Violent Cross: A Theology of Revolution and Peace* (London: Macmillan, 1968), p. 41. cf. *Gaudium et Spes*, §80.
12 Sowle Cahill, *Love Your Enemies*, p. 207.

13 'A Just War? Article Sent to the *Catholic Herald*', 27 February 1976, in Northern Ireland Political Collection, Linen Hall Library, Belfast, *Addresses on Peace in Northern Ireland, 1976–1983*, vol. 2, P13579.

14 Pius XI, *Ubi Arcano Dei Consilio*, 23 December 1922, §11, http://w2.vatican.va/content/pius-xi/en/encyclicals/documents/hf_p-xi_enc_23121922_ubi-arcano-dei-consilio.html (accessed 12 August 2019).

15 Maryann Cusimano Love, 'What Kind of Peace Do We Seek? Emerging Norms of Peacebuilding in Key Political Institutions', in Robert J Schreiter, R Scott Appleby and Gerard F Powers (eds.), *Peacebuilding Catholic Theology, Ethics, and Praxis* (New York: Orbis, 2010), pp. 56–91, 57.

16 *Gaudium et Spes*, §78.

17 Himes, *Christianity and the Political Order*, p. 333.

18 *Pacem in Terris*, §167. See also Himes who argues that 'In accord with the Catholic principle of mediation the bishops at Vatican II maintain that it is not divine action alone that brings about God's reign but God acting through, with and in us.' *Christianity and the Political Order*, p. 234.

19 Levine, *Religion and Politics in Latin America*, p. 42.

20 Paul VI, 'If You Want Peace, Work for Justice', World Day for Peace Message for 1972, 8 December 1971, http://w2.vatican.va/content/paul-vi/en/messages/peace/documents/hf_p-vi_mes_19711208_v-world-day-for-peace.html (accessed 12 August 2019).

21 *Gaudium et Spes*, §78.

22 Johan Galtung, 'Violence, Peace, and Peace Research', *Journal of Peace Research*, 1969, vol. 6, no. 3, pp. 167–191. For an understanding of the difficulties of implementing such a definition of peace even in a seemingly successful peace process as Northern Ireland, see Maria Power, 'Building Peace in Northern Ireland', in Maria Power (ed.), *Building Peace in Northern Ireland* (Liverpool: Liverpool University Press, 2011), pp. 1–17.

23 *Gaudium et Spes*, §57.

24 George E Ladd, *The Gospel of the Kingdom* (Grand Rapids, MI: Eerdmans Publishing Co, 1959), pp. 13–23. This concept has become popularised within Catholic 'popular' spirituality, see for example James Martin, *Jesus: a Pilgrimage* (New York: Harper, 2014), pp. 170–171.

25 Gustavo Gutiérrez, 'The Option for the Poor Arises from Faith in Christ', *Theological Studies*, 2009, vol. 70, pp. 317–326, 323.

26 RH Brinton, *Christian Attitudes Toward War and Peace* (New York: Abingdon Press, 1960); Ernst Troeltsch, *The Social Teaching of the Christian Churches*, 2 vols. (New York: Harper and Row, 1960).

27 Paul VI, *Opening Speech to the Second Session of the Vatican Council*, 29 September 1963, https://w2.vatican.va/content/paul-vi/it/speeches/1963/documents/hf_p-vi_spe_19630929_concilio-vaticano-ii.html (accessed 12 August 2019), trans. Ana Elvia Carrasco Bustillos.

28 *Gaudium et Spes*, §3.

29 Maria Power and Christopher Hrynkow, 'Transforming the Centre: Popes on Inter-Religious Dialogue as a Path to Multi-Track Peacebuilding', *International Journal for Peace Studies*, 2018, vol. 23, no. 2, pp. 33–47.

30 Paul VI, *Evangelii Nuntiandi*, 8 December 1975, §21, http://w2.vatican.va/content/paul-vi/en/apost_exhortations/documents/hf_p-vi_exh_19751208_evangelii-nuntiandi.html (accessed 12 August 2019).

31 John Fullenbach, *The Kingdom of God: The Message of Jesus Today* (Eugene, OR: Wifp and Stock, 1995), p. 4.

32 Rowan Williams, 'Transforming Words, Transforming Relations', "Making all things new? Evangelii Gaudium and Ecumenical Mission", St John's College,

University of Cambridge, 29 June–1 July 2015, http://evangeliigaudium.co.uk (accessed 1 January 2017).

33 Simone Weil, *Waiting for God* (New York: Harper Modern Classics, 1951, 2009), p. 85.
34 Andrew Greeley, *The Catholic Imagination* (Los Angeles: University of California Press, 2001), p. 16.
35 John Paul Lederach, *The Moral Imagination: The Art and Soul of Building Peace* (Oxford: Oxford University Press, 2005), p. ix.
36 *Gaudium et Spes*, §4.
37 Power and Hrynkow, 'Qualified Advocacy for JustPeace'.
38 Leonardo Boff, *Virtues for Another Possible World* (Eugene Oregon: Wifp and Stock, 2011).
39 Power and Hrynkow, 'Qualified Advocacy for JustPeace'.
40 Elise Boulding, *Cultures of Peace: The Hidden Side of History* (Syracuse: Syracuse University Press, 2000), p. 29.
41 David Tracy, *The Analogical Imagination* (New York: Crossroads, 1982).
42 Paul VI, *Ecclesiam Suam*, 6 August 1964, §42, http://w2.vatican.va/content/paul-vi/en/encyclicals/documents/hf_p-vi_enc_06081964_ecclesiam.html (accessed 12 August 2019).
43 See Martin, *Jesus: a Pilgrimage*, pp. 195–223 for a commentary on this issue.
44 *Gaudium et Spes*, §72, and Second Vatican Council, *Lumen Gentium*, 21 November 1968, §31, www.vatican.va/archive/hist_councils/ii_vatican_council/documents/vat-ii_const_19641121_lumen-gentium_en.html (accessed 12 August 2019).
45 'Third Conference of Catholic Prison Chaplains', Domantine, Newry, 19 October 1988 in Northern Ireland Political Collection, Linen Hall Library, Belfast, *Addresses on Peace in Northern Ireland, 1987–1988*, vol. 4, P13581.
46 See for example a 1973 speech made by Daly where he stated that 'man's [sic.] being in the world is a moral and spiritual mission, to continue and complete the creation itself by charity and justice.' Cahal B Daly, 'The Christian in Politics', Speaker's Club, Clonmel, 26 May 1973, *Addresses on Peace in Northern Ireland, 1968–1975*.
47 Cahal B Daly, 'Christianity and Politics', St Thomas' Parish Church, Belfast, 24 October 1993 in Northern Ireland Political Collection, Linen Hall Library, Belfast, *Addresses on Peace in Northern Ireland, 1993–1996*, vol. 7, P13584.
48 Paul VI, *Populorum Progressio*, 26 March 1967, http://w2.vatican.va/content/paul-vi/en/encyclicals/documents/hf_p-vi_enc_26031967_populorum.html, §§ 29, 30, & 32 (accessed 12 August 2019).
49 'The Politics of Peace', Address at Longford on World Day of Peace, 1 January 1978, Northern Ireland Political Collection, Linen Hall Library, Belfast, *Addresses on Peace in Northern Ireland, 1976–1983*, vol. 2, P13579. Cf. 'Witnessing the struggle: struggling to witness, Lecture given under the auspices of the Irish School of Ecumenics in Heythrop College, London', 24 November 1984, Northern Ireland Political Collection, Linen Hall Library, Belfast, P10469.
50 'The Role and Responsibility of the Churches in the Northern Ireland Crisis.'
51 Cahal Daly, *Mass and the World of Work* (Dublin: Irish Messenger Publications, 1981), p. 30.
52 See for example *Gaudium et Spes* §§ 1, 4, 9, 29, 34, & 39.
53 *Gaudium et Spes*, §4.
54 Mt 16:4.
55 Dennis P McCann, 'Signs of the Times', in Judith A Dwyer (ed.), *The New Dictionary of Catholic Social Thought* (Collegeville: Liturgical Press, 1994), pp. 881–883.

56 For an articulation of this in practice and the tensions that it can sometimes cause, see Kate Hennessy, *Dorothy Day: The World Will Be Saved by Beauty. An Intimate Portrait of My Grandmother* (New York: Scribner, 2017), p. 74.

57 Paul VI, *Octogesima Adveniens,* 14 May 1971, http://w2.vatican.va/content/paul-vi/en/apost_letters/documents/hf_p-vi_apl_19710514_octogesima-adveniens.html, §37 (accessed 13 August 2019).

58 Cited in Bernard P Dauenhauer, *Paul Ricoeur: The Promise and Risk of Politics* (Lanham, MD: Rowman and Littlefield, 1998), p. 116.

59 Maria Power, 'Alternative Possible Futures: Unearthing a Catholic Public Theology for Northern Ireland', in Christopher R Baker and Elaine Graham (eds.), *Theology for Changing Times: John Atherton and the Future of Public Theology* (London: SCM, 2018), pp. 158–174.

60 Johan Verstvaeten, 'Towards Interpreting the Signs of the Times, Conversation with the World, and Inclusion of the Poor: Three Challenges for Catholic Social Teaching', *International Journal of Public Theology*, 2011, vol. 5, pp. 314–330, 317.

61 Robert McAfee Brown, *Gustavo Gutiérrez: An Introduction to Liberation Theology* (Maryknoll, NY: Orbis, 1990), p. 51.

62 José Inocencio Alas, *Land, Liberation, and Death Squads: A Priest's Story, Suchitoto, El Salvador, 1968–1977,* trans. Robin Fazio and Emily Wade Hill (Eugene, OR: Resource Publications, 2017); Robert Lassalle-Klein, 'Jesus of Galilee and the Crucified People: The Contextual Christology of Jon Sobrino and Ignacio Ellacuria', *Theological Studies*, 2009, vol. 70, pp. 347–376.

63 Kevin Burke (ed.), *Pedro Arrupe: Selected Writings* (New York: Orbis, 2005), p. 84.

64 The preferential option for the poor was a phrase first used by Fr Pedro Arrupe SJ, Superior General of the Society of Jesus from 1965–1983, in a 1968 letter to the Jesuits of Latin America. This term was then developed by the Dominican Fr Gustavo Gutiérrez (n. 1928–) in his 1971, *The Theology of Liberation: History, Politics, Salvation,* trans. Sister Cardidad Inda and John Eagleson (London: SCM, 1974). However, it has been implicit in papal teachings since Leo XIII, *Rerum Novarum,* 15 May 1891, §23, 29, http://w2.vatican.va/content/leo-xiii/en/encyclicals/documents/hf_l-xiii_enc_15051891_rerum-novarum.html (accessed 25 March 2019), with these ideas further developed in John XXIII, *Mater et Magistra,* 15 May 1961, §157, http://w2.vatican.va/content/john-xxiii/en/encyclicals/documents/hf_j-xxiii_enc_15051961_mater.html (accessed 13 August 2019), *Gaudium et Spes,* §63, and *Populorum Progressio,* §23, 53, & 75. It was first explicitly articulated in 1987 by John Paul II in *Solicitudo Rei Socialis,* §§ 39 & 42 John Paul II, *Solicitudo Rei Socialis,* 30 December 1987, §42, http://w2.vatican.va/content/john-paul-ii/en/encyclicals/documents/hf_jp-ii_enc_30121987_sollicitudo-rei-socialis.html, accessed 13 August 2019), and further emphasised in *Centesimus Annus* when he stated that 'love for others, and especially for the poor, is made concrete by promoting justice.' John Paul II, 1 May 1991, trans. Donders, www.cctwincities.org/wp-content/uploads/2015/10/Centesimus-Annus-The-Hundredth-Year.pdf, §58 (accessed 13 August 2019). It was embraced as a true Catholic obligation during Benedict XVI's papacy (2005–2013) in the Holy See, *The Compendium of the Social Doctrine of the Church* (Vatican City: 2004), §182, www.vatican.va/roman_curia/pontifical_councils/justpeace/documents/rc_pc_justpeace_doc_20060526_compendio-dott-soc_en.html (accessed 13 August 2019). More recently, Francis (2013–) re-emphasised its importance to the mission of the church in his 2013 apostolic letter, *Evangelii Gaudium,* 24 November 2013, §§186–212, http://w2.vatican.va/content/francesco/en/apost_exhortations/documents/papa-francesco_esortazione-ap_20131124_evangelii-gaudium.html (accessed 13 August 2019).

65 'Identifying and Facing the Challenges in the Local Situation, Corrymeela Community and the Irish School of Ecumenics', 10 May 1989 in *Addresses on Peace in Northern Ireland, 1989–1990*.

66 JR Palanque, *Saint Ambroise et l'empire romain* (Paris: de Boccard, 1933), p. 336 ff.

67 Gustavo Gutiérrez, *The Power of the Poor in History*, trans. Robert R Barr (London: SCM, 1979), p. 44.

68 Burke, *Pedro Arrupe*, p. 87.

69 McAfee Brown, *Gustavo Gutiérrez*, p. 52.

70 Tissa Balasuriya, 'Benedict XVI's *Deus Caritas Est* and Social Action', in Philomena Cullen, Bernard Hoose and Gerard Mannion (eds.), *Catholic Social Justice: Theological and Practical Explorations* (London: T & T Clark, 2007), pp. 41–62, 48.

71 *Gaudium et Spes*, §76.

72 'The Role and Responsibility of the Churches in the Northern Crisis' Address to Dublin University History Society, 8 May 1975, *Addresses on Peace in Northern Ireland, 1968–1975*.

73 *Gaudium et Spes*, §72.

74 'The Role and Responsibility of the Churches in the Northern Crisis'.

75 Brown, *Gustavo Gutiérrez*, p. 51.

76 Gutiérrez, 'The Option for the Poor', p. 318.

77 John Paul Lederach, *Building Peace Sustainable Reconciliation in Divided Societies* (Washington, DC: United States Institute of Peace Press, 1997), p. 39.

78 Gutiérrez, 'The Option for the Poor', p. 325.

79 Maria Power, *From Ecumenism to Community Relations: Inter-Church Relationships in Northern Ireland 1980–2005* (Dublin: Irish Academic Press, 2007), p. 139.

80 *Populorum Progressio*, §64.

81 *Populorum Progressio*, §54.

82 *Gaudium et Spes*, §4.

83 'Installation of Bishop Cahal B Daly in the See of Down and Connor', Address before the Final Blessing, 17 October 1982, Northern Ireland Political Collection, Linen Hall Library, Belfast, PH2184.

84 Mt 5–7, and Lk 6:20–49. For a discussion of the Sermon on the Mount and its relationship to understandings of the Kingdom of God, see Rodger Charles SJ, *Christian Social Witness and Teaching: The Catholic Tradition from Genesis to Centesimus Annus*, vol. 1 (Leominster: Gracewing, 1998), pp. 28–50; and Joseph A Grassi, *Informing the Future: Social Justice in the New Testament* (New York: Paulist Press, 1989); Benedict XVI, *Jesus of Nazareth*, trans. Adrian J Walker (London: Bloomsbury, 2007), pp. 46–99.

85 Jn 13:34.

86 St Ignatius of Loyola, *Personal Writings Reminiscences, Spiritual Diary, Select Letters Including the Text of The Spiritual Exercises*, trans. Joseph A Munitiz and Philip Endean (London: Penguin, 2004), p. 329.

87 Cahal Daly, 'Christ and the Irish Crisis', *The Furrow*, 1972, vol. 23, no. 7, pp. 399–404, 399.

2 The Church as Peaceable Kingdom

****

'There are no quick or dramatic ways to peace'[1] Daly told a congregation in Derry during a homily given in 1992. This was because peace, with its interplay of personal, communal, and structural elements, is the epitome of the 'already, but not yet.' The message of peace lies at the very heart of the Gospel, and it was peace in the fullest sense of the word that Daly preached in Northern Ireland.

> The New Testament understanding of peace carries all the rich reso-
> nances of the Hebrew 'Shalom'. It includes of course, the meaning of
> absence of war and violence, but it includes much more besides – it
> means fullness of well being, spiritual, mental, physical, it means proper
> relationships between man and woman with one another and the mar-
> ried couple with God; it means respect for God's plan for human flour-
> ishing and his plan for the whole of creation.[2]

Peace was therefore about creating both the internal and external conditions necessary for each person to flourish and reach their full potential. In short, it was 'a peace founded on the incomparable dignity of the free human being.'[3] This form of peace could be achieved if the people of Northern Ireland committed themselves to achieving such human flourishing through non-violent means; action based upon the knowledge and acceptance that 'the seeds of peace which Christ's Holy Spirit has planted in the world are potent but they are tiny; they are easily blown away by the winds of hatred or devoured by the hawks of violence.'[4]

Daly taught that, as a result of Christ's sacrifice through the crucifix-
ion for us, peace was already a reality in the world: 'The peace of God's kingdom begins with me and must be spread with me. It is a peace which has already been won for us by Christ. Peace is the future which God has promised to us.'[5] The sinful nature of society with its direct, structural, and cultural violence[6] leading to widespread injustice and the complicity of Christians in its creation, meant however, that 'peace does not just happen,

it has to be made.'[7] This future could only be achieved by Christians using their moral imaginations to create a society which would fulfil the vision of the Peaceable Kingdom as defined by Christ in the Gospels. But because peace 'depends on right relations with God, and when these relations have been violated by sin peace needs their reparation by repentant seeking of God's forgiveness and reconciliation with him.'[8] This meant that Christians had to place as much focus on their interior relationship with God as they did on the restructuring of society. One of Daly's main tasks in seeking the Peaceable Kingdom was to prepare the laity to create the conditions in which it could become manifest and to teach them of their moral responsibility to do so.[9] Such conditions were both interior and exterior, and focused upon developing an equilibrium between the relationship that Christians had with God, the relationships that they had with one another (mainly through ecumenical contact), and the manner in which they acted together to make the Christian Church the prototype of the Peaceable Kingdom. The foundation stone of all of this work was a process of conversion which would result in the creation of a new Christian identity in Northern Ireland. It was here more than anywhere that Daly was speaking to all Christians, rather than just Catholics.

Creating a new identity in the image of God's love

In the opening days of Jesus's ministry in his hometown of Nazareth, he proclaimed that 'the time is fulfilled and the kingdom of God has come near; repent and believe the good news.'[10] Luke's Gospel expands further on the meaning of this 'good news', telling us that Jesus read the following verses from Isaiah 61 to those gathered at the synagogue in Nazareth: 'The Spirit of the Lord is upon me, because he has anointed me to bring good news to the poor. He has sent me to proclaim the release to the captives and recovery of sight to the blind, to let the oppressed go free, to proclaim the year of the Lord's favour.'[11] Jesus continues, saying 'Today this scripture has been fulfilled in your hearing.'[12] Through this exchange with the worshipers in the synagogue, Jesus defines his mission as one of conversion: Conversion of the individual into a person who focuses upon the will of God and conversion of society into a kingdom worthy and emblematic of God's love for the world. It is no surprise then, that Daly, with his emphasis on the creation of the Peaceable Kingdom, saw the need for the wholesale transformation of Northern Ireland. 'Our Christian faith is a call for continuous conversion of ourselves and of our society, conversion never completed, never finished but never abandoned, never defeated and daily renewed.'[13] Individuals, communities, societies, and political structures needed to undergo a metamorphosis that would lead to a more just way of living and, peace and reconciliation and ultimately the creation of the Peaceable Kingdom.

To begin this process of wholesale conversion, the individual had to undergo a 'spiritual revolution' described by St Paul[14] in his letter to the

Ephesians thus: 'to be renewed in the spirit of your minds, and to clothe yourself with the new self, created according to the likeness of God in true righteousness and holiness.'[15] In practice within the context of Northern Ireland this meant focusing on the promises and responsibilities of baptism, ultimately creating a new identity in the image of God's love. This signified that:

> We Christians have to <u>become</u> the Christians which we are. We still fall far short of achieving, or rather permitting Christ to achieve in us the "Christening", "<u>Christening</u>", of ourselves, our thoughts, our emotions, our attitudes and judgements; and of our society, to which we are called by our own baptism.
>
> "Christians are not born as such, they become such". The phrase is still relevant to today. After two millennia of Christianity, we are still only pagans in the process of conversion.[16]

The key element missing in this process of becoming Christian in Northern Ireland was the type of love which is the whole of Christian life. Without such love, one cannot be a Christian.[17] Without this love, the visible church-community cannot be identified and the counter-community necessary for the establishment of the Peaceable Kingdom cannot be created.[18] As Daly put it:

> Our Lord expects his followers to live by a standard of love which is distinct from that which is commonly thought sufficient. His followers are to love their enemies. He said that they must model their love for each other on God's love for all men and women. A love which reaches out to bad people as well as good, to enemies as well as friends.[19]

This love is agape,[20] the purist form of love, the very love revealed by Jesus through his death on the cross – a sacrifice which redeemed humanity. Agape, then, comes from God and is His gift to humanity.

Anders Nygren in his study of *The Christian idea of love through the ages: Agape and Eros* defines it thus:

> [Agape] is spontaneous, unconditional, theocentric, self-giving and self-sacrificial: in other words, we can love others and God, with a love of agape in which we reject all self gain and interest and surrender ourselves to others and love them purely for themselves.[21]

St Paul in his letter to the Philippians instructs members of the church in Philippi to 'do nothing from selfish ambition or conceit, but in humility regard others as better than yourselves. Let each of you look not to your own interests, but to the interests of others.'[22] Such an attitude of love can only come from God, and can be found within a circle of encounter with God which involves prayer, dialogue with the other, the creation of mutual understanding, and service. Through this both the interior (one's relationship with God) and exterior (one's relationship with others) are transformed, resulting in the bonds necessary to build the Peaceable Kingdom.

All of this is founded upon Christ's ministry and sacrifice on the cross which shows that to be a Christian is to take risks; think, for example, of Mary's 'yes' to God[23] or of Christ's challenge to the money lenders in the temple.[24] As CS Lewis puts it in *The Four Loves*, 'Christ did not teach and suffer that we might become, even in the natural loves, more careful of our own happiness.'[25] Christians, thus, must develop characteristics and behaviours which run counter to the prevailing norms in society. The characteristics which make up the Christian character are set out in the Beatitudes and St Paul's definition of love in his first letter to the Corinthians,[26] and are frequently spoken of by Daly as the virtues needed to bring peace to Northern Ireland.[27] Thus, the Beatitudes ask Christians: to be poor in spirit or humble-hearted; to be meek or gentle-hearted; to hunger for righteousness; to be merciful; to be forgiving and compassionate; to be authentic; and to be peacemakers.[28] To this Daly added the fruits of the Holy Spirit: love, joy, peace, patience, kindness, generosity, faithfulness, gentleness, and self-control.[29] Daly acknowledged the difficulty inherent in living such virtues, reassuring people that:

> St Paul is not speaking here to an elite group of saints but to ordinary Christians like ourselves. He is not speaking of the heroic virtue required of saints but about the daily test and struggle of every Christian; for a Christian is by definition a person who tries to have in all spheres of life, including politics and human relations, the same mind as Jesus Christ. This is after all what being a Christian means.[30]

But through the adoption of such attitudes and behaviours, Christians could become 'dynamic forces for creative change',[31] creating the conditions necessary for the Peaceable Kingdom to emerge. In such an endeavour, Christians are not alone: to be a Christian is to take risks safe in the knowledge of God's love and the efficacy of Jesus's sacrifice on the cross. Above all, Daly argues, agape grounds Christians in hope which will give them the strength to continue their work for the Peaceable Kingdom:

> Christian faith and hope are not just the feeling that things will some how work out for good in the end. They are the certainty that things have already worked out for good; for sin has already been defeated by the cross and resurrection of Christ, hostility has been overcome, reconciliation is already a fact.[32]

Such hope, Daly tells us a decade later, is 'aware of stubborn realities of realpolitik, but refuses to be discouraged by obstacles and set backs or to desist from try again and beginning again.'[33]

In a conflict which Daly argued was largely about issues of identity[34] and in which loving your enemy was potentially dangerous, the adoption of such attitudes and behaviours would be a difficult but ultimately fruitful task, giving people the strength and perspective required to encounter the 'other' and work to challenge and change the structures of society. Such a spiritual revolution would:

> inaugurate a whole new way of relating to persons and to communities long regarded as hostile to people's whole sense of identity, persons and communities long felt to be alien, to be outsiders, seen not as belonging. Repentance meant a whole new way of defining our own identity, whether cultural or national or even religious, defining it in dialogue with others and in respect for others rather than suffer isolation.[35]

As the parable of the Prodigal Son[36] shows, anyone 'can break away from the most entrenched identity.'[37] Daly used the term 'metanoia' to describe this process.

According to Alan J Torrance, metanoia

> denotes the transformation of our orientation towards God and also towards the world – the reconciliation and reconstitution of our dysfunctional modes of thought.
>
> [It] denotes a new redeemed orientation towards God and the world that is so radically discontinuous with the old that it is described in terms of the reconstitution of our identities – our being 'born again' to participate in a 'new humanity' whereby we are given 'eyes to see' and 'ears to hear' what we could not otherwise recognise or appropriate.[38]

Through the process of metanoia, Christians repent and become the people that God wills them to be, flourishing as human beings and creating a society in which all are equal and have their dignity respected.[39] 'However, long it may take, we must patiently work to reform our stubborn prejudices, our bitter memories, our recalcitrant hearts, into the shape of Christ's kingdom of justice and peace.'[40] Such a transformation could only take place through prayer, both individual and communal.

Prayer

The task that the ministry of Jesus sets the Church is the conversion and subsequent salvation of *both the individual and society*. The salvation of the individual cannot be achieved without a concern for one's neighbour, the inevitable consequence of which is a regard for justice and peace, which in turn cannot be achieved without due attention being paid to one's inner spiritual development. For Daly the link between these two elements of the Christian life was prayer.

Daly explained the power and importance of prayer thus:

> Prayer is in fact God working in us. We are conscious of the effort
> needed in order to pray – the effort to attend to the presence of God,
> the effort to concentrate, the effort to be still, to be sincere with God.
> Awareness of our effort could deceive us into thinking that prayer is our
> doing. In fact, prayer is something God is doing for us, something God
> is giving to us. Prayer is a gift from God to us.
>
>   . . .
>
>   Prayer is therefore the most powerful force that we can bring to bear
> on any situation. Prayer is indeed the power of God working through us
> in a given situation. *When we pray we are letting God create and trans-
> form ourselves first, and then the world through us.* When we pray,
> God is allowing us to share in his power, to share in his work.[41]

Ideally, the commitment to both the prayer and the action for justice necessary for the establishment of the Peaceable Kingdom needed to be made
simultaneously. Although this symbiotic relationship is not always imme-
diately possible, the relationship between the two should be circular rather
than linear.[42] The peace activist, Daniel Berrigan SJ, sums the relationship
up thus:

> Some people today argue that equanimity achieved through inner spirit-
> ual work is a necessary condition for sustaining one's ethical and politi-
> cal commitments. But to the prophets of the Bible, this would have
> been absolutely foreign language and a foreign view of the human. The
> notion that one has to achieve peace of mind before stretching one's
> hand out to one's neighbor is a distortion of our human experience and
> ultimately a dodge of our responsibility. Life is a roller coaster and one
> had better buckle one's belt and take the trip. This focus on equanimity
> is actually a narrow minded, selfish approach to reality dressed up in the
> language of spirituality.[43]

Prayer thus sustains, nourishes, and inspires action, whilst action brings
new meanings to prayer, especially the experience and understanding of the
message of the Gospels which were the foundation stone of Daly's moral
imagination. This crucial relationship is explored in the closing part of this
section, but first we discuss what Daly meant by prayer and how he con-
nected its practice to conversion and ultimately salvation, both individual
and communal, in Northern Ireland.

The meaning and purpose of prayer

Daly taught that the imitation of Christ was the ultimate purpose of Christian life. Prayer was fundamental to this task. In a 1972 article on 'Prayer

in the Modern World,' he stated that 'St Luke shows Christ's whole life as spent in an atmosphere of prayer. Indeed he interprets Christ's whole mission in terms of a theology of prayer.'[44] The task of prayer, and the laity's engagement with it, was twofold: first, to prepare people for salvation and second, to form them as social and political actors working to secure the Peaceable Kingdom. These two tasks were to be achieved through witness, fostering a sense of community, and discernment.

Acts of witness

Daly was particularly prolific when it came to asking for intercessory prayer from the people of Ireland – nearly all of his public addresses conclude with an exhortation for the Christians of Northern Ireland, both Catholic and Protestant, to pray. During the initial stages of the conflict, from c. 1968 to c. 1982, the context in which this prayer was set was unremitting violence with very little hope for a political settlement. Daly's discourse on prayer reflected this. He believed that the conflict could not be brought to an end without the intervention of prayer: 'Politicians will work with all the more urgency when they realise that ultimately peace is God's first, and that the world with all its wisdom and experience cannot give it.'[45] The means for such a transformation was a prayer of witness through which Christians petitioned God for peace and most importantly allowed Him to act through them: 'God must act in this situation, if peace is to come; but God can act only if we want Him to and allow Him to act. Prayer is the condition of God's all-powerful action for peace.'[46] This allows God to draw us closer into his salvific plan for both the individual and the world.

Prayer was thus both a means of witness to the temporal realm and petition to the spiritual. The importance of this witness was crucial as it enabled Christians to demonstrate to those engaged in violence that the majority of people wanted peace:

> Our best way of imitating him today is to join our prayers and our conviction and our efforts with those brave women and men who march and work and suffer for peace in Ireland. It is a Christian task, a Christian duty. Christ's work in the world is essentially peace-making – making peace between men and God and between man and man.[47]

Initially, intercessory prayers requested by Daly focused mainly upon the perpetrators of violence that 'God may touch the hearts of both loyalist and republican paramilitaries, that they may turn from the ways of death and destruction and heartbreak and may give their people peace';[48] and the victims and their families that they be comforted in their grief and forgive.[49] The effects of the violence on communities who were 'suffering, frightened, and sometimes angry' was also recognised through the use of prayer.[50] The prayer of the Church therefore was not one of acceptance but one of challenge to the situation in which it found itself. Thus, in the Northern Irish context the focus was on an end to violence and addressing the issues that had initially caused the conflict.

From the 1990s onwards, the Catholic Church instituted (along with the Catholic churches in England and Wales, and Scotland) a series of 'Days of Prayer for Peace.' These were intended to support the embryonic and fragile peace process in Northern Ireland which suffered a number of disruptions before the signing of the Good Friday Agreement in 1998. Through such intercessory prayer, it was expected that Christians would bear witness for peace by demonstrating their belief in God, gratitude for His gifts to the world and the tools that he provided for creating the Peaceable Kingdom upon the earth, as evidenced in the Sermon on the Mount which represented Christ's vision for society.

Prayer could also change and challenge relationships – something which was crucial in Northern Ireland. In a conflict based upon socio-economic disparities and differing political aspirations, communal acts of intercessory prayer were an important bonding and bridging mechanism both within and between groups. Prayer was therefore not just an individual act but its communal praxis played an important role in the establishment of the Peaceable Kingdom. When undertaken publicly, communal prayer was an act of prophetic witness which could sometimes provoke strong opposition. For instance, a Good Friday cross-community walk of witness and prayer service on the Shankill Road attended by 1500 people 'came under attack from a crowd who pelted them with eggs and stones on the Lanark Way junction' as they processed behind a banner proclaiming 'Christ is our Peace'.[51] Such acts could, however, have the opposite effect, something noted by Daly in a homily in July 1996: 'People present in the Lower Ormeau Road in Belfast on the "twelfth" have told me of the extraordinarily calming effect which came from people praying the rosary together at a time of high emotion and tension.'[52] The commonalities underlying these two events were the expression of hope that they represented and the opportunity that they gave people to reach out to one another. By engaging in such public acts of witness, both inter and intra communal, those involved were providing a glimpse of an alternative possible future in which violence and confrontation would not be the main forms of communication.

Fostering a sense of community

Communal acts of worship were also crucial, fostering within individuals a desire to work for the Peaceable Kingdom. For Catholics, the communal aspect of prayer was emphasised most compellingly through the Mass. For Daly, the Mass was at the centre of this prayer for peace and was crucial in forming community: 'Around the altar of this Holy Mass we have present to us all that is needed for the peace of the world. We receive here our mission to make a peace with one another first and then to spread peace throughout the world.'[53] The Eucharist and therefore the Mass[54] is 'the source and summit of the Christian life.'[55] It is through the celebration of the Mass that the community of the Church is formed and in which Catholics unify with heaven:

> The Eucharist is the efficacious sign and sublime cause that communion in the divine life and that the unity of the People of God by which the Church is kept in being. It is the culmination both of God's action sanctifying the world in Christ and of the worship men offer to Christ and through him to the Father in the Holy Spirit.
>
> Finally, by the Eucharistic celebration we already unite ourselves with the heavenly liturgy and anticipate eternal life, when God will be all in all.[56]

In Daly's writings concerning the role of prayer in the conflict in Northern Ireland, the importance of the Mass was threefold: it allowed for witness but it also provided spiritual nourishment and strength, and reaffirmed the mission for peace handed down to us through the Gospel. For example, when writing of the Creed,[57] Daly stated that 'It is then that we "stand up to be counted" and say out loud exactly what we believe, and what we exactly believe; namely, that we believe exactly what God has spoken'[58] through the Gospels. Mass provided Christians with the strength required to 'suffer for peace'[59] and gave people the necessary tools to work for peace and acted as a reminder of its importance for Christian living:

> In Mass, . . . we shall pray before Holy Communion: "Lamb of God, you take away the sins of the world, grant us peace". Before we receive Our Lord, we shall exchange with one another the sign of peace; for only those who are at peace with one another, only those who are reconciled with their brothers and sisters in mutual forgiveness and love, can fittingly receive the Lord of peace. Only they who have His Spirit of peace can receive, and thus be built up into, His body.[60]

A homily, based upon prayerful reflection, played a central role in this relationship between prayer and action for peace: 'preaching is a means of drawing others into a conversation with God.'[61] It also gave people who would otherwise be unaffected by the conflict a means of focusing on the issue of peace and reconciliation, promoting solidarity across boundaries such as geography, denomination, and class by focusing people upon the needs of others. Through this a love of neighbour can be developed. Finally, the mission of creating the Peaceable Kingdom is handed to the people through the final words spoken to the congregation of 'The Mass is ended. Go forth in peace.'[62]

According to Gustavo Gutiérrez, this led to a new spirituality where prayer and the person, and community were all dependent upon one another:

> God [is not] unrelated to human history. On the contrary, if it is true . . . that one must go through humankind to reach God, it is equally certain that "passing through" to that gratuitous God strips me, leaves me naked, universalises my love for others, and makes it gratuitous. Both movements need each other dialectically and move towards a synthesis. This synthesis is found in Christ; in the God-Man we encounter God and humankind. In Christ humankind gives God a human countenance and God gives it a divine countenance. Only in this perspective will we be able to understand that the "union with the Lord," which all spiritually proclaims, is not a separation from others; to attain this union, I must go through others, and the union, in turn, enables me to encounter others more fully.[63]

Such a process can be painful, forcing people to understand and face their own role in history.[64] Thus, prayer and redemptive suffering combine, allowing 'ministerial solidarity'[65] to emerge as people prayed for one another's needs. Daly emphasised this forcefully in the 1970s:

> Our suffering can be redemptive. It can be reconciliatory. But it will be so only to the extent that we "suffer with" each other as if the other's suffering were our own. "Suffer with" is the strong and original meaning of "sympathise". Catholics must, in this strong sense, sympathise with Protestant sufferings, fears, insecurities; Protestants must sympathise with Catholic insecurities, fears, sufferings. This is how we "complete in our flesh what is lacking in Christ's afflictions" for the sake of all our Churches.[66]

Such empathy or compassion is fuelled by prayer, restores the humanity of the 'other', and focuses the Christian upon the needs of the community, leading on to action for justice and peace.

Redemptive Suffering

It is in Isaiah 53 that Christians are taught that suffering is redemptive: 'but he was wounded for our transgressions, crushed for our inequities; upon him was the punishment that made him whole, and by his bruises we were healed,'[67] and this theme recurs frequently in Daly's writings, especially during the 1980s and 1990s when the conflict seemed relentless. Suffering was a means of spiritual nourishment: drawing the individual closer to God, preparing them for the Heavenly city, developing their prayer life, and ultimately promoting the compassion and reconciliation needed for the

Peaceable Kingdom to emerge. Suffering and the hope that emerges from it were demonstrations of faith and of God's power in the world. The mission of a Christian was to imitate Christ, and the endemic violence and injustice brought the people of Northern Ireland an opportunity to do so: 'The people of Cappagh and Galbally have the great consolation of knowing that their sorrow and suffering are not in vain. They are united with the sufferings of Christ for the salvation of the world.'[68] However, such 'redemptive suffering' was wider than a personal experience of conversion; rather it brought with it the hope of salvation:

> For us it is the Passion of Christ which most clearly manifests His Divine nature. The Passion best reveals Christ's oneness with His eternal Father, His union with the Father's will. The Passion most strongly manifests Christ's infinite love for His people. The Passion forms one single whole with Christ's resurrection and His ascension into glory at the Father's right hand. He triumphs over His enemies, the powers of evil, through weakness and suffering and apparent defeat. It is through humiliation and abandonment that he attains to glory.[69]

This notion of mission in line with Christ is key to the Church's teachings on suffering. Suffering is seen as a means of displaying fidelity to Christ and God's redeeming mercy to the world.[70] It therefore had a missionary characteristic. This had been clearly illustrated by the Catholic Church's first systematic reflection on the Church's teachings on suffering, undertaken by John Paul II (r. 1978–2005) in 1984. In it he stated:

> The motif of suffering and glory has a strictly evangelical characteristic, which becomes clear by reference to the Cross and the Resurrection. The Resurrection became, first of all, the manifestation of glory, which corresponds to Christ's being lifted up through the Cross. If, in fact, the Cross was to human eyes Christ's emptying of himself, at the same time it was in the eyes of God his being lifted up. On the Cross, Christ attained and fully accomplished his mission: by fulfilling the will of the Father, he at the same time fully realized himself. In weakness he manifested his power, and in humiliation he manifested all his messianic greatness. Are not all the words he uttered during his agony on Golgotha a proof of this greatness, and especially his words concerning the perpetrators of his crucifixion: "Father, forgive them for they know not what they do"? To those who share in Christ's sufferings these words present themselves with the power of a supreme example.[71]

Thus, as both Daly and John Paul II demonstrate, through their suffering the people of Northern Ireland could fulfill their mission of imitating Christ and bring His message of peace and reconciliation to the world.

However, this teaching also had a strongly personal element contained within it as suffering brought people closer to Christ:

> Suffering is also an invitation to manifest the moral greatness of man, his spiritual maturity. Proof of this has been given, down through the generations, by the martyrs and confessors of Christ, faithful to the words: "And do not fear those who kill the body, but cannot kill the soul."[72]

Daly's discourse emphasised the reliance of people upon God, and demonstrated to them that their suffering was one element of this. However, this was not to be a passive suffering which would merely be accepted; instead it was to lead people closer to God and assist in the process of discernment which was so crucial to action.

Discernment

The keys to this process of discernment were persistence, perseverance, and formation. Taking inspiration from the Gospel,[73] Daly frequently reminded people that prayer rarely remained unanswered: 'We can have total confidence that He will hear our cry for peace, when we have prayed enough and worked enough to deserve it.'[74] Thus, one of the key themes to emerge in his writings was that of perseverance or persistence as he argued that 'the only way really to fail in faith or in prayer is to stop trying.'[75] Daly insisted that the Christians of Northern Ireland should be tenacious in their attitude to prayer: 'Persist in prayer to the point where God is simply weary of listening to us and just has to give us what we ask! That is the spirit in which we must pray for peace.'[76] The need for perseverance in prayer was a means used by God to increase people's faith and develop their vision for peace; in the words of St Augustine: 'The whole life of a good Christian is holy desire. . . . [B]y delaying fulfilment of desire God . . . expands the soul, and by this expansion he increases its capacity.'[77] Similarly, in one of his earliest writings on the relationship between perseverance and prayer produced in 1977, Daly states:

> Our perseverance in prayer is a test of the earnestness of our prayer. Our earnestness in prayer is measured also by what we are prepared to <u>do</u> to cooperate with God in bringing about an answer to our prayer. There is no genuine prayer without effort on our part to put our 'muscle', as it were, at God's disposal for the purpose for which we pray. Prayer is not so much an effort by us to change God's mind as a willingness by us to let God change our minds and change our lives, so we will allow His will to be done to us and through us, "on earth as it is in Heaven".[78]

Here, the relationship of prayer to the conflict in Northern Ireland was laid bare: Prayer transformed the individual and his or her relationship with God, providing people with the spiritual freedom and strength required to *act* for peace and to become full members of the Church. The Church thus had a dual mission: to prepare people for salvation in the heavenly city, whilst working to proclaim and realise the message of the Gospel with its focus upon peace in the earthly city. This was achieved through the medium of prayer.

The creation of the Peaceable Kingdom on earth is both an internal and external act – both a private and public declaration of a belief in God's salvific plan for the world, and an agreement to adhere to the ethical standards established by Jesus's ministry. To work for the establishment of the kingdom requires the development of an outward-looking spirituality which is at once a way of life and a hope for the future, both in terms of salvation and the temporal realm. Benedict Viviano describes this understanding of the kingdom thus:

> The Kingdom of God . . . is a new, future divine breaking into history already present in sign, anticipation and momentary ecstasy, especially in the ministry of Jesus himself, yet in its fullness still to come. This divine act will be of a social rather than individual character and will have as its immediate political manifestations justice and peace. As well it will involve a new and greater outpouring of God's Holy Spirit upon those who enter this kingdom.[79]

This has implications for a believer's prayer life as 'the faithful who pray this prayer [e.g. the Our Father] are not an inward looking circle praying merely for their own needs.'[80] Prayer is therefore not meant to be a comfortable experience; rather it brings Christians face to face with the problems of society. Furthermore, in his teachings on prayer, Jesus gives us instructions to 'stand where he stands'[81] to better focus on the will of God, and through this the realisation of the Peaceable Kingdom on earth and salvation. Jesus expresses this through the words of the Our Father, 'Your Kingdom come. Your will be done, on earth as it is in heaven.'[82]

Christians were expected to lead an integrated life in which the religious, moral, and political were combined. According to Daly, 'Christianity is not about explaining the world, but about changing it. It is not about explaining human existence but about making us new creatures.'[83] To establish the Peaceable Kingdom, this 'making of new creatures' required intense spiritual work. Such an integrated vision of the role of Christianity within society demanded a well-rounded spirituality, and this could not be achieved without the regular practice of prayer. Prayer was the means through which Christians discerned how to act: 'prayer for peace and work for peace are inseparable from one another and are in a sense the interior and the exterior of one single reality.'[84] One could not exist without the other. Furthermore,

prayer was the mechanism through which the exercise of the moral imagination focused on the realisation of the kingdom was triggered. As Rowan
Williams tells us:

> Only when we have begun with that affirmation, that imagining of a
> world in which God's lights are coming through, only then do we start
> asking for what we need. And what do we need? We need sustenance,
> mercy, protection, daily bread, forgiveness; we need to be steered away
> from the tests that we are not strong enough to bear.[85]

However, for such a vision to be achieved, the individual had to be formed:
moving their prayer from one of desperation to one of freedom and creating
an interior state from which positive action could be discerned and subsequently flow. In *Spirituality and Justice*, Donal Dorr argues that there are
two types of petitionary prayer: the prayer of desperation and the prayer of
freedom. This could also be defined as conditional and unconditional prayer.
In desperation, the Christian will often plead with God to gain acquiescence
to his or her requests in what Daly called 'a sad caricature of prayer'[86] or as
Miroslav Volf suggests, 'to enlist God's help in critical situations seems to
reduce God to a performance enhancing drug.'[87] He or she will put conditions in place with which God is expected to comply. As Dorr argues:

> There is little or no freedom in the prayer of desperation. It is rather the
> cry of one who is in urgent need. The person who prays in this mode is
> one who has been deprived of the freedom of spirit that ought to char-
> acterise our relationship with God. It is important to note this element
> of deprivation – generally an unjust deprivation. The one who prays the
> prayer of desperation is somebody who is prevented from being fully
> human. This means that, ideally, nobody should ever have to pray in
> this way; for all our prayer should be made in freedom.[88]

Furthermore, in engaging in a prayer of desperation, Christians are distort-
ing their relationship with God by setting limits on how He can help them:
Jesus 'could do no deed of power there, except that he laid his hands on a
few sick people and cured them. And he was amazed at their unbelief.'[89]
This is not to say that such prayer has little or no meaning. In fact, quite the
opposite is true; even Christ cried out in desperation.[90] Thus, although the
prayer of desperation strips the person of their dignity, it can start a process of transformation through which freedom is achieved. This is because
as Dorr argues, 'Crying out is already the first step in changing things, in
breaking the silence of oppression.'[91]

Prayer is encountering God and learning of His will for us. It provides
the hope necessary to carry on when the situation is intolerable. Thus,
'the goal of prayer should be to take charge of one's own history, to make
a choice in conformity with the saving will of God who has acted and

continues to act in history.'[92] The resultant prayer of freedom recognises the dignity of the entire person and enables them to develop a trusting relationship with God. In short, it strengthens the Christian's faith in, and relationship with, God, whilst allowing them to understand who they are before God. In prayer, 'God's grace meets us and acts in human history, an essential task of living out the spiritual life is discerning God's will within it.'[93] Radcliffe further adds to this when he suggests, 'We do not pray so as to manipulate history and bend it to our will, but because God wishes us to receive things in accordance with our prayers and so recognise them as gifts.'[94] The reception and recognition of such gifts provides Christians with the assurance to ask for more. Thus, although the prayer of freedom requires an understanding that God may say no to the request, it provides Christians with the confidence that they will receive what they need, when they need it. This is because 'the more you grow in faith, the more what you want shifts into alignment with God's will for you.'[95] A faith based on prayer according to the Christian tradition, therefore, makes all things possible: 'Ask, and it will be given to you; search, and you will find; knock, and the door will be opened for you.'[96] Petitionary prayer of the type advocated by Daly was central in facilitating this move from desperation to freedom.

> When we pray – and we often find it hard to pray – we should remember that the Holy Spirit is praying within us and with us; He knows our needs and our longings better than we know them ourselves; He prays infinitely better than we ever could, the prayers we would ourselves love to be able to pray; and we have the assurance that our prayers, enveloped in the prayer of the Holy Spirit, will be answered because they will be "according to the mind of God" (cf Rm 8:26–27).[97]

It enabled people to commence a process that would eventually lead to action, but this action would be based firmly upon the will of God, thereby ensuring the mission of the Church through the promotion of the Gospel message of peace and reconciliation. It allowed an interior state of peace to be achieved which was a prerequisite for the exterior state of peace.

Daly therefore sought to use prayer to prompt people to broaden their outlook and seek a practical mysticism which would allow a better integration of Christianity and spirituality into their everyday lives:

> It is a unique feature of the Christian faith that it refuses any separation between believing, worshiping and living. The unity and continuity is, of course, perpetually threatened because of innate human weaknesses. One-sided emphasis can be put on one or other of these three elements of the Christian whole. At times, orthodoxy of belief could be stressed in a manner that made Christian living[98] seem of secondary importance. In our time it is perhaps more likely that Christian moral action and

social commitment would be regarded as the one thing necessary, and rightness of belief as a secondary matter.

But in the true Christian vision no one of these elements can be separated from the others. Creed, prayer and ethics; orthodox faith, true Christian prayer and right moral living are one. We must restore our sense of the unity of this triad, a unity so strongly marked in the New Testament and the tradition of the Church.[99]

However, such a balance could only be achieved by discernment. It was only through prayer that the Christian could enter into this process and achieve what Radcliffe calls 'spontaneity' – a fundamental element of freedom.[100] This process is intimately linked to a prayer of freedom and ultimately leads to a form of action which springs from the very core of one's being. As noted earlier, persistence or perseverance is very much part of this process because, as St Thomas Aquinas tells us: 'The Holy Spirit makes us plead inasmuch as he causes the right desires in us. Pleading is a certain unfolding of our desires, and the right desires arise from the ardour of love, and this is produced in us by the Holy Spirit.'[101] Thus, by entering into a dialogue with the Holy Trinity through petitionary prayer, the Christian is put in touch with his or her deepest desires and comes to understand what they 'ought to pray for'.[102] It is here that God resides, and it is from the 'core of one's being' that action emerges.[103] It is from prayer that the strength to act even against seemingly insurmountable odds emerges, as Dorothy Day demonstrates when speaking of her 'Adventures in Prayer':

> I felt so strongly my nothingness, my powerlessness to do anything about this recognition of my own hardness of heart, it drove me to the recognition that in God alone was my strength. Without him I could do nothing. Yet I could do all things in him who strengthened me.[104]

These transformations in turn lead to an understanding of the place of virtue, morals, or ethics in the Christian life, the place where the integration of faith and action ultimately reside.[105]

Prayer and action

When it comes to the creation of what Ellacuría calls a 'contemplative in the action of justice',[106] context is everything, and both prayer and action must seek solutions to the problems facing society. Gutiérrez, although writing in a Latin American context, provides an excellent definition of this process that can easily be applied to Northern Ireland: 'as faith puts one in right relationship with God through the grace of internal justice. It also calls a person to seek external justice through the promotion of good works, through changing structures that oppress, through empowering the lowly.'[107] The mission of the Christian churches was to 'have a healing and elevating impact on the dignity of the person, by the way in which it strengthens the seams of human society and imbues the everyday activity of men with a deeper meaning and importance.'[108] Thus described, the task of the Church was now both spiritual *and* social.[109] As well as focusing upon spiritual salvation, Christians were expected to 'devote themselves with all their being to the glory of God and the service of their neighbour'; labours which would result in 'an abundant harvest of good.'[110] Faith as *Gaudium et Spes* taught[111] was to be integrated into everyday life. During the twentieth century, the Catholic Church produced many contemplatives in the action of justice. For example, Simone Weil's 'mystical consciousness only intensified and deepened her attention to the invisible and powerless in history and society.'[112] Daniel Berrigan SJ speaks of spending days in prayer before undertaking his many ploughshare actions,[113] and Dorothy Day 'in all her activities, even as she marched on picket lines or went to jail, she was strengthened by the constant discipline of prayer.'[114] This combination of spiritual and social therefore created an ideal which Daly termed 'lived Christianity' where the responsibilities of each were held in mutually enhancing tension, with contemplative and communal prayer, and analysis and action, acting to develop the whole person, and through them facilitate a reordering of society based upon the Kingdom of God. It was this integration of faith with everyday life which made Daly's reimagining of a temporal Peaceable Kingdom possible.

The creation of the Peaceable Kingdom was both a way of life and a hope for the future. This creates a tension in the Christian life which can be lessened and ultimately resolved through prayer. However, such practical mysticism whilst fueled by individual prayer and contemplation must be combined with an obvious effort on the part of churches to be a model of the Peaceable Kingdom within the communities they serve.

The nature of the church-community

By virtue of their baptism, Christians become members of a church-community. Christians can only be Christians in community with one another. This is because according to Philip Vielhauer:

> The goal of the ways of God is not the pious individual, but the one, holy, Catholic church, in the pregnant and radically eschatological sense of the New Testament; it is the church's creation and preservation, its promote and realisation, that Paul describes as *oikodomein*.[115]

On being christened then, Christians become Jesus's representatives on earth and must carry on his salvific mission. Consequently, 'All who belong to the body of Christ have been freed from and called out of the world. They must become visible to the world not only through their communal bond evident in the church-community's order and worship, but also through the new communal life among brothers and sisters in Christ.'[116] In the context of Northern Ireland, this meant working for peace. Daly was determined that Christians in the region should become what Gerald Lohfink has called a 'contrast community'[117] as it is only through collective effort on the part of *all Christians*, not just Catholics,[118] that the Peaceable Kingdom can be built. This was because:

> The antisocial and corrupt system of a dominant society cannot be attacked more sharply than by the formation of an antisociety in its midst. Simply through its existence, this new society is a much more efficacious attack on the old structure than any programmes, without personal cost, for the general transformation of the world.[119]

But first, they must coexist peacefully with one another. This Daly argued could be achieved by a dual approach creating the 'right relationships'[120] that make up one of the two arms of the justice so crucial to the foundation of the Peaceable Kingdom. Thus, to act as an example of the Peaceable Kingdom and a contrast community within Northern Irish society, Christian churches had first to address issues in their structural relationships as well as think about the manner in which Christians, both clerical and lay, dialogued with one another. There were two issues in particular which attracted Daly's attention: sectarianism and ecumenism.

Sectarianism

Sectarianism has always been a feature of Irish identity, and was Daly argued one of the key causes of the conflict in Northern Ireland. As Marianne Elliott argues:

> Sectarianism was there before modern nationalism developed, and the political division of Ireland was the consequence of sectarianism, rather than the cause of it. If sectarianism had not been so deep-rooted, the Northern Ireland Troubles would not have happened. They happened because both sides acted as the stereotypes said they would.[121]

The role of religious belief, expression, and doctrine alongside religious stereotyping in the creation and maintenance of sectarianism is seen as a crucial element in its definition. And it is here that religion[122] and politics most closely intersect in Northern Ireland, creating a negative mix of the two that lead to prejudice and violent conflict. Sectarianism therefore is both personal and structural and is 'really embedded in the whole culture.'[123] John Brewer's definition of sectarianism supports this but further emphasises the religious components:

1   Sectarianism refers to a whole cluster of ideas, beliefs, myths, and demonology about religious difference which are used to make religion

a social marker, to assign different attributes to the various religious groups, and to make derogatory remarks about others.

2   Sectarianism is not just a set of prejudiced attitudes but refers to behaviour, policies, and types of treatment that are informed by religious difference.[124]

It is thus a pastoral issue as it 'always involves religion'.[125]

The Protestant and Catholic churches, and Daly in particular, had a complex relationship towards sectarianism, caused in part by an inability, or perhaps unwillingness, to see the link between it and their institutions. Sectarianism was, according to Daly, a misuse of religion, 'the frame of mind that exploits denominational differences to promote a sense of superiority, a denial of rights, a justification of conflict.'[126] This definition, created as part of a report for the Joint Group on Social Questions,[127] concurs with Daly's belief that the conflict in Northern Ireland was not religious but was rather caused by structural injustice – a viewpoint which he later changed.[128] Sectarianism was 'quite distinct from religion'[129] despite evidence to the contrary.[130] However, Daly viewed the adverse consequences of sectarianism: violence, injustice, and a lack of democratic representation and structures, as something to be exposed and denounced.[131] It was thus an issue, which needed to be understood and combatted, and was one of the most enduring themes of Daly's discourse, both explicitly and implicitly. He argued that it was one of the core elements preventing Gospel values from embedding within society and thwarting the subsequent establishment of the Kingdom of God. A clear role for the churches, both Catholic and Protestant, therefore needed to be developed in order to meet the challenge that it posed to their ministry.

Daly saw the solution to sectarianism as an ecumenical matter. On this, more than any issue, he spoke to *all* the churches in Northern Ireland, signalling his acceptance of the plurality of religion there.[132] The sectarian nature of the conflict was a key argument for the promotion of ecumenism in Northern Ireland. Working to combat sectarianism was one of the positive actions that the churches could take together to improve society and end the conflict. Initially, Daly framed this in structural terms, arguing that the 'evangelical and moral infrastructure of the political order' could be prevailed upon to 'work for [sectarianism's] eradication.'[133] He thus suggested that the churches undertake a supporting role in society, persuading social agencies to work for sectarianism's eradication, thereby seeing their function as moral educators using the Gospel as a template for a society rather than examining their own role in its development. In doing so, he married their effectiveness to that of the agencies he sought to educate: a solution that in many ways abdicated responsibility from the state as well as the church for this issue.

By the mid-1980s, however, after a sustained period of speaking out against sectarian violence at funerals and in the public square in a manner that was motivated by the search for truth,[134] a sea change in Daly's under-standing of the matter can be seen. Sectarianism was now 'a disgrace to a community of Christians',[135] and Daly began to see it as a personal as well as structural matter – the eradication of which the churches, as communities of believers rather than institutions, should take responsibility for:

> The persistent anti-Roman element in much popular Protestantism is not unimportant in community conflict in the North. The Catho-lic Church must pay serious attention to it and earnestly seek ways in which it might be lessened and eventually removed. Catholic bishops, clergy, and laity must be particularly sensitive to this problem, and must do everything possible, in their words and by their lives, to witness to the true nature and authentic teaching of the Catholic Church.
>
>   Anti-Catholic prejudice is not, however, a problem to be solved by Catholics alone. The existence and the persistence of this prejudice is a problem also for the Protestant churches. They have a Christian respon-sibility to seek to become more accurately informed about the Catholic Church, its self-understanding, its teaching, its beliefs, its worship, and its practices, and to help their members to "represent the condition [of Catholics] with truth and fairness".[136]

In a process reminiscent of the individual and collective praxis of Libera-tion theology and which had been called for by *Unitatis Redintegratio*,[137] Christians were being asked to develop a greater self-awareness: 'We Catho-lics and Protestants must both make determined efforts to identify the ele-ments in our own community's behaviour which cause suspicion or fear or prejudice in the minds of the other community.'[138] Such an examination of conscience leading to personal repentance would also be communal 'so that Catholic and Protestant Churches may be able to speak the truth about one another and to one another in love, and that the disagreements which persist may at least be based upon accurate understanding.'[139] He was to reiterate this suggestion in his response to the 1993 Document on Sectarianism,[140] stating that 'there is a great need for repentance and conversion, at an indi-vidual level and at community level, beginning with ourselves.'[141]

This would bring about change, which would come through mutual understanding, a concept first mooted by Daly in 1988: 'Each community and each Christian communion must try to accept the others as the oth-ers understand and define themselves.'[142] This mutual understanding and acceptance could only be achieved by dialogue (a theme that was to recur throughout Daly's bishopric and once more highlighted the influence of Vat-ican II on his thinking) and regular interaction:

> Contact on a regular basis can lead to trust and even friendship and friendship can dissolve mistrust and suspicion and prejudice. . . . Social contact is not to be despised; it can break the ice. But we should all try

to move on from there to a more serious kind of contact, when gradually deeper misunderstandings may be clarified or removed and where we can talk honestly with one another and speak the truth as we see it to one another, but in love.[143]

Through such a process of mutual understanding and dialogue, combined with a renewed self-awareness, Christians would be working towards the creation of the Peaceable Kingdom by providing an authentic example of personal and communal reconciliation crucial to the creation of peace in Northern Ireland. Daly was thus reorienting the mission of the Catholic Church in two ways: first, by encouraging ecumenism, and second, by showing himself to be committed to the new model of church-state relations which defined the church as an influencer and expected it to assist in the transformation of the world, starting with itself, before going on to work as a prophetic voice. Sadly, the effectiveness of this is questionable. As Daly himself commented in 1999 during the Drumcree crisis:

> Many of us in the Churches genuinely thought that sectarianism was lessening. We are dismayed to find out how little real progress has been made at grassroots level, and at how deeply ingrained sectarianism still is in Northern society. We perhaps overestimated the effects on public opinion at large of the cordial relations which have so long and so visibly existed between the Church leaders and many of the clergy in all the churches.[144]

Ecumenism and reconciliation

In both Matthew's and Luke's versions of the Sermon on the Mount, Jesus places emphasis upon the need for constant introspection, insight, and self-understanding if one is going to criticise or offer advice to another: 'Why do you see the speck in your neighbour's eye, but do not notice the log in your own eye?'[145] In a society riven by division, to which churches and faith-based organisations sought to act as a moral imagination, this teaching took on a heightened urgency. As early as 1975, Daly was calling for action based upon this Gospel teaching, arguing in a speech given to participants in the Ballymascanlon talks[146] that 'the church must be undergoing a continual self-examination and purification in order to rid herself of any compromise with the ideologies and powers of the world.'[147] Such a comment was not meant to encourage an isolationist stance within such conversations but rather promoted an almost Jesuitical level of self-examination allowing for the self-understanding and discernment necessary for meaningful dialogue with 'the other' to emerge.[148] Churchmen and women needed to rid themselves of sectarianism as well as the hubris and triumphalism that had characterised past public and private manifestations of religion in Ireland.[149] Additionally, the sectarianism, motivated in part by religious beliefs and misunderstandings, that fuelled the conflict in Northern Ireland, and which damaged relations between the Protestant and Catholic churches, bestowed any contact between their representatives with a sensitivity and pressure that was far beyond the norm found in most European countries.[150] Such disordered relationships prevented the personal and communal transformations required for the establishment of the Peaceable Kingdom. If leaders such as Daly were to offer alternative ways of living to the people of Northern Ireland, then the issue of the 'plank' had to be meaningfully and publically addressed by the Protestant and Catholic churches because, as Daly himself argued, 'mutual understanding, respect and acceptance between Christians must surely begin among the clergy.'[151] He put this even more plainly in 1988, stating that 'we cannot be credible to the world unless we live reconciliation ourselves, as well as preaching it.'[152] Only once such conditions were starting, and more importantly were being seen to be fulfilled, could the churches offer the sort of prophetic vision necessary to revolutionise society in Northern Ireland – a task mandated to them through the teachings of Christ and based upon a contextual reading of His teachings.[153] For Daly, himself a committed ecumenist, the answer to this challenge was to be found in inter-church dialogue:

> The very adversity of the times provides a new urgency for ecumenism as it provides a new call to deeper Christian faith and life. Let us have no doubt that ecumenism is an indispensible element in that Christian life and faith. Christians are summoned to ecumenism because it is a command of the Lord. Ecumenism is one irreplaceable element in the profound and radical change which Ireland needs if it is to be worthy of its Christian name.[154]

For the Peaceable Kingdom to be established, relationships had to resemble the cross upon which Jesus had died to atone for humanity's sins, both horizontal and vertical, focusing on love of neighbour through relationships with the 'other' as well as love of God through the search for personal salvation.

Ecumenical contact then provided an opportunity for relationships to be healed and reconciliation to be practised not only to achieve the Christian unity emphasised by Jesus[155] and reiterated by St Paul,[156] but also as a prototype of the Peaceable Kingdom:

> The Churches should be providing a model to the wider community in that which is an essential defining characteristic of the Christian Gospel, namely that is the Gospel of reconciliation. St Augustine said that the church is the reconciled world. *The church should be that section of humanity which is already reconciled and therefore can be a reconciling influence in the human community*. Unless the churches are working positively and courageously for reconciliation between themselves and

within society, then they are failing the Gospel of Christ. It is not that Christianity is failing but that we are failing to be fully Christian.[157]

Such witness was vital to Daly's endeavours to create peace in Northern Ireland through the establishment of the Kingdom of God within communities. The churches were to act as a microcosm of the behaviours and attitudes that needed to be developed within wider society if a meaningful peace, in which relationships were based upon love of God and the resultant love of neighbour rather than an unenthusiastic tolerance of the other, was to be fostered and maintained.

Ecumenical dialogue carried a heavy burden in Northern Ireland and was subject to criticism from many quarters.[158] Not only was it required to deal with issues of doctrinal importance but it was also expected to act as a proxy for the peace process, with the leaders of the churches in Northern Ireland achieving agreement in areas where politicians could not. Such criticisms vastly overestimated the authority of Irish religious institutions which were collectively facing the challenge of secularisation[159] and latterly the child abuse scandals and the collusion of the Catholic hierarchy in their concealment. There were therefore a number of obstacles that needed to be overcome if ecumenical relationships were to provide a reconciling exemplar to Northern Irish society. Daly sums these up thus:

> What motivated the Irish hierarchy in first proposing a Ballymascanlon-type meeting was, I believe, the fear that ecumenism could become identified exclusively with a number of specific practical problems (such as mixed marriage) supposed to be capable of rapid resolution by a change in the rules made by the appropriate authority; and the fear that this would both be an over – simplification of these problems themselves and would be an impoverishment of ecumenism in general.[160]

Ecumenism was not a 'public relations exercise'[161] but rather involved taking part in hard, and often painful, conversations, the avoidance of which was more often than not counter-productive. Neither were such conversations exercises in 'generalised benevolence', the negative consequences of such a style of interaction Daly summarised thus:

> Ill-informed geniality (what *Humani Generis* referred to as "false irenicism") does the ecumenical cause no good. The Catholic who tries to soft-pedal the issue of papal infallibility for diplomatic reasons, or has convinced himself that the dogma is not very important in the articulation of Catholic truth, is simply not a responsible representative of the faith he has called upon to understand and communicate.[162]

Participants were therefore not 'wasting time discussing academic theology'[163] when they could have or should have been discussing the conflict

in Northern Ireland; rather it was the methods employed and their consequences for personal and communal transformation that offered the prototype of the Peaceable Kingdom and opportunities for peace in Northern
Ireland, not the content of the discussion.

> Mutual understanding and respect at religious level will lead to a com-
> mon desire for understanding at the level of communities. It will predis-
> pose efforts, studies, consultations and conversations, designed to reveal
> how the two communities feel about themselves and about one another,
> to uncover and understand their reciprocal hopes, fears, aspirations and
> resentments.[164]

Ecumenical dialogue was not a dilution of faith or a solution to the situation
in Northern Ireland by itself, but instead was a means of understanding,
deepening, and enriching participants' faith in a way that would allow them
'to replace their oppositional identity with an identity based on a firmer
knowledge of their own and the "other's" belief system.'[165]

   The value of ecumenism then was not only a move towards Christian unity,
but the example that it set for the spiritual formation of the person, both in
their relationship with God and their relationships with the communities in
which they lived and worked. Through a reordering of both relationships the
Peaceable Kingdom could begin to emerge. If such peace was to be achieved,
it could only be done in relationship with the 'other'. Daly therefore wanted
inter-church relationships to become a habitual way of acting or a virtue for
Christians and within his lifetime they did for many. On a personal level,
therefore, inter-church contact and dialogue was an essential element in the
spiritual renewal that was needed to enable peaceful relationships to emerge.
'Our discussions about the situation cannot be and are not public relations
exercises. They concern our private relationship with God, our personal
standing under the judgement of God.'[166] This spiritual renewal allowed for
the confidence necessary to engage and reconcile with people perceived as
different. Such confidence was a grace bestowed by God in return for trust in
His will which created an openness to difference and allowed for an appreciate of the value and contribution of divergent belief systems:

> Ecumenism is closely linked with conversion and with spiritual renewal.
> As we Catholics ourselves, as individuals and in our parish communi-
> ties, become converted to Christ and renewed in our relationship with
> him, we shall at the same time become more conscious of the presence
> of Christ in our Protestant and fellow Christians and the work of Christ
> in the Protestant Churches. We shall come to see the signs of Christ's
> truth and power and grace in the lives of Protestants and to praise and
> thank Christ our Lord for them. Nothing that Christ has given to other
> Christian Churches or has done for other Christian communities can
> leave a Catholic indifferent or unmoved.[167]

Such mutual understanding, openness, and trust could, however, only be achieved by ecumenical dialogue which 'should be providing a model for the political dialogue for peace. The churches must give the lead in showing how communities can not only co-exist, but can grow together in love, in acceptance of their differences, in respect for different but sincerely held beliefs.'[168]

Dialogue and the creation of reconciled relationships[169]

The church-community had to perfect itself, before trying to perfect others.[170] Whilst the ecumenical movement showed some evidence that this was occurring, this was, Daly suggested, essentially a clergy-led movement which jarred with his own theology of church.[171] The church-community could not be inward looking, addressing only its own needs and interests. Rather, Daly argued that its focus must be outwards and that everyone, and Christians in particular, were responsible for creating the conditions necessary for peace and reconciliation in Northern Ireland.[172] In 1983, he framed this in terms of the church-community and its role in society:

> The churches should be providing a model to the wider community in that which is an essential defining characteristic of the Christian Gospel, namely that is the Gospel of reconciliation. . . . The church should be that section of humanity which is already reconciled and therefore can be a reconciling influence in the human community. Unless the churches are working positively and courageously for reconciliation between themselves and within society, they are failing the Gospel of Christ. It is not that Christianity is failing but that we are failing to be fully Christian.[173]

Whilst in 1994, he appealed to individuals, stating that 'there is an overwhelming moral imperative obliging *everyone* in our society to do everything in his or her power to bring about peace.'[174] Here, the dualism of Daly's teachings, with its emphasis upon personal as well as communal transformation and repentance, was clearly explained. In stating that 'Unless we are reconciled with one another, we cannot be reconciled with God' (Matthew 5:24–5),[175] Daly was in effect expressing the entire mission of his bishopric: the establishment of the Peaceable Kingdom through reconciled relationships. An individual could only achieve transformation and therefore salvation with the help of a reconciled community, and the community could only reflect the Kingdom of God through the efforts of individuals. Only then could the Peaceable Kingdom emerge.

Relationships built upon the trust and honesty created through dialogue were fundamental then, if the church-community was going to create a new community, just as Christ had done,[176] which was based upon the example set by the New Testament. This dialogue would be based upon a deep and

genuine encounter, the result being the establishment of a contrast community, the members of which acted in opposition to the sectarian society
in which they lived and worked. Such reconciled relationships, both within
the church and within wider society, could be achieved through a dialogue,
or as Daly put it, 'we must talk with one another more',[177] which would
allow those involved to 'accept each other as we are, in our differences.'[178]
The resultant paradigm shift would create a change in thinking and living,
motivating those involved to serve one another and society more widely in
the name of peace. Stephen B Bevans and Roger P Schroder, in their study of
Prophetic Dialogue, defined dialogue and set its parameters thus:

> Dialogue can be understood as the practice of, openness to, fairness and
> frankness with, respect for, sincerity toward and appreciation of people
> of other Christian churches or other religious ways, those who hold a
> commitment to a particular ideology (eg Marxism), those for whom
> faith commitment is meaningless (eg secularists), or those who have no
> faith at all.[179]

The end result of such encounters should, according to Daly, be twofold 'to
exorcise the evil of sectarianism from our society'[180] and that all Christians,
by ridding themselves of the fear of the other through dialogue, exhibit the
fruits of the Holy Spirit in their relationships: love, joy, peace, patience,
kindness, generosity, faithfulness, gentleness, and self-control.[181] However,
before the question or process of dialogue could be approached, each person
had to address the most fundamental question posed in the Gospel: am I a
loving neighbour even to my enemy?

Who is my neighbour?

The issue of relationships with the 'other' or one's neighbour was fundamental to nurturing reconciliation and establishing the Peaceable Kingdom,
and it was therefore central to the purpose, scope (both in terms of membership and discussion topics), and method of dialogue in Northern Ireland.
Daly recognised the inherent parallels in the teachings of Jesus, pointing out
in 1992 that:

> The removal of barriers of hostility between Jew and Samaritan seems
> to have remarkable relevance to the situation here. The Samaritans had
> broken away from both the political and religious unity of the Jewish
> nation, and were despised, excluded, avoided, feared, and even hated
> by the Jews on both counts. Relations between the Samaritans and Jews
> were always tense; and each territory was unfriendly and sometimes
> dangerous to visitors or intruders from the other. Interface tensions
> heightened around times of the great religious and national feasts of
> the respective communities. Periodic outbursts of communal violence

marked the relationships between them. One does not need to point to the parallels with our local situation.[182]

He went on to state:

> Down all the Christian centuries, the term "Samaritan", once an expression of loathing, has been a synonym for charity and goodness. Jesus totally changed the use of words by radically transforming the relationship between Jews and Samaritans, marking the two divided people into one "new creation" in Christ. The power of Jesus Christ to make peace and to unite is not lesser now.[183]

As Jesus taught, and Daly constantly emphasised, the solution to this was to be found in following Jesus's example by building strong and meaningful relationships with the 'other,' most importantly engaging with those who were 'the moral equivalent of lepers'.[184] These relationships were to be founded in (the purist form of) love (agape) and a desire to understand and mitigate the fear associated with difference which was fuelling the conflict in Northern Ireland. The crucifixion of Christ had overcome all barriers and left a world in which reconciliation should have been the norm:

> The heart of the saving work of Jesus was reconciliation; reconciliation of men and women with God and reconciliation of men and women with one another. The most insuperable barriers in the time and culture of Jesus were those dividing Jew and Gentile and those dividing Jew and Samaritan. Both of these are dramatically abolished by the death and resurrection of Jesus Christ and by the work of His Holy Spirit.[185]

Christians through their baptism were expected to embody this new paradigm. Any form of sectarianism or conflict was therefore unthinkable. As Dietrich Bonhoeffer affirmed, 'The church-community can never consent to restrictions of its service of love and compassion toward other human beings.'[186]

Northern Ireland was a society characterised by barriers both physical and psychological which were dangerous to cross. But the answer given by Jesus to the lawyer's question in Luke 10:29, 'and who is my neighbour?' along with his creation of a new community that knew no boundaries or outcasts,[187] challenged Christians to set standards for cross-community contact in the region. The parable told by Jesus in response to the lawyer 'shows love compassionately aiding not only an unknown neighbour, but a known enemy – and the hands of love are those of a Samaritan!'[188] Through this story Jesus was teaching us how to be in relationship with one another. In pointing out this test of their faith to Christians in Northern Ireland, Daly was showing them how their development had to be carried out in relationship with others who stood on the other side of seemingly insurmountable barriers. The process of changing understandings of the concept of neigh-bourliness was itself as important as the action of engaging across deeply entrenched barriers. Here, the intersection of the cross (God [the vertical] and neighbour or community [the horizontal]) becomes real: 'the love of God and the love of one's neighbour converge in the encounter with the other'[189] and the mandate given at baptism is enacted and a new community is created.

The process of dialogue

But this cannot be done without first reaching out to the other. In his study of the 'Woman at the Well',[190] Brent C Neely demonstrates how Jesus effec-tively provided Christians with a 'how to' guide for dialogue:

> For Jesus, simple avoidance of the woman at the well (not to mention Samaria itself) would have been quite advisable. Instead, he taxes him-self, he humbles himself; he takes the initiative; he asks *her* for some-thing. In this dialogue Jesus crosses the line without preconditions, with extraordinary sensitivity and confidence, meeting her at the point of need. In the interchange over Gerizim and Jerusalem, Jesus is confi-dently grounded in truth, truth he uniquely embodies. He knows him-self, his people, his God. Yet, his eschatological vision explodes narrow and nationalist agendas of *every* pedigree (Samaritan or Judean): ulti-mately even Jerusalem is not the point. The Messiah invites her into full fellowship, in spirit and truth, as a Samaritan daughter of YHWH. Reconciliation on every level of being.[191]

But as Knud Jørgensen points out, 'reconciliation is never ahistorical',[192] and must be placed within context with appropriate methods. Daly did this with confidence in his writings and sermons, asking: 'How can mutual understanding of the other community's point of view be attained otherwise than by dialogue? How can a middle ground be explored, otherwise then through dialogue between both parties?'[193] The key here is the term 'mutual understanding' which Daly constantly used and which was part of the lexi-con of cross-community relationships in Northern Ireland, and it is through the example of a dialogical method provided by Jesus that Daly's use of dialogue to achieve this was articulated. The roots of conflict, in particular the Troubles, are to be found in 'the realms of emotion and feeling, fear and suspicion . . . they are not fully amenable to rational explanation of remov-able by rational argument.'[194] The only way to overcome fear and suspicion is to meet with those that you fear and despise which involves enacting change within yourself:

> The Samaritan, the foreigner, makes himself the neighbour and shows me that I have to learn to be a neighbour deep within and that I already

have the answer in myself. I have to become like someone in love, someone whose heart is open to being shaken up by another's need. Then
I find my neighbour, or – better – then I am found by him.[195]

However, coming to understand God's love both for oneself and for others,
thereby moving towards reconciliation, is a task that in the context of a conflict based upon identity requires practical action. This change, according to
Daly, can only be achieved through friendship with members of the 'other'
community, arguing in 1985 that 'when friendships are formed across the
community divide, people can come to trust and respect each other to the
point where difficulties can be honestly faced without risk to the friendship.'[196] Through such friendships, developed through working together
on community development or social action schemes, inter-church prayer
groups, faith discussion groups, or courses on political or social issues, people can begin to understand and demythologise the other: 'meetings of this
kind greatly help people in each community to understand and to sympa-
thise with the feelings and apprehensions of the people in "the other community" and can dispel many fears and misconceptions.'[197] This does not,
however, mean assimilation into one overarching identity or religion. As
Tom Hannon, leader of the Cornerstone Community in Belfast, and one of
the interviewees for my earlier work on inter-church relations in the region,
described it: 'People coming together to pray and share their faith and to
work together doesn't make them into an amorphous mass. We still maintain our identities but we work together.'[198]
    The value of dialogue lies in truly seeing and listening to the other:

> The more deeply we see the goodness of the other, the more we are natu-
> rally inclined to empathise and care for them, and the more we care for
> them, the more we will not want to hurt or harm them. We will know
> the damage that our self-centredness, pride, and antipathy can do, and
> we will naturally be inclined to move away from these things – attrac-
> tive as they can sometimes be – for the *sake of the other*.[199]

It is only through acceptance developed through dialogue that sectarianism
can be eradicated.

Conclusion

The Church, both as an institution and as a collection of believers, needed
to act as a contrast community before its teachings could be taken seriously. Daly comprehended the power of the mote and the beam, and its
special relevance for the Northern Irish context, and this was therefore his
starting point in the creation of the Peaceable Kingdom. Individuals had to
be formed and introduced to the methods of creating an alternative possible future before the hard work of transforming society could begin. Daly
understood and taught that prayer, both contemplative and communal, was

the key to such formation, and he therefore saw this as the starting point of his vision for Northern Ireland. By promoting a reliance upon, and acceptance of, the will of God amongst the laity, Daly was allowing the mission of the Church to emerge. This mission was twofold: not only did it involve the creation of a contract community which acted as an example of the Peaceable Kingdom, but also Daly argued that this should place an emphasis upon the creation of new communities. Mutual understanding, acceptance of the other, a rejection of sectarianism, and an agreement that justice should lie at the heart of all Christian activity would characterise such communities. Only then could the structural injustice, which provided the foundation stone for much of the direct violence in Northern Ireland, be tackled.

Notes

1 'Homily by Cardinal Cahal B Daly', Mass in St Eugene's Cathedral, Derry 1 March 1992 in Northern Ireland Political Collection, Linen Hall Library, Belfast, *Addresses on Peace in Northern Ireland, 1991–1992*, vol. 6, P13583.

2 'The Roots of Peace in the New Testament', Conference on Religion and Violence, Religion and Peace, Auschwitz, Poland, 18–20 May 1998 in Northern Ireland Political Collection, Linen Hall Library, Belfast, *Addresses on Peace in Northern Ireland, 1997–2001*, vol. 8, P13585.

3 'Fourteenth World Day of Peace: Freedom to Trust', Longford, 1 January 1981 in *Addresses on Peace in Northern Ireland, 1976–1983*.

4 'Seek Peace and Pursue It', Homily during Seventh Annual Peace Week, Carmelite Church, 10 March 1981, *Addresses on Peace in Northern Ireland, 1976–1983*.

5 'Reach Out to the Poor' World Day of Peace, St Malachy's Church, Armagh, 1 January 1993 in *Addresses on Peace in Northern Ireland, 1993–1996*, cf. 'The peace which Jesus gives is the peace which he has achieved by his death on the cross accepted voluntarily by Him as a sacrifice of atonement for human sins a sacrifice which we recall and make sacramentally present in our Eucharist, where we have really present to us the body 'given up' for us and the blood 'shed for us and for all so that sins may be forgiven.' 'The Roots of Peace in the New Testament'.

6 Direct violence means that people are murdered; structural violence means that people die as a result of poverty whilst 'cultural violence makes direct violence look, even feel right, or at least not wrong.' Johan Galtung, 'Cultural Violence', *Journal of Peace Research*, 1990, vol. 27, no. 3, pp. 291–305, 291.

7 'Seek Peace and Pursue It'.

8 'The Roots of Peace in the New Testament'.

9 *Gaudium et Spes*, 7 December 1965, §43. See also 'The Role and Responsibility of the Churches in the Northern Crisis', Address to the Dublin University History Society, 8 May 1975, *Addresses on Peace in Northern Ireland, 1968–1975*.

10 Mk 1:15.

11 Lk 4:18–19. cf. Isa 61, 1–2.

12 Lk 4:21.

13 'Fourteenth World Day of Peace: Freedom to Trust', Daly supports this comment with a reference to Rev 21:5, 'He who was seated on the throne said, "See, I am making all things new." '

14 Daly said of St Paul: 'Our desire as Christians should be the same as St Paul that Christ should be proclaimed, that the witness to Christ should be strong in our growingly materialistic modern world. The dominant concern of churches must be with Christ.' 'Preaching the Reconciled Word,' Ecumenical Service in

the Church of the Holy Redeemer, Bray, 20 January 1998 in *Addresses on Peace in Northern Ireland, 1997–2001.*

15 Eph 4:23–24. cf. Rom 13:14, and Gal 3:27.

16 'Northern Ireland Prison Chaplains Association', Address at AGM, Stormont, 1 May 1985 in Northern Ireland Political Collection, Linen Hall Library, Belfast, *Addresses on Peace in Northern Ireland, 1984–1986,* vol. 3, P13580.

17 1 Cor 13:2. 'And if I have prophetic powers, and understand all mysteries and all knowledge, and if I have all faith, so as to remove mountains, but do not have love, *I am nothing.*' Emphasis added.

18 Jn 13:34–35. 'I give you a new commandment that you love one another. Just as I have loved you, you also should love one another. By this everyone will know that you are my disciples, if you have love for one another.'

19 'Peace and Reconciliation in Northern Ireland', Archbishop's House, Birmingham, 7 November 1995 in *Addresses on Peace in Northern Ireland, 1993–1996.*

20 'In Christian theology there are three words to say "love": eros, phillia and agape. The New Testament privileges agape as the Christian way par excellence to be understood as Christian love and also as the definition of God Himself, as says the 1st Letter of John 4:8 "God is love" The word used there is agape.' Maria Clara Lucchetti Bingemer, 'The Journey of Etty Hillesum from Eros to Agape', in KAD Smelik (ed.), *The Ethics and Religious Philosophy of Etty Hillesum: Proceedings of the Etty Hillesum Conference at Ghent University, Jan 2014* (Leiden, Boston: Brill, 2017), pp. 68–89, 68–69.

21 Anders Nygren, *Agape and Eros,* trans. Philip S Watson (London: SPCK, 1953) summarised in Lucchetti Bingemer, 'The Journey of Etty Hillesum from Eros to Agape' p. 69.

22 Phil 2:3–4.

23 Lk 1:26–38.

24 Mt 21:12–17; Mk 11:15–19; Lk 19:45–48; and Jn 2:13–16.

25 CS Lewis, *The Four Loves* (London: Geoffrey Bles, 1960), p. 148.

26 Mt 5:3–11 and 1 Cor 13:4–8.

27 Inter alia: 'Mercy, Justice and Peace', Ardagh and Clonmacnois Diocesan Pilgrimage to Knock, 6 September 1981 in *Addresses on Peace in Northern Ireland, 1976–1983;* 'A Call to Commitment', St Patrick's Eve Service, St Anne's Cathedral, Belfast, 16 March 1987 in *Addresses on Peace in Northern Ireland, 1987–1988;* 'Community Conflict: Christ's Answer', Contribution to "Opinion-Makers" Series, 15 April 1990 in *Addresses on Peace in Northern Ireland, 1989–1990;* and 'Peace for God's Family', World Day of Peace, St Malachy's Armagh, 1 January 1994 in *Addresses on Peace in Northern Ireland, 1993–1996.*

28 Summarised from Robert Spitzer SJ, *God So Loved the World: Clues to Our Transcendent Destiny from the Revelation of Jesus* (San Francisco: Ignatius Press, 2016), p. 23.

29 Gal 5:22–23. See 'Peace for God's Family'.

30 'Peace for God's Family'. Cf. Phil 2:5.

31 'Mercy, Justice and Peace'.

32 'A Call to Commitment'.

33 'God: the Master of the Impossible', Armagh Diocesan Mass for Peace, St Patrick's Cathedral, Armagh, 21 July 1996 in *Addresses on Peace in Northern Ireland, 1993–1996.*

34 See for example 'From the White Paper to a New Beginning', 23 March 1973 in *Addresses on Peace in Northern Ireland, 1968–1975* for an exposition of his views on the causes of the conflict.

35 'Towards a True and Lasting Peace', Fitzroy Presbyterian Church, Belfast, 26 November 1995 in *Addresses on Peace in Northern Ireland, 1993–1996.* Cf.

'I believe that a mighty task of conversion and repentance awaits us in each of our Northern communities. Conversion is an individual struggle; but it must also be a community struggle. Communities traditionally hostile to one another and suspicious of one another, communities who have each mutually suffered at the hands of some members of the other community, must undertake the task of reaching out to one another in forgiveness and in friendship. Our two communities must each begin to learn to trust the other. The Christian must be ready to take the first step, and then be prepared to go the extra mile.' 'Peace for God's Family'.

36 Lk 15:11–32.

37 Spitzer, *God So Loved the World*, p. 99.

38 Alan J Torrance, 'Forgiveness and Christian Character: Reconciliation, Exemplarism and the Shape of Moral Theology', *Studies in Christian Ethics*, 2017, vol. 30, no. 3, pp. 293–313, 308.

39 'Reconciliation in a Northern Ireland Perspective', For Christian Democracy, 9 January 1991 in *Addresses on Peace in Northern Ireland, 1991–1992*.

40 'Northern Ireland: Peace or Disaster', Statement at Beginning of All-party Talks, 9 June 1996 in *Addresses on Peace in Northern Ireland, 1993–1996*.

41 'Peace: A Gift from God, A Task for Man', World Day of Peace, Longford, 1 January 1982 in *Addresses on Peace in Northern Ireland, 1976–1983*. Emphasis added.

42 See for example the life of Jewish mystic Etty Hillesum whose prayer life gave her the courage to act during the Nazi pogroms in the Netherlands. Etty Hillesum, *An Interrupted Life: The Diaries and Letters of Etty Hillesum 1941–43*, trans. Arnold J Pomerans (London: Persephone Books, 1999). My thanks to Amber Giles for bringing this mystic and writer to my attention.

43 'Daniel Berrigan on Contemporary Developments in American Spirituality', *Tikkin*, September--October 1998, vol. 13, no. 5, p. 48.

44 Cahal Daly, 'Prayer in the Modern World', *Review for Religious*, 1972, vol. 31, no. 6, pp. 901–914, 906.

45 'Reconciliation: The Path to Peace', Address to Mark the World Day of Peace, 1 January 1975, *Addresses on Peace in Northern Ireland, 1968–1975*.

46 'Reconciliation: The Path to Peace'.

47 'Justice through Peace', Celebration of the 750th Anniversary of the Death of St Francis of Assisi, 4 October 1976, *Addresses on Peace in Northern Ireland, 1976–1983*. cf. We can show our desire for peace – as you have done by marching in silent witness here today. We can think peace, speak peace, make peace, as all the Churches in Ireland have asked us to do this Christmastide. We can be prepared to suffer for peace – to suffer criticism, opposition, unpopularity for peace. Christ did more He smuggled, not bombs and arms, but love and peace, forgiveness and reconciliation into mankind's City of Hate. And they crucified him for it. But that is how he became our peace.' 'Blessed are the Peace-Makers', Address at the conclusion of the peace walk organised by 'Stand Against Violence Everywhere', Navan, 22 December 1974, *Addresses on Peace in Northern Ireland, 1968–1975*.

48 'Funeral Mass for Jim McCartney', St Paul's Church, Belfast, 13 March 1989, *Addresses on Peace in Northern Ireland, 1989–1990*.

49 For examples of this see: 'Peace Through Tolerance' World Day of Peace 1988, St Anne's, Derriaghy, 3 January 1988; 'The Challenge to Christian Conscience', Recent Events in West Belfast, 22 March 1988; and 'Funeral Masses for the Three Victims of the "Avenue Bar" Shooting', Holy Cross Church, Ardoyne, St Malachy's Church, Finaghy, and St Patrick's Church, Donegall St, Belfast, 18 May 1988, all in *Addresses on Peace in Northern Ireland, 1987–1988*.

50 'Statement: Fear and Anger in both Communities', 28 October 1993, *Addresses on Peace in Northern Ireland, 1993–1996.*
51 My thanks to Karin S Tate and Gabriele Penna, who took part in this procession, for sharing their memories of the event with me.
52 'God: Master of the Impossible'.
53 'Sermon for "World Peace Day"', St Mel's Cathedral, 1 January 1969, *Addresses on Peace in Northern Ireland, 1968–1975.*
54 See Holy See, *Catechism of the Catholic Church* (1994), §1328–1332 www.vati can.va/archive/ENG0015/_INDEX.HTM (accessed 21 August 2019) for explanations of the various names given to this sacrament.
55 Paul VI, *Lumen Gentium*, 21 November 1964, §11, www.vatican.va/archive/ hist_councils/ii_vatican_council/documents/vat-ii_const_19641121_lumen-gen tium_en.html (accessed 21 August 2019).
56 *Catechism of the Catholic Church*, §1325–1326.
57 The Creed is recited after the Homily in Mass. Radcliffe describes the Creed thus: 'In the Creed we declared our belief in God the Creator, expressing our gratitude for his gifts.' p. 92. For a full explanation of the Creed see Timothy Radcliffe OP, *Why Go to Church? The Drama of the Eucharist* (London: Bloomsbury, 2008), pp. 64–91.
58 Cahal Daly, *We Believe* (Dublin: Catholic Truth Society, 1969), p. 7.
59 'Blessed are the Peace-Makers'.
60 'Seek Peace and Pursue It'.
61 Cahal Daly, *Steps on my Pilgrim Journey: Memories and Reflections* (Dublin: Veritas, 1988), p. 64. For a full explanation of the role of the Homily in the Mass see Radcliffe, *Why Go to Church?* pp. 42–52.
62 *Layman's Daily Missal, Prayer Book and Ritual* (London: Burns and Oates, 1966), p. 889.
63 Gutiérrez, *A Theology of Liberation*, p. 119.
64 Gutiérrez, *The Power of the Poor in History*, p. 106.
65 Donal Dorr, *Spirituality and Justice* (Maryknoll, NY: Orbis Books, 1985), p. 247.
66 Cahal Daly, *Peace the Work of Justice: Addresses on the Northern Tragedy, 1973–79* (Dublin: Veritas, 1979), p. 35.
67 Isa 53:5.
68 'Masses in Donaghmore and Cappagh', 24 March 1991 in *Addresses on Peace in Northern Ireland, 1991–1992.* Other examples of Daly's writings on redemptive suffering can be found in 'Looking to the Future', Lecture under the auspices of the Irish School of Ecumenics, Columbanus Community of Reconciliation, Belfast, 21 November 1988, *Addresses on Peace in Northern Ireland, 1987–1988,* and 'Gospel Values in a Situation of Conflict: Northern Ireland', Parliamentary Wives' Christian Group, London, 14 March 1990, Northern Ireland Political Collection, Linen Hall Library, Belfast, P7647.
69 'Masses in Donaghmore and Cappagh'.
70 Jn 9:3 'he was born blind so that God's works might be revealed in him.'
71 John Paul II, *Salvifici Doloris*, 11 February 1984, §22, http://w2.vatican.va/con tent/john-paul-ii/en/apost_letters/1984/documents/hf_jp-ii_apl_11021984_sal vifici-doloris.html (accessed 21 August 2019).
72 *Salvifici Doloris*, §22, cf. 'It will be the bishop's task to raise up from among his own people, especially the sick and those oppressed by hardship, some souls to offer prayers and penance to God with a wide – open heart for the evangelization of the world.' Paul VI, *Ad Gentes, On the Mission of the Church,* 7 December 1965, §38, www.vatican.va/archive/hist_councils/ii_vatican_coun cil/documents/vat-ii_decree_19651207_ad-gentes_en.html (accessed 21 August 2019).

73 For example, 'For mortals it is impossible, but for God all things are possible', Matt 19:26, and 'All things can be done for the one who believes.' Mark 9:23.
74 'Peace is Mightier than the Bomb', Address for 1979 World Day of Peace', 1 January 1979, *Addresses on Peace in Northern Ireland, 1976–1983*. Cf. 'Peace: A Gift of God, A Task for Man' World Day of Peace, Longford, 1 January 1982, *Addresses on Peace in Northern Ireland, 1976–1983*, and 'Prayer in the Modern World', p. 13.
75 'Homily at Closing Mass for "World Watch '85"', Carnlough, 28 July 1985 in *Addresses on Peace in Northern Ireland, 1984–1986*. Cf. 'The Politics of Peace'.
76 'Prayer Power for Peace', St Malachy's Church, Armagh' 18 August 1991, *Addresses on Peace in Northern Ireland, 1991–1992*.
77 St Augustine, *Homilies on the First Letter of St John*, cited in Radcliffe, *Why Go to Church?* p. 95.
78 'Peace and the Sacredness of Human Life', New Year Address in Longford to mark the Tenth Annual World Day of Peace, 1 January 1977, *Addresses on Peace in Northern Ireland, 1976–1983*.
79 Benedict Viviano, *The Kingdom of God in History* (Wilmington, DL: Michael Glazier, 1988), p. 149.
80 Kenneth E Bailey, *Jesus Through Middle Eastern Eyes: Cultural Studies in the Gospels* (London: SPCK, 2008), p. 117.
81 Rowan Williams, *Being Christian* (London: SPCK, 2014), p. 63.
82 Mt 6:9–10.
83 *Mass and the World of Work*.
84 'Peace: A Gift of God, A Task for Man'.
85 Williams, *Being Christian*, pp. 63–64.
86 'Prayer in the Search for Peace', Cathedral Church of St Mary and St Boniface, Plymouth, 27 November 1998, *Addresses on Peace in Northern Ireland, 1997–2001*.
87 Miroslav Volf, *A Public Faith: How Followers of Christ Should Serve the Common Good* (Grand Rapids, MI: Brazos Press, 2011), p. 25.
88 Dorr, *Spirituality and Justice*, p. 227.
89 Mk 6:5–6.
90 Mt 27:46. 'And at about three o'clock Jesus cried with loud voice. . . . "My God, my God, why have you forsaken me?"'
91 Dorr, *Spirituality and Justice*, p. 228.
92 J Matthew Ashley, 'Contemplation in the Action of Justice: Ignacio Ellacuría and Ignatian Spirituality', in Kevin F Burke and Robert Lassalle-Klein (eds.), *Love That Produces Hope, the Thought of Ignacio Ellacuría* (Collegeville, MN: Liturgical Press, 2006), pp. 144–168, 147.
93 Daniel G Groody (ed.), *Gustavo Gutiérrez Spiritual Writings* (Maryknoll, NY: Orbis, 2011), p. 36.
94 Radcliffe, *Why Go to Church?* p. 93.
95 Williams, *Being Christian*, p. 63.
96 Lk 11:9.
97 'God: Master of the Impossible'.
98 The term 'Christian living' is one that Daly uses frequently. Through it he develops an ideal of what the kingdom should look like and argues that it is only through the 'lived Gospel' that Christians can gain credibility within society: 'Christian living is simply a way of believing; indeed it is the authentic way of Christian believing. Christian living is the Creed spelt out in actions and habits of action. It is the practice of the Gospel.' 'Listening to God in the City', St Thomas Parish Church, Belfast, 14 January 1990, *Addresses on Peace in Northern Ireland, 1989–1990*. See also 'Christmas and the Cry of the Poor', St Pater's Cathedral, Belfast, 13 December 1987, *Addresses on Peace in Northern Ireland, 1987–1988*.

99   Cahal Daly, *Christian Authority and Christian Responsibility* (Hoddesdon: Crux Publications, 1971), p. 1.
100 Timothy Radcliffe OP, *What Is the Point in Being a Christian?* (London: Bloomsbury, 2013), pp. 41–46.
101 Cited in Paul Murray OP, *Aquinas at Prayer: The Bible, Mysticism and Poetry* (London: Bloomsbury, 2013), p. 101.
102 Dorr, *Spirituality and Justice*, p. 225.
103 Radcliffe, *What Is the Point of Being a Christian?*, p. 43.
104 Robert Ellsberg (ed.), *Dorothy Day: Selected Writings* (Maryknoll, NY: Orbis, 2005), p. 181.
105 Mic 6:8.
106 Ashley, 'Contemplation in the Action of Justice', p. 154.
107 Groody, *Gustavo Gutiérrez*, p. 35.
108 *Gaudium et Spes*, §40.
109 As Gerald O'Collins SJ puts it: 'The two constitutions on the church approved by the council understood the church to be the "sacrament" or visible and holy sign of what the invisible Christ does (*Lumen Gentium*), and to be a servant church of repentant sinners who embrace a ministry of justice and peace for the whole of humanity (*Gaudium et Spes*). *Lumen Gentium* saw the church as the sacrament of what Christ has done and is doing through the Holy Spirit to bring together all human beings into the kingdom of God.' *Living Vatican II: The 21st Council for the 21st Century* (New York: Paulist Press, 2006), p. 148.
110 *Lumen Gentium*, §40.
111 *Gaudium et Spes*, §43.
112 Alexander Nava, *The Mystical and Prophetic Thought of Simone Weil and Gustavo Gutiérrez: Reflections on the Mystery and Hiddenness of God* (New York: State University of New York Press, 2001), p. 9.
113 John Dear, *Daniel Berrigan SJ Essential Writings* (Maryknoll, NY: Orbis Books, 2009), p. 178.
114 Ellsberg, *Dorothy Day*, p. xx.
115 Cited in Gerhard Lohfink, *Jesus and Community: The Social Dimension of Christian Faith*, trans. John P Galvin (Philadelphia: Fortress Press, 1984), p. 102.
116 Dietrich Bonhoeffer, *Discipleship*, trans. Barbara Green and Reinhard Krauss, Dietrich Bonhoeffer Works, vol. 4 (Minneapolis: Fortress Press, 2003), p. 234.
117 Lohfink, *Jesus and Community*, p. 122.
118 He did, however, argue that: 'Catholics have special responsibilities in respect of ecumenical outreach at this time. Individually and collectively, each of us and each of our communities must become active agents of reconciliation, especially with our Protestant neighbours. For a variety of historical and theological reasons, the Roman Catholic Church seems to inspire fear and suspicion in the minds of some Protestants. Some of this is undoubtedly the result of sectarianism, which is still an active and evil force in our society, even though the churches are officially committed to eliminating it, some of this sectarianism is still sadly being disseminated from some platforms and even from a few pulpits.' From 'Peace Process to Peace', O'Carolan Harp Festival, Keadue, Official Opening Address, 6 August 1995 in *Addresses on Peace in Northern Ireland, 1993–1996*.
119 Lohfink, *Jesus and Community*, p. 147.
120 Grassi, *Informing the Future*, p. 152.
121 Marianne Elliott, *When God Took Sides: Religion and Identity in Ireland* (Oxford: Oxford University Press, 2009), p. 4.

122 In the discourse surrounding sectarianism, 'religion . . . indicated the complete spectrum of religious expression and not simply doctrine. It includes attitudes, values, forms of worship, language, community structure, and outreach.' Joseph Liechty and Cecelia Clegg, *Moving Beyond Sectarianism: Religion, Conflict, and Reconciliation in Northern Ireland* (Dublin: The Columba Press, 2001), p. 113.

123 Joseph Liechty, 'The Nature of Sectarianism Today', in Trevor Williams and Alan Falconer (ed.), *Sectarianism, Papers of the 1994 Corrymeela Ecumenical Conference* (Dublin: Dominican Publications, 1995), pp. 9–29, 19.

124 John D Brewer, 'Sectarianism and Racism, and their parallels and differences', *Ethnic and Racial Studies*, 1992, vol. 15, no. 3, pp. 352–364, 359.

125 Liechty, 'The Nature of Sectarianism Today', p. 14.

126 Cahal Daly and Eric Gallagher, *Violence in Ireland: A Report to the Churches* (Dublin: Veritas, 1976), p. 71.

127 See Power, *From Ecumenism to Community Relations*, pp. 19–20.

128 'Northern Ireland: Is There a Way Forward?' Address to 'Challenge 90' Course for Business Leaders, Millisle, 21 September 1988, *Addresses on Peace in Northern Ireland, 1987–1988*.

129 'The Role and Responsibility of the Churches in the Northern Crisis'.

130 Elliott's *When God Took Sides* provides ample evidence to the contrary as does John D Brewer and Gareth Higgins, *Anti-Catholicism in Northern Ireland, 1600–1998: The Mote and the Beam* (London: Macmillan, 1998).

131 'The Role and Responsibility of the Churches'.

132 See Second Vatican Council, *Unitatis Redintegratio: Decree on Ecumenism*, §4, 21 November 1964, for Vatican II's teaching on this matter. www.vatican.va/ archive/hist_councils/ii_vatican_council/documents/vat-ii_decree_19641121_ unitatis-redintegratio_en.html (accessed 13 August 2019).

133 'The Role and Responsibility of the Churches'.

134 See for example 'Witnessing the Struggle: Struggling to Witness'.

135 'Peace: A Better way to Justice'.

136 'Northern Ireland: Risk and Opportunity for the Churches'.

137 'Catholics, in their ecumenical work, must assuredly be concerned for their separated brethren, praying for them, keeping them informed about the Church, making the first approaches toward them. But their primary duty is to make a careful and honest appraisal of whatever needs to be done or renewed in the Catholic household itself, in order that its life may bear witness more clearly and faithfully to the teachings and institutions which have come to it from Christ through the Apostles.' *Unitatis Redintegratio: Decree on Ecumenism*, §4.

138 'Address for the Week of Prayer for Christian Unity'.

139 'Address for the Week of Prayer for Christian Unity'.

140 The Working Party on Sectarianism, *Sectarianism: A Discussion Document* (Belfast: Department of Social Issues of the Irish Inter-Church Meeting, 1993).

141 'Response to the Discussion Document on "Sectarianism"', Irish inter-Church Meeting, Newry, 8–9 October 1993, *Addresses on Peace in Northern Ireland, 1993–1996*.

142 'Northern Ireland: Is There a Way Forward?'

143 'The Response of the Churches', Facing up to Sectarianism, Conference of the Four Church Leaders, 1 December 1992, *Addresses on Peace in Northern Ireland, 1991–1992*.

144 'Peace Is Still Possible'.

145 Mt 7:3; cf. Lk 6:41.

146 The Ballymascanlon talks were an early iteration of the Irish Inter-Church Meeting, see Power, *From Ecumenism to Community Relations*, pp. 20–25.
147 'The Role and Responsibility of the Churches in the Northern Crisis'.
148 Phil 1:8–11.
149 Rom 12:16.
150 Much of this pressure centred on demands that any inter-church or ecumenical talks act as a proxy peace process.
151 Cahal Daly, 'Ecumenism in Ireland Now: Problems and Hopes', *Irish Theological Quarterly*, 1978, vol. 45, no. 1, pp. 3–27, 13.
152 'Looking to the Future'.
153 'We all have a responsibility as Christians in the face of this situation. Our responsibility is one with our response to the words of Christ in the Gospel.' 'Peace to St Patrick's Sons', Holy Year Celebration in St Mel's Cathedral, Longford, 18 March 1974 Cf. 'what all we churchmen need to aspire to today is not survival but prophecy. Prophets have never been noted for referring back to assemblies or consulting flocks.' 'Response to Auditor's Paper at Trinity College Theological Society, Dublin', 2 November 1972, both in *Addresses on Peace in Northern Ireland, 1968–1975*.
154 'Ecumenical Service in the Octagon of the University of Ulster at Coleraine', Address for Week of Prayer for Christian Unity, 22 January 1986 in *Addresses on Peace in Northern Ireland, 1984–1986*.
155 Jn 13:35.
156 1 Cor 12:12.
157 'Building Bridges in a Divided Community', St Anne's Cathedral and Servite Priory, Benburb, 22 and 23 March 1983 in *Addresses on Peace in Northern Ireland, 1976–1983*. Emphasis added.
158 See Maria Power, 'Of Some Symbolic Importance But Not Much Else: The Irish Inter-Church Meeting and Ecumenical Dialogue in Northern Ireland Since 1980', *Journal of Ecumenical Studies*, 2008, vol. 43, no. 1, pp. 111–123, for an exposition of these arguments.
159 Daly, 'Ecumenism in Ireland Now', p. 7. Daly also cites the influence of secularisation in improving inter-church relationships when he said, 'We have come increasingly to see that what distinguishes all Christians from an unbelieving secular world is incomparably more important than what divides us from one another.' 'Hope in Our Land', Address in College Chapel, Trinity College Dublin, 15 November 1989 in *Addresses on Peace in Northern Ireland, 1989–1990*. Such sentiments were a common theme in the interviews conducted for Power, *From Ecumenism to Community Relations*.
160 Daly, 'Ecumenism in Ireland Now', p. 4.
161 'The Role and Responsibility of the Churches in the Northern Crisis'.
162 Robert McAfee Brown, *The Ecumenical Revolution: An Interpretation of the Catholic-Protestant Dialogue* (London: Burns and Oates, 1967), p. 67 cited in Daly, 'Ecumenism in Ireland Now', p. 5.
163 Daly, 'Ecumenism in Ireland Now', p. 6.
164 'The Role and Responsibility of the Churches in the Northern Crisis'. The validity of such a comment was shown by Power, *From Ecumenism to Community Relations*.
165 Maria Power, 'Getting to Know the Other: Inter-church Groups in Belfast and the Peace Process', in Marianne Elliott (ed.), *The Long Road to Peace in Northern Ireland*, 2nd Edition (Liverpool: Liverpool University Press, 2007), pp. 192–206, 193.
166 'The Role and Responsibility of the Churches in the Northern Crisis'.
167 'Hope in Our Land'. cf. 'ecumenism, if it is authentic, instead of weakening our own faith and tradition will deepen and strengthen them.' 'Dialogue for

Peace', Address for World Day for Peace, 1 January 1983, *Addresses for Peace in Northern Ireland, 1976–1983.*

168 'Dialogue for Peace'.

169 Interestingly, such dialogue and its role in creating reconciled relationships did not extend to support for integrated education in Northern Ireland, and it is for this reason that I have not included a section on the topic. A study of the reasons behind the Catholic Church's reluctance to support the integrated education movement in the region is much needed.

170 In 1988 Daly argued that 'We cannot be credible to the word unless we live in reconciliation ourselves, as well as preaching it.' 'Looking to the Future'.

171 '[E]cumenism is therefore a Christian duty. Ecumenism cannot be left for specialists to do for us; we all have a responsibility; we cannot discharge our responsibilities by setting up committees and pointing to them as a sufficient sign of our commitment; or by drawing up reports and then doing nothing about them or by waiting until the 'others change'; or by saying 'it's up to them' to make the first move; or by deferring action until the ecumenical or political climate is more favourable, or until our own people, or our own clergy, are less likely to protest and resist. So far as ecumenism is concerned 'now is the acceptable time', 'Ecumenical Service in the Octagon of the University of Ulster at Coleraine'.

172 In this he was supported by St Paul who in his letter to the Romans reminded the community their responsibility to live faithfully to the teachings of Jesus. He admonished them: 'For if God did not spare the natural branches (who failed in the work of reconciliation), perhaps he will not spare you.' Rom 11:21.

173 'Building Bridges in a Divided Community'.

174 Day of Prayer for Peace in Bosnia and Ireland', St Patrick's Cathedral, Armagh, 23 January 1994 in *Addresses on Peace in Northern Ireland, 1993–1996.* Emphasis added. Cf. 'Reconciliation through dialogue leading to the establishment of mutually agreed structures of justice and lasting peace is an urgent task facing all Christians in this country at this time.' 'A Time for Conversion', Lenten Message, Lent 1987 in *Addresses on Peace in Northern Ireland 1987–1988.*

175 'Northern Ireland Prison Chaplains' Association'.

176 As Bevans and Schroeder tell us: 'Jesus' method was one of dialogue. . . . Jesus remembered in the Gospels as a man of dialogue, open to foreigners, to people of a non-Jewish background like the Samaritan woman (the story is a model of dialogue) and the Canaanite woman, responsive to the pleas of the centurion, or Jairus and blind Bartimaeus.' Stephen B Bevans and Roger P Schroder, *Prophetic Dialogue: Reflections on Christian Mission Today* (New York: Orbis, 2011), p. 25.

177 'Dialogue for Peace'.

178 'Letter to a Northern Protestant', For Publication in the *Irish Times,* June 1979 in *Addresses on Peace in Northern Ireland, 1976–1983.*

179 Bevans and Schroder, *Prophetic Dialogue,* p. 21.

180 'Building Bridges in a Divided Community'.

181 Gal 5:22–23. Daly reflects on these and their relationship to dialogue and reconciliation in 'Renewed Heart for Peace', Address for World Day of Peace 1 January 1984 in *Address on Peace in Northern Ireland, 1984–1986.*

182 'Community Conflict'.

183 'Community Conflict'. Cf. 'Let us remember that Jesus changed the very meaning of the term 'Samaritan". . . . In Christ therefore there is neither Jew nor Gentile; both are reconciled to become one new thing in Christ.' 'Towards a True and Lasting Peace'; and Gal 3:28.

184 NT Wright, *Jesus and the Victory of God* (London: SPCK, 2012), p. 267.

185 'Community Conflict'.
186 Bonhoeffer, *Discipleship*, p. 236.
187 'The four Gospels make clear that Jesus exhibited great affection, understanding, compassion and self-sacrifice for His friends and disciples. But He went far beyond His circle of friends, and even beyond the wider circle of those who are easily loved – even beyond the much wider circle of those who are acceptable. He sought out the poor, outcasts, and even the most egregious sinners. Jesus wanted to be a healing, reconciling and compassionate force for those who were in the greatest need of His and the Father's love.' Spitzer, *God So Loved the World*, p. 91.
188 Willard M Swartley, *Covenant of Peace: The Missing Peace in New Testament Theology and Ethics* (Grand Rapids, MI: William B Eerdmans Publishing Company, 2006), p. 146.
189 R Zimmerman, 'The Etho-poietic of the Parable of the Good Samaritan (Lk 10:25–37). The Ethics of Seeing in a Culture Looking the Other Way', *Verbum et Ecclesia*, 2008, vol. 29, no. 1, pp. 269–292, 280.
190 Jn 4:1–26.
191 Brent Neely, 'Jesus at the Well (John 4:4–42): Our Approach to the "Other"', *Theology*, 2018, vol. 121, no. 5, pp. 332–340, 336.
192 Knud Jørgensen, 'Mission as a Ministry of Reconciliation: Hope in a Fragile World', *Transformation*, 2014, vol. 31, no. 4, pp. 264–272, 268.
193 'Thoughts on Drumcree', 10 July 1998 in *Addresses on Peace in Northern Ireland 1997–2001*.
194 'Northern Ireland: Risk and Opportunity for the Churches', Conference on the Role of the Churches in British-Irish Relationships, 26 November 1985 in *Addresses on Peace in Northern Ireland, 1984–1986*.
195 Benedict XVI, *Jesus of Nazareth*, p. 197.
196 'Northern Ireland: Risk and Opportunity for the Churches'. Daly describes friendship thus: 'Friendship is a special kind of relationship. It has been said that true friendship either finds its partners equal or feels driven to create equality between them.' 'Reach Out to the Poor', World Day of Peace, St Malachy's Church, Armagh, 1 January 1993 in *Addresses on Peace in Northern Ireland, 1993–1996*.
197 'Northern Ireland: Risk and Opportunity for the Churches'.
198 Power, *From Ecumenism to Community Relations*, p. 137.
199 Spitzer, *God So Loved the World*, p. 30.

3   Social and economic justice

Daly believed that the creation of a just society was the only way to establish the Peaceable Kingdom in Northern Ireland. In a sermon outlining his support for the Birmingham Six, Daly quoted German Lutheran theologian and committed ecumenist, Jürgen Moltmann, who argued 'Peace is not the absence of violence but the presence of justice. It is justice which creates peace, not vice-versa, and so every act of justice is an act of peace.'[1] He reiterated this belief in his autobiography ten years later:

> There has never been any doubt in my mind but that peace and justice are inseparable and that the only viable way to peace in the North is through working for justice and for deprived communities and thus demonstrating that there are effective, non-violent ways of effecting change in the direction of justice, whereas violence only destroys the work of justice. The past thirty years has brought ample proof of this.[2]

In Northern Ireland, the tensions and inherent difficulties with conscience forming and future creating were at their strongest in the pursuit of social and economic justice. Most people abhorred paramilitary and state violence, and understood that the creation of just political structures could bring about a cessation of that violence, but many of those living in Northern Ireland did not witness the 'wastelands of human dignity'[3] that were poverty, marginalisation, and deprivation as a part of their day-to-day existence, and therefore were not, or did not want to be, aware of the issues that were fuelling the conflict. As Robin Eames, Church of Ireland Archbishop of Armagh (1986–2006), commented: 'They are not fighting each other on the Malone Road. . . . There are two communities here, one is involved in violence, suffering, unemployment and injustice. The demarcation is class.'[4] Daly commented upon this challenge in a 1991 Address to the Institute of Directors: 'Yet, for the most part, people in affluent sectors, living in private residential areas, were largely unaware of these conditions and *undisturbed* by them.'[5] The need for consciousness building was stronger here than in any other area explored by Daly in his work on Northern Ireland. To tackle inequality and eradicate it, thereby bringing Northern Irish society up to the standards of the Peaceable Kingdom, people had to first accept that it existed, before finding meaningful and durable solutions.

Daly's priesthood was characterised by a commitment to what he called in his autobiography, 'the social justice imperative'.[6] By using such a phrase, Daly demonstrated that social justice was something to be built, an integral part of the 'lived Christianity' – that blend of conversion and action which was the only means of achieving salvation. Before his ordination on 22 June 1941, Daly was a member of a group of seminarians and later priests who, inspired by the church's teachings on social justice, tried to keep the spirit of *Rerum Novarum* (1891), 'alive and incarnate in their ministries.'[7] Whilst in the seminary at Maynooth (1937–1941), Daly was a member of a study group that would later become Christus Rex.[8] This was an integral part of his formation: 'We had the desire and we saw the need to continue this interest after ordination, convinced that this was a vital need for the Ireland of our time and an integral part of the proclamation of the Gospel which we were ordained to live and preach.'[9] Daly believed and taught that the church stood on the side of the poor, stating, for example, in 1986 that: 'No doubt must be left in people's minds as to where the church stands. It stands on the side of the poor. Increasingly, the church must be seen to be the champion of the poor, the voice of the men and women and children in deprived sectors of society.'[10] Daly saw his primary role as consciousness building, considering this as one of the main routes through which clergy could contribute to the development of the Peaceable Kingdom.[11] He stated this plainly in 1988, saying: 'The church must strive to make her members and the general public more aware of the reality and extent of poverty in our midst.'[12] This message regarding poverty, deprivation, and marginalisation, as his work – be it sermons, speeches, pamphlets, or newspaper articles – was not restricted to those living in his diocese but was designed to make everyone from politicians to their constituents aware of the poverty within the region, and start them factoring these issues into their political and social action. This, Daly argued, was the primary role of members of the clergy: motivating the laity to work towards a peaceful society, and the creation of the Peaceable Kingdom.[13]

Daly's framework for social justice

The fundamental principle upon which Daly defined the parameters of his consciousness raising was the inherent and God-given dignity of the human person.[14] The promulgation of *Pacem in Terris* by John XXIII in 1963 marked a turning point in Catholic teachings on human rights and dignity. Hehir has argued that this document is 'unmatched as a moral and political statement in defence of the human person.'[15] Human rights (which flowed from the concept of human dignity) became 'a way to describe and secure proper participation in the life of the community'[16] for all members of society. Human rights were a roadmap for human flourishing. This encyclical stresses: the rights to life and worthy standard of living, including rights to proper development of life and to basic security (§11); the rights of cultural and moral values, including freedom to search for and express opinions, freedom of information, and right to education (§ 12–13); rights to religion and conscience (§14); rights to choose one's state in life, including rights to establish a family and pursue a religious vocation (§15–16); economic rights, including right to work, to a just and sufficient wage, and to hold private property (§18–22); rights of meeting and association (§23); right to emigrate and immigrate (§25); and political rights, including right to participate in public affairs and juridical protection of rights (§26–27). But the encyclical also outlines the following duties: To acknowledge and respect rights of others (§30); to collaborate mutually (§31); to act for others responsibly (§39); and to preserve life and live it becomingly (§42). As we shall see, each of these elements provided the foundation of Daly's consciousness raising and future creating throughout the course of his ministry.

Acknowledgement of the inherent dignity of each human being leads to a radically equal society, capable of enabling each person to flourish and contribute to the creation of the Peaceable Kingdom. His thinking on the concept was rooted in the New Testament, and he cited this passage from St Paul's Letter to the Galatians on more than one occasion to support his arguments: 'There is no longer Jew or Greek, there is no longer slave or freeman, there is no longer male or female; for all of you are one in Jesus Christ.'[17] Whatever one may think of the Catholic Church's record on human rights, especially with regard to women and in Ireland, this passage does provide justification for the creation of a programme of radical equality within a society that seeks to base itself upon the structures and values of the Peaceable Kingdom. Daly recognised this, and all of his work on social justice was in effect, as this quotation from Lent 1983 shows, a clarion call for the establishment of a society based upon human dignity and rights: 'Let this be the year of the great return to the Gospel call to hunger and thirst for justice – a justice which is not merciless vengeance but a justice filled with love and mercy, and with respect for the rights and dignity of others.'[18] For Daly, this was based upon a preferential option for the poor, marginalised, and deprived. Citing St Paul's letters to the Corinthians and Romans,[19] he argued that 'if the church is credibly to proclaim the kingdom, she must aspire towards the blessing which our Lord pronounced on the poor.'[20] In doing so, he was demonstrating that social justice was the fundamental element in the creation of the Peaceable Kingdom.

In calling for the creation of such a programme, Daly was strongly supported by both the teachings of the New Testament and Catholic social teaching. From the moment Mary first spoke the words of the Magnificat to her cousin Elizabeth, Christians have been concerned with social justice: 'He has brought down the powerful from their thrones, and lifted up the lowly; he has filled the hungry with good things, and sent the rich away empty.'[21] Her words found a fuller articulation in the teachings of Jesus, who demonstrated a preference for the poor and marginalised in his ministry, developing the fiat upon which the church was founded and which Daly used as the main source and inspiration for his teachings.[22] The poor, marginalised, and deprived are seen by the Magisterium as the primary recipients of the Good News, with for instance, the Congregation for the Doctrine of the Faith stating in 1986 that:

> Jesus proclaims the Good News of the Kingdom of God and calls people to conversion. "The poor have the good news preached to them" (Matt 11:5). By quoting the expression of the Prophet, Jesus manifests his messianic action in favour of those who await God's salvation. Even more than this, the Son of God who has made himself poor for love of us wishes to be recognized in the poor, in those who suffer or are persecuted: "As you did it to one of the least of these my brethren, you did it to me".[23]

The pursuit of social justice is therefore an indispensable part of the church's mission and is a major element in evangelisation.[24] Throughout the twentieth century, the Catholic Church raised issues that were of concern to both the personal and communal expressions of faith, and which when taught in unison with one another, created a social morality for the church which was just as important, if not more so, than the personal, sexual, and reproductive morality that it was (and still is) popularly known for, especially in Ireland. These included but were not restricted to: the distribution of wealth; economic planning; poverty; international development; the rights of workers and trade unions; unemployment; and living conditions, all of which were underlined by the inherent dignity of the human person. Through such teachings, the public nature of the Catholic Church changed. In teaching that 'social stability cannot be given a higher priority than social justice',[25] it moved away from the notions of statehood that it still occasionally clung to despite the loss of the Papal States under Pius IX (r. 1846–1878). This movement allowed the establishment of a more prophetic stance centring upon the creation of a vision for society 'concerned primarily with the "welfare of the city" (Jer 29:7). In doing so, it was responding to the agenda of the world and contributing critically and constructively (in word and action) to a flourishing public square,'[26] providing a vision of the Peaceable Kingdom which the laity were expected to enact.

The phrase 'social justice' means many things to Catholics, but from the perspective of the teaching authority of the twentieth-century Church, it has found its expression in Catholic social teaching.[27] The development of this body of thought has evolved since Leo XIII's pontificate (r. 1878–1903) toward a focus upon structural change.[28] A critical point was reached when Pius XI highlighted the crucial distinction between personal injustice (both the perpetration of injustice and the lived experience of poverty, marginalisation, and deprivation) and structural injustice (the wider inequalities within society which allow personal injustices and suffering to continue), and their interplay with one another.[29] From the papacy of Paul VI onwards, the attitudinal change required of those perpetrating and suffering personal injustice and the need for structural change were taught in a mutually enhancing tension with each other. It was at the intersection of personal conversion and structural change that the motivation to work for the establishment of the Peaceable Kingdom was to be found. For instance, as the following passages demonstrate, whilst *Populorum Progressio* emphasises the need for structural change over the requirement for attitudinal change, it also teaches that individuals have a duty to reflect upon the consequences of their behaviour for such structures and act by adjusting their behaviours accordingly. Thus, §66 of this encyclical emphasises structure by stating that 'Human society is sorely ill. The cause is not so much the depletion of natural resources, nor their monopolistic control by a privileged few; it is rather the weakening of brotherly [sic.] ties between individuals and nations.' Whilst, §37 focuses upon attitudinal change in the service of social justice by instructing that:

> There is no denying that the accelerated rate of population growth brings many added difficulties to the problems of development where the size of the population grows more rapidly than the quantity of available resources to such a degree that things seem to have reached an impasse. . . . It is for parents to take a thorough look at the matter and decide upon the number of their children. This is an obligation they take upon themselves, before their children already born, and before the community to which they belong – following the dictates of their own consciences informed by God's law authentically interpreted, and bolstered by their trust in Him.[30]

Such a tension, however, brings two crucial concepts to the fore: solidarity and subsidiary, without which social justice (from a Catholic perspective) can never be achieved.

The concept of solidarity compels people to take into account the effect of their actions on others, asking them to strive to promote the common good, whilst standing and working *with* the poor and marginalised rather than myopically focusing on their own desires and needs. Through acting in such a manner, individuals thus come to see themselves as part of a community and organise its power structures accordingly. The human rights fundamental to the Peaceable Kingdom were to be found in solidarity with the other, as full personhood, the ultimate aim of Catholic teaching, 'can only be achieved through self-donation to others.'[31] Such an aim could only be accomplished through participation in community, as Daly put it in 1989: 'the *entire community* must be conscious of its collective responsibility for the poor in its midst.'[32] This was a fundamental element of Catholic understandings of, and teachings on, human rights: the person could never flourish outside of the community. Person, community, and society were in relationship with one another; none could be realised without the others. 'Persons can live in dignity only when they live in a community of freedom, that is in a community in which both personal initiative and social solidarity are valued and embodied.'[33] Catholic teachings on human rights were thus neither individualistic nor collectivist. Religious freedom was central to this and provided the Church with a mandate to engage with public life. This was because 'it comes within the meaning of religious freedom that religious communities should not be prohibited from freely undertaking to show the special value of their doctrine in what concerns the organization of society and the inspiration of the whole of human activity.'[34] In such a critique of society, the political, the social, and the economic all combined to underline the dignity of the human person in order to address inequality.

Subsidiarity affirms the idea that each person has the right to shape their own destiny rather than it being solely subject to external forces. When at all possible, therefore, power and decision-making processes should be exercised at the lowest possible level. In 1987, Daly defined subsidiarity thus: 'the poor must not be merely objects of research and of planning. . . . They must be motivated agents of their own amelioration. Their dignity as persons must be respected. Their intelligence and sense of their own problems must be deployed.'[35] Taken together these two concepts act as a check upon each other, by ensuring that power is distributed fairly throughout society, thereby promoting social justice and the vision of the Peaceable Kingdom.

Fundamentally these two teachings are about responsibility, both personal *and* communal, a theme that Daly constantly emphasises when speaking about matters relating to social justice. As a consequence, social justice is a pastoral praxis, a foundational element of the evangelical mission of the church, which all members must engage with according to their vocation and skills. Here, the personal and the communal are so intimately linked, that a person cannot find salvation without addressing the influence of both personal spirituality, and the welfare of others and the place of social justice in their lives. This was the 'Lived Christianity' that was so crucial to Daly's work on Northern Ireland. It was the personal and structural change that would allow human flourishing to become the societal norm. Christians were expected to feel and express moral outrage at the situation of the poor and marginalised and, most importantly, to do something about it. Working for social justice, alongside exercising the democratic right to vote, was the means through which this moral outrage could be brought to bear upon the structures of society and was, alongside peace, Daly's ultimate goal for Northern Ireland. It was the work that would enable injustices to be rectified through the creation of the Kingdom on earth.

A person's faith was thus not complete without this combination of prayer and praxis which allowed the binary of personal and communal salvation, so important to Daly, to come to fruition. Such praxis, however, like the prayer discussed in Chapter 2, was not to be 'blind action,' rather it was based upon 'theoretical understanding and . . . [was] guided by practical reasoning. . . . Praxis [was] not merely manipulative action, suggesting a crude utilitarianism, but [was] governed by wisdom and moral reasoning.'[36] This would allow Christians to bear witness to their faith in authentic terms which could enable meaningful societal change. Such a public expression of faith furthermore has the potential to radically affect the participant's personal relationship with God in two ways. First, by deepening their knowledge and understanding through dialogue, a point is made potently by a Christian quoted in Elaine Graham's book on public theology: 'There is nothing challenging in having deep thoughts all by oneself. What is interesting is doing this work in community, where other people might call you on stuff, or heaven forbid, disagree with you.'[37] Solidarity with the poor, and the encounter with the face of the suffering Christ that it implies, is therefore a source of spiritual nourishment for Christians. As Gutiérrez points out 'discipleship allows us to see our lives in relation to the will of God and sets goals for us to strive for and realise through a daily relationship with the Lord which implies relationship with the other person.'[38] Personal spiritual and communal social progress is therefore completely inseparable, as Paul VI taught 'the individual cannot develop unless the community develops.'[39] Thus, prayer and praxis become entwined, moving the individual not only towards personal salvation but allowing them a central role in the transformation of society.

In concert with Paul VI's exhortation that local bishops adapt the teaching of the Magisterium for their milieu,[40] in his writings on social justice, which formed a fundamental element of his vision of the Peaceable Kingdom, Daly concentrated on four key areas: the economy, prisoners, housing, and community development. Although the tone of these writings was somewhat theoretical in the 1970s, his translation to Down and Connor, one of the most deprived and violent dioceses in Ireland, in February 1982 brought with it a new perspective that enhanced his vision of an alternative possible future in which a Peaceable Kingdom had been achieved.

The economy, the state, private capital, and the roles, rights, and responsibilities of the individual

Daly's translation to the Diocese of Down and Connor brought with it a new understanding of the issues facing the people of Northern Ireland. Before this, a distance, both intellectual and emotional, can be sensed in Daly's writings about the conflict. He sought and, for the most part, achieved a critical distance that enabled him to fulfil his role as teacher and pastor guiding the laity and empowering them to use their knowledge to create specific solutions to the issues of the time as *Gaudium et Spes* had taught. On his move to Down and Connor in 1982, his work became more grounded in the lived realities of conflict, and his teachings on justice became more urgent and detailed. This approach showed an evolution and sensitivity to both physical and political context that owed much to developments such as liberation theology and the subsequent teachings of John Paul II. There is, therefore, an underlying tension in Daly's writings on justice and the economy which is hard to reconcile. Whilst, in his more abstract writings and sermons on the economy, the role of the teacher can clearly be seen as he seeks to shape consciences and ask the critical questions needed to form a more just society; at times, he advocates for the Catholic community in a manner that pays mere lip service to his commitment to parity of esteem between the nationalist and unionist communities, moving into providing the prophetic voice regarding the plight of the nationalist community, demanding rather than requesting action.

The economy, work, and unemployment: aid from the British government

Although he was to later focus upon the role of private capital and workers in promoting justice in Northern Ireland, Daly's initial approach to the issue of the economy was state-centred and for the most part remained so until 1998. Given the circumstances in Northern Ireland this is unsurprising. The economy was dominated by the public sector and relied heavily upon subsidies for its survival.[41]

That said, his stance on the issue of economic development did evolve in the 30 years between 1968 and 1998, and the influence of the Church's teachings on justice, if not the minutiae of its economic understandings, can be discerned. Three concepts dominated his ideas in this regard: justice, equality (which was closely related to human dignity), and fairness. Each of these were fundamental elements in the creation of the Peaceable Kingdom in Northern Ireland. Initially critical of both the Unionist and British governments' economic policies, his translation to West Belfast signaled an evolution in his thought and attitude. From the early 1980s he became increasingly prophetic as he sought to achieve a fair dispensation for the people of West Belfast that was based upon the creation of an economy with equality of opportunity for all, whist continuing to hold the government's actions up to scrutiny.

As far as Daly was concerned, Unionist rule, and especially its economic policy, had been a fundamental cause of the conflict in Northern Ireland. As a consequence, the nationalist community's 'noviceship to violent protest was generations of unemployment and social deprivation.'[42] When responding to accusations that the people of West Belfast had somehow chosen socio-economic depravation, Daly argued that 'West Belfast has not chosen to become a "ghetto". Its great concentration of Catholic people is the result in large part of official government housing policy under the old Stormont regime.'[43] Most of Daly's ire, however, was reserved for the British government which had a 'grave moral obligation'[44] to 'right . . . the wrongs'[45] and inequalities of Unionist rule. This articulation of economic justice was fundamental to the vision of a peaceful and integrated Northern Ireland articulated by Daly. He argued that 'the nationalists of the six counties, in whom decades of second-class citizenship have bred suspicion and cynicism, will begin to believe in a New Ulster only when they see all Ulster being developed in the interest of *all* Ulstermen.'[46] Daly was to be disappointed and made his displeasure known through his stance on the issue of West Belfast and its economic future.

Daly's advocacy for West Belfast was an expression of the preferential option for the poor, vulnerable, and marginalised. At the end of a visitation to the area in 1985, he described his impressions:

> My first reaction is one of unbounded admiration for the people of St Peter's in the area commonly known as the 'Lower Falls'. This area is far too often misrepresented by the media and misjudged by public opinion. It has become associated in people's minds with violence, rioting and unrest. In particular, the name 'Divis' is made to seem synonymous with lawlessness and crime. It would seem that some who live in other parts of the city would almost hesitate to visit that area.
>
> These attitudes are totally unjustified. They are a slur on the good people who live here. . . . Society owes them respect and even admiration. Government and public agencies owe them amends for decades of misplanning, broken promises, and neglect.[47]

According to Daly, West Belfast with its 73% unemployment rate (a figure he himself calculated from unofficial statistics) was facing a 'crisis',[48] and he was vociferous in advocating for the community there. The massive socio-economic balance had to be redressed, and he repeatedly argued that 'West Belfast is in danger of becoming a great pool of deskilled labour.'[49] He believed that the government needed to take action before West Belfast lost 'its capacity for economic recovery.'[50] This was not a political crusade. Rather, it was based upon the concept of the preferential option for the poor, vulnerable, and marginalised. In a homily given at St Luke's Church, Twinbrook, he framed his actions in the following terms: 'I wish to speak of [Christ's] concern [for] his people – his concern for their human rights, their dignity as persons, their right not to be denied the opportunity to fulfil their potential as human beings and as Christians.'[51] In short, Daly felt that the people of West Belfast were being prevented from flourishing and that action needed to be taken to ensure that this community gained equality of opportunity.

In common with most churches and religious organisations in the UK at the time, Daly initially looked to the state for solutions to these problems but, as we shall see, did explore other options. Indeed, he argued that the lack of co-ordinated government economic policy alongside security concerns in West Belfast was exacerbating and compounding the issues facing communities, allowing deprivation to feed into an already worsening conflict. In 'Lower Falls Road: a wronged but forgiving people', he cited the Belfast Areas of Need Planning Team who stated in 1978 that: 'The Government is giving the highest priority to the creation of new employment opportunities in West Belfast generally and future employment prospects of those living in Divis will largely depend of these efforts.'[52] His reaction was blunt: 'Seven years of deepening recession later, could the people of West Belfast be blamed for being sceptical about official declarations and promises? It would surely be hard to expect them to have confidence in the political will of Government to tackle the disastrous economic problems of the area.'[53] He therefore called upon the government to facilitate industrial development within the area, and to fund a programme of infrastructural redevelopment, urban renewal, to ensure that public services and amenities were of a high standard, and most importantly given the high rate of unemployment to develop training relevant to the needs of the economy. This was because 'there must be no grounds for any perception that the people of West Belfast are being held collectively responsible for IRA violence or are being collectively penalised for it; whereas in truth they are its first victims and chief suffers.'[54] West Belfast, he was to comment, 'has been allowed to take on all the appearances of urban blight and industrial wasteland. It has fallen behind almost all comparable areas in terms of arterial roads and approach roads. . . . The environmental neglect serves as a deterrent to potential industrial investors and is depressing and demoralising for the inhabitants.'[55]

Many of the issues being faced by the people of West Belfast were due, Daly argued, to a lack of understanding on the part of planners, ministers, and civil servants – a view shared by those in government at the time who sought to address the lack of contact between deprived communities in general and the government. A senior civil servant, Sir Kenneth Bloomfield described the government's strategy thus:

> One of the useful things we did was to put really promising people out in the localities. That was very important. You can have people dealing with issues that have very little contact with the people. One of the better things we did was get really promising youngish men and they're going to right out there working with the local community and feeding back to the centre what the community needs. It effected some improvements, I wouldn't put it higher than that, these are not problems to be solved in a decade I'm afraid, they really are very deeply entrenched. At least there's some manifestation of the government caring about these concerns. This is a tiny little place really, but Stormont can feel very remote and I think to be a presence in places like Ballymurphy can be very important.[56]

All of these changes would be a prelude for inward investment to the area (which had been neglected by the industrial development board), the achievement of which was one of Daly's highest priorities, and were linked to his opinions on private capital, which is discussed shortly. Daly therefore called upon businesses to ensure that their locations reflected the employment needs of the region, especially as much industry was publically subsidised.

Daly's writings on West Belfast represent a microcosm of his attitude towards the economy and the British government's mismanagement of it. He frequently criticised the government, seeing their economic policy as much a barrier to peace as the IRA's violence. Initially, Daly argued that the British government needed to act in a manner which would counteract Unionist policy: 'British economic aid must have a calculated political trust in a contrary, balancing direction.'[57] This alongside co-ordinated development of the border regions would convince nationalists of their place in the new Ulster whilst reassuring Unionists that their concerns about a stealth reunification of Ireland were unfounded. British intransigence and lack of political will to do anything more than suppress violence in Northern Ireland became more apparent throughout the 1980s. Daly consequently began to consider the moral implications of public spending more closely. He saw this as a matter of conscience for both those in government and those receiving public subsidies: 'all public economic policy must have a social dimension, a commitment to fairer shares for all.'[58] In the interests of justice, Daly argued that the government should keep tighter controls on those businesses receiving public subsidies. He stated that 'so much enterprise is now dependent on public finance that private employers have to be prepared to accept public checks on freedom in the urgent interests of community justice and social peace.'[59] This, he believed, could be achieved through legislation designed to ensure equality.

Daly was keen to address the structural problems that he believed had initially caused the conflict. A disparity in employment figures between the Protestant and Catholic communities was evident throughout the period of the Troubles. This has variously been attributed to geographical, demographic, industrial, and educational factors. The effect of each of these has been downplayed by Tony Gallagher. For instance, when speaking of the demographic factors, the argument for which was based upon the higher birth rates within the Catholic community which led to higher unemployment rates, he pointed out that:

> Those who attempt to make the connection seem to overlook that time lag between birth and labour market entry – a period which becomes longer as children stay longer in full-time education. The further we go back in the post-war evolution of the Northern Irish population, the stronger the share of Catholics in both the child and the adult working age-groups; yet the excess unemployment was always there. This is another reason why it is not legitimate to blame Catholic fertility for the present heavy imbalance (Eversley, 1989, p 221).[60]

However, as is often the case, perception is more important than reality, especially in arenas of conflict. The evidence to support the argument that direct and indirect discrimination was a feature of the employment market in Northern Ireland is not unequivocal, 'but the evidence is of such an extent that it would be foolish to ignore it as an issue.'[61] In the immediate period following the outbreak of the conflict, there was a widespread acceptance that Catholics had been discriminated against by Protestants, leading to inequality of opportunity for the community. In his 1968 survey, Richard Rose had found that three quarters of Catholics believed that they had been treated unfairly in terms of employment, whilst three quarters of Protestants disagreed with this assertion.[62] By 1990, Curtice and Gallagher found that 63% of Protestants and 84% of Catholics believed that there was some prejudice against Catholics in Northern Ireland, whilst 61% of Protestants and 62% of Catholics believed there was some prejudice against Protestants.[63] A distinction was made between direct and indirect discrimination: Sarah Nelson found that indirect discrimination was a feature of life in Northern Ireland, a practice justified by the need to 'look after one's own' in a hostile environment. It was argued that 'history provides several sound reasons why one community should not trust to the goodwill of the other; the present conflict has provided more, and an infinite number of bitter memories . . . Protestants and Catholics are people who fought one another.'[64] Such views were, according to Nelson, most prevalent in the 1970s, and by 1976, legislation had been put in place to prevent discrimination in employment practices, the discussions leading up to which had been framed in terms of indirect and direct discrimination. The Fair Employment Act (Northern Ireland) 1976[65] made discrimination in employment illegal, but the Fair Employment Agency created to enforce this 'found itself caught between those who felt it was an unnecessary sop to Catholics and those who felt it was a toothless tiger.'[66] This was followed in 1989 by the second Fair Employment (Northern Ireland) Act which introduced compulsory workforce monitoring, discouraged informal recruitment, and promoted objective recruitment and selection procedures. In 1990, the community composition of the monitored workforce was 65.1% Protestant and 34.9% Catholic which represented a shortfall of around 4% in the Catholic share of the workforce.[67]

Daly recognised unfair employment practices as a problem both in terms of perception and reality. From the 1980s onwards, he concentrated a good deal on the development of fair employment practices. This was rooted in pastoral concern and demonstrated his commitment to the creation of an equal society in which the dignity of all, both Catholic and Protestant, was respected. 'If you create jobs and keep trying to improve the fair employment legislation then *everybody* will benefit.'[68] Once more, Daly related such inequality to violence: 'economic injustice and paramilitary violence are quite obviously casually inter-related.'[69] He therefore saw fair employment combined with job creation as a path to peace. Again his focus was on the state, and in 1989, he argued that 'there is immediate need for commitment and effective action, both on the part of government and its agencies and on the part of the private sector, for the redressing of this imbalance over a reasonable period of time.' Furthermore, schemes such as the Fair Employment legislation, should be 'welcomed by all fair-minded citizens and especially by Christians.'[70] He also supported a number of faith-based fair employment initiatives, especially when they were ecumenical.[71]

However, Daly, like the other Northern bishops, was sceptical of the efficacy of the MacBride Principles launched in November 1984. These principles were a corporate code of conduct for US companies undertaking business in Northern Ireland.[72] Although Daly himself never condemned them, he stated in 2002 that the 'attitude of the Northern Bishops towards MacBride he said was one of suspicion because they were afraid that it might possibly lead to disinvestments.'[73] Daly explained the stance taken thus: 'There was a serious shortage of jobs, and therefore an acute need for overseas investment, and, in particular, American investment, in the North of Ireland.'[74]

Unemployment

Daly was translated into the Diocese of Down and Connor in the middle of an economic recession. The 1980s saw steep rises in unemployment throughout the UK, but these were particularly acute in Northern Ireland. By 1989, 15.7% of people in Northern Ireland were unemployed compared with 10.2% in Scotland, and 6.6% in England and Wales. Daly's diocese was particularly badly affected, with half of all those unemployed in Northern Ireland throughout the 1980s residing in Belfast. Even here, unemployment was not evenly distributed, with the Westminster constituencies of Belfast West and Belfast North having significantly higher unemployment rates than Belfast South or Belfast East. There was also a clear unemployment gap between the nationalist and unionist communities, with Catholic unemployment standing at twice that of Protestants.[75] Such high levels of unemployment were of particular concern to Daly who argued in several places that 'the official figures manifestly fall far short of the real unemployment rates.' He goes on to provide his own estimates:

> Unofficial but reliable local surveys in a number of west Belfast parishes indicate unemployment rates of upwards of 60 per cent and in one or two cases as high as 80 per cent of the working population. Of the 13,000 to 15,000 unemployed persons in Catholic west Belfast, more than half have been unemployed for more than a year.[76]

Daly was concerned about unemployment on a number of levels, and his discourse once more highlights his desire to create a society embedded in in the values of the Peaceable Kingdom, with human flourishing and social justice at its heart. His thoughts on this matter also demonstrate the binary nature of this plan as he aimed to form both the individual and society, preparing people for the Kingdom both in heaven and on earth.

When Daly first arrived in Down and Connor, his initial concerns about unemployment were related to the escalation of paramilitary violence. The vicious circle of violence and poverty was a recurrent theme in his writings. So, for example, in his 1983 World Day of Peace sermon he stated, 'Deprivation feeds violence. Violence increases deprivation.'[77] He was also concerned about the unemployment gap between the nationalist and unionist communities which, although lessening, was still significant and had the potential to fuel conflict.[78] These relationships to him were givens, and outside of condemnations of the IRA and their 'revolutionary activity' were not something he dwelt on a great deal. Instead, he used his speeches on unemployment to promote pastoral solutions both at a micro and macro level, which were aimed at improving society through the use of the concepts of solidarity and subsidiarity, as well as developing the individual.

Although the relationship of unemployment to the conflict was clear, Daly placed more emphasis upon both the personal and communal aspects of the matter. He wanted the impact of unemployment upon the dignity of the human person to be understood and most importantly, acted upon. Here the influence of Catholic social teachings, and in particular those of *Gaudium et Spes* are evident: Human dignity, the protection of which was *the* fundamental task of the church, lay at the heart of this. A just, and therefore peaceful, society could not be achieved whilst so many were unemployed and were therefore not only being stripped of their rights but also a fundamental element of what it means to be human. His words in a 1984 sermon to young people are emblematic of the tone of this:

> When we speak of unemployment, we are not speaking simply of a shortage of personal income. We are talking also about lack of purpose and of meaning in daily life. We are talking of a person's status and standing in society. . . . It would be difficult to exaggerate the demoralising consequences of unemployment.[79]

Again, in 1989, he stated that:

> To have a job is to be an adult, to begin to have one's own earned money and to have some control over one's own life. . . . Not to have a job and never to see hope of a job is to be drawn close to hopelessness. It feeds the spirit of resentment and rebellion.[80]

To be unemployed therefore created a 'sense of hopelessness and worthlessness'[81] and a society that allowed up to 40% of its working-age population to be jobless was failing in its responsibilities to human flourishing by dehumanising such people.[82] In his role as pastor and teacher, he argued that developing the economy and creating jobs would allow a more just society to emerge based upon positive conceptions of peace. This, however, was not the sole responsibility of the British government but of everyone who had a duty to practice what was in effect a preferential option for the unemployed.

The inspiration for this can be seen in *Rerum Novarum*, the founding document of the Catholic social canon. Written in 1891 by Pope Leo XIII as a response to 'the changed relations between masters and workmen; [and] the enormous fortunes of some few individuals, and the utter poverty of the masses',[83] this encyclical sought to outline the rights and duties of capital and labour. In doing so, it started a tradition within the Catholic Church which sought to read the signs of the times, and to bring the institution's wisdom to bear upon the most pressing temporal matters. Daly took this language of rights and duties, and deployed it alongside the concepts of subsidiarity and solidarity introduced by John Paul II to provide teaching on the issue of unemployment which would create a more just and peaceful society. In his early years in Down and Connor, he focused upon the government, and later economic regeneration, as a means of alleviating poverty and unemployment. But from the late 1980s onwards, in line with teaching from John Paul II, he began to advocate that those in employment had a duty towards the unemployed; by 1996, Daly was speaking in terms of a social mortgage taken out to fund an individual's membership of society.

In a 1975 speech to the Longford Chamber of Commerce, Daly outlined his vision for the role of business in society. 'Commerce,' he stated, 'is one of the acts of peace. It flourishes in a soil of justice.'[84] Daly's understanding of the role of the economy and business in the achievement of justice and peace was profound and moved beyond the paradigm of statism that dominated both Irish and global faith-based discourses on the issue during this period. He argued that justice and peace could only be achieved through a concerted effort being made by the whole of society, from this a positive, and therefore longer-lasting, peace would emerge which would provide the foundation stones of the Peaceable Kingdom. Waiting for the government to implement political structures was futile and enabled violence to thrive, creating a vicious circle of violence and intransigence. Instead, whilst undertaking the prophetic and teaching roles handed to bishops at the Second Vatican Council, he sought to encourage business people to exercise their lay vocation and provide leadership to society. Daly's dual mission was inherent in this: by creating business leaders who engaged in 'deep and searching moral thinking'[85] regarding their economic practices, not only would the individual's conscience be developed but so also would a society more closely modelled on the Sermon on the Mount, thereby creating the Peaceable Kingdom. A sustainable justice and peace embedded within the principles of dignity would be the result should these practices be adopted.[86] Such thinking closely mirrored that of the Magisterium and developed in line with that of subsequent papal teachings.

The rights and responsibilities of capital, and the social mortgage

Most of Daly's writings on the economy centred upon the rights and responsibilities of capital, ideas that were founded upon the Catholic Church's
teachings on private property and the ownership of wealth. Daly's teachings
in this regard focused on the appropriate use of capital, the dignity and
rights of labour, and in the wake of the economic recession of the late 1980s,
posing a challenge to the orthodoxy of the market. In the Peaceable Kingdom, money would serve society rather than dominating it, as is presently
the case. By embedding the Church's teachings on this matter within the
mind-sets of Christian businessmen and women, Daly could not only form
their consciences by helping them to become 'self-critical' and self aware,[87]
but also create a more equal society in which a focus on human flourishing
was the norm.

Since *Rerum Novarum*, the Catholic Church has accepted and indeed
promoted the right to private property. This encyclical taught that 'the fact
that God has given the earth for the use and enjoyment of the whole human
race can in no way be a bar to the owning of private property . . . the limits
of private possession have been left to be fixed by man's own industry, and
by the laws of individual races.'[88] Successive popes have upheld this right.
However, with rights come responsibilities. As *Mater et Magistra* stated,
'The right of private property is rooted in social responsibility.'[89] By the
late 1960s, the concept (but not the term itself) of a 'social mortgage' was
starting to appear in papal teachings. For example, *Populorum Progressio*
stated that:

> The right to private property is not absolute and unconditional.
>
> No one may appropriate surplus goods solely for his own private use
> when others lack the bare necessities of life. In short, "as the Fathers
> of the Church and other eminent theologians tell us, the right of pri-
> vate property may never be exercised to the detriment of the common
> good." When "private gain and basic community needs conflict with
> one another," it is for the public authorities "to seek a solution to these
> questions, with the active involvement of individual citizens and social
> groups."[90]

John Paul II used the term 'social mortgage' for the first time in 1979,
cementing its place in Church teachings with *Sollicitudo Rei Socialis* in 1987
when he wrote:

> It is necessary to state once more the characteristic principle of Christian
> social doctrine: the goods of this world are originally meant for all. The
> right to private property is valid and necessary, but it does not nullify
> the value of this principle. Private property, in fact, is under a "social
> mortgage," which means that it has an intrinsically social function,

based upon and justified precisely by the principle of the universal des-
tination of goods. Likewise, in this concern for the poor, one must not
overlook that special form of poverty which consists in being deprived
of fundamental human rights, in particular the right to religious freedom and also the right to freedom of economic initiative.[91]

Such teaching placed a strong emphasis upon justice, and in particular the
preferential option for the poor and its relationship to the common good. As
the 1937 Encyclical, *Divini Redemptoris*, had put it: 'Now it is of the very
essence of social justice to demand from each individual all that is necessary
for the common good.'[92] It drew attention to the fact that human beings
are designed to live in community and therefore must be committed to the
betterment and benefit of *all* within the community. Those without private
property must not be left to fend for themselves, a teaching which Daly
was to foreground in his work on housing. It was incumbent upon those
with material goods to provide for the needs of those who found themselves
without enough to meet their basic needs. This in itself was crucial to the
creation of a peaceful society. As Maslow has demonstrated with his hierarchy of needs, until those such as shelter and security are achieved, higher
needs such as community relations, in the case of Northern Ireland, will
not be addressed.[93] Or in other words, absolute needs must be met before
relative needs can be addressed. In such situations, the needs of others must
come before profit: money must be made to serve society.

Gaudium et Spes had reiterated a concern about the huge inequalities
between rich and poor, and it was this issue which motivated and underlined
Daly's discourse surrounding the concept of 'social responsibility' or the
term 'social mortgage' which he first used in 1987. In the 1970s, he merely
observed the phenomenon of the abuse of capital and greed, stating, for
example, in 1976 that:

> Some of our owners and disposers of wealth could be suspected of cling-
> ing to outdated notions of the absolute right of money to follow the
> magnet of the highest available immediate return on investment; even if
> this means a steady flow of money out of the country and a deadly loss
> of vitally needed investment in this country.[94]

This was followed by an appeal to conscience and a statement that a re-
evaluation of the economy needed to take place in light of technological
changes.

By the late 1980s, as a consequence of his direct experience of minister-
ing to the people of West Belfast, his tone changed and he became more
direct about the responsibilities of capital. The right to private property or
wealth 'is always conditioned by the rights of others to a fair share of the
world's resources . . . systems which foster and maintain an unjust distribution of resources and opportunities are morally indefensible.'[95] The premise

of his argument was based upon the fact that such wealth is not created in a vacuum and therefore does not belong entirely to its 'owners'. Therefore, social mortgage payments were a 'matter of justice and not just a matter of expediency'.[96] Social mortgage payments fall into two categories: the public and the private. Public elements include the payment of taxes, regulation of private property by the state, and mandates such as a just or living wage. Private arrangements include businesses employing those without private property, such as rehabilitated persons, charitable donations, and the creation of enterprise plans which allow employees to gain a share of the business.[97] For Daly, the large subsidies given to businesses in Northern Ireland should have prevented the hoarding of private property:

> Society, through government and the tax-payer, already makes a large financial input to wealth creation and to profit and capital accumulation. Government does this through heave contributions in subsidy, grant-aid, tax remission etc. In the complex structure of modern society, the concept of purely private ownership, or exclusively private capital or indeed of undiluted free enterprise, has to be qualified.[98]

Therefore, 'the social dimension in the generation of profits must be acknowledged in the disposal of them.'[99] By the late 1980s, much of Daly's hope for the future of Northern Ireland was focused on the private sector – a belief which chimed with the Conservative government's policy at the time but which was motivated more by a disenchantment with government policy and the knowledge that investment and the resulting jobs could end the vicious circle of deprivation and violence that existed in Northern Ireland than a love for neo-liberalism and the market. Employers had to create jobs. In 1987, for example, Daly stated that 'the opportunities and incentives now being offered to industrialists in both parts of Ireland to maximise employment create for them corresponding and serious moral obligations towards job creation.'[100] The creation of jobs would lead to peace. Once more, the relationship of the individual and the community was clear: an individual should not be motivated by profit. Rather, service to the community combined with 'a reasonable return on investment', or what Daly also terms 'a just profit',[101] was the correct incentive for business activity within the Peaceable Kingdom. Thus, whilst Daly was not going as far as to promote a social enterprise–style economy for Northern Ireland or indeed one based upon the economy of communion, he was arguing that a mixed economy based upon human flourishing offered the prospect for peace in the region.

Such ideas were supported by his views on neo-liberalism. In 1992, Daly gave a sermon in which he criticised free-market capitalism. In it he observed that:

> A new economic orthodoxy seems to be triumphant, the orthodoxy of the market. Market forces are erected into some kind of absolute norm

of all economic behaviour, if not of political policy. Whatever the market dictates must be accepted, even if this means mass unemployment. More than one authoritative voice has claimed over recent years that mass unemployment is a "price worth paying". This is a harsh and unfeeling orthodoxy.[102]

Whilst some Catholic economists have argued that such an economic orthodoxy is indeed compatible with Catholic social teaching, as it leads to 'trickle down economics,'[103] free-market capitalism or neo-liberalism as Pope Francis (r. 2013–) has recently pointed out counteracts the development of the common good and cannot therefore be supported by the Church.[104] Such an ideology puts profit above people and has allowed capital to control the way in which humans were treated both in the workplace and in society as a whole. The social teaching of the Christian churches, including the Catholic Church and the World Council of Churches, provided a counter to this. Instead, Daly argued that the market should be characterised thus:

> The market operates as a result of human choices and decisions. These are moral choices and moral decisions and must be governed by the moral law of justice, love and compassion. Left to themselves, market forces favour the wealthy, the strong and the powerful, and hurt or even crush the poor, the weak and the powerless. A Christian society must provide safety nets of justice and compassion to protect the weaker sectors from the destructive consequences of uncontrolled market forces. Healthcare and social welfare budgets and educational services must build in special provisions to protect the poor and the weak from the harsh consequences of the market. The market is a proper mechanism for economic exchanges, but it is not a criterion of moral values.[105]

However, in employing the concept of solidarity relating to the development of the Northern Irish economy, Daly was expecting everyone, and not just the owners of capital, to take responsibility and contribute.

The role of workers

Workers too had rights and responsibilities. Daly spoke vociferously of their rights which were 'morally binding' on the part of the employer.[106] The 1980s were characterised by industrial action on the part of workers; a right firmly upheld by the Catholic Church. It taught that a strike could be viewed as legitimate when all of the following conditions are met:

1   Every other method for the resolution of disputes has been ineffectual;[107]
2   It is necessary to obtain a proportionate benefit;[108]
3   It is peaceful;
4   The goal is directly related to working conditions;
5   The goal is in accord with the common good;

6   It must never be forgotten that, when essential community services are in question, they must in every case be ensured, if necessary by means of appropriate legislation.[109]

Nevertheless, striking is 'an extreme means' that 'must not be abused.'[110] It thus follows that a strike is immoral when any of the following is true:

1   The chances of a resolution via negotiation have not been reasonably exhausted;
2   The benefit sought is not proportionate to the losses inflicted by the strike;
3   It is violent;
4   The goal is not directly related to working conditions, or
5   The goal is not in accord with the common good.[111]

In common with Catholic social teaching, Daly also firmly believed in the worker's right to strike, although once more his reasoning was framed in terms of morality and individual conscience demonstrating Daly's commitment to spiritual as well as temporal formation. In a 1981 pamphlet, he stated that 'we need as Christians to inform our consciences properly about the morality of strikes and the conditions for a just strike.' He then goes on to list the conditions set forth in the Bishops' Pastoral on Justice which include questions such as 'is it sure that a real injustice is present? Is the injustice grave enough to justify the loss and the damage likely to be caused? Is there a proper proportion between the loss about to be inflicted and the lawful end pursued? Have all efforts been made to reach settlement by negotiation, and have these efforts failed?'[112] Daly also argued that workers were entitled to just wages:

> Wage levels and wage claims should be related to justice. Instead, they seem to be decided by power and the determination to use power regardless of the consequences for others and for the country. . . .
>   There is often a real choice facing workers today. It is a choice between higher wages and more jobs. Higher wages for some workers make job losses more likely for others.[113]

Fundamental to this was the dignity of the human person, which when combined with the teachings of solidarity and subsidiarity, formed an ethic of work. Essentially the workplace was a community in which each person – worker, manager, owner – would play a role in securing human flourishing. In doing so, they would secure both personal and communal salvation, and create the conditions necessary for the creation of the Peaceable Kingdom by developing business models based upon society's needs rather than fuelling a culture of materialism, resulting in the formation of an underclass.

Just as solidarity between the rich and poor was crucial, so too was that between those in work and the unemployed. In 1987 and again in 1989, Daly argued that 'those with jobs are a privileged minority'.[114] This was a reflection of the Irish Bishop's Conference 1977 pastoral on Justice which had taught that 'we should all have the country's high unemployment figures on our conscience'[115] and reinforced teachings on social sin that were also prominent in Daly's writings.[116] In terms of personal responsibility therefore, Daly was firm in his argument that the employed had duties and obligations towards the jobless:

> The reality of unemployment, like the reality of poverty, can easily subside into the penumbra of public consciousness. We learn to live with problems – particularly when they are other people's problems. Vaguely we may feel and occasionally loudly say that <u>somebody</u> should do <u>something</u> about unemployment. We do not feel it is our affair. Meanwhile, we have "our own" interests to defend, "our own" living standards to protect.
>
> But unemployment is a problem for us all and should be a concern for all of us.[117]

Daly therefore argued for the creation of social solidarity by which he meant that every member of society had to take responsibility for social and economic problems within Northern Ireland. This had a particular class dimension to it in which echoed *Rerum Novarum* regarding the responsibility of capital to labour: 'excess accruing profits should be ploughed back into new jobs, and the performance of industrialists should be monitored to ensure that the promised new jobs will effectively be created.'[118] The middle classes were also asked to respect their obligations towards human flourishing. Daly therefore asked that people make 'social mortgage' payments. This concept was based upon the idea that 'it rests on the principle that it is one thing to have a right to the possession of money and another to have a right to use it as one wills.'[119] In doing so, Daly was placing a great emphasis upon economic regeneration which again could be carried out at both a macro and micro level, and which served to create the justice necessary for a peaceful society to emerge.

Community development and urban regeneration

But economic regeneration alone could not create the conditions necessary for the Peaceable Kingdom to be realised. This was one part of a jigsaw which when complete would present a picture of a society where human dignity and flourishing were at the heart of all decisions made. Daly argued that the social problems facing communities, which inevitably led to a slide into violence, needed to be tackled at their source. In the service of human dignity and subsidiarity, this process should involve the community itself, the members of which should be encouraged to stand in solidarity with one another. He was commenting on this in a prescient manner as early as 1975, seven years before his translation into Down and Connor and before many of the most socio-economically deprived parts of the UK slid into a period of intense rioting in the early 1980s:[120]

> There are other more indirect but no less real connections between the erosion of local community control and democracy and the propensity towards violence. Communities which feel that decisions affecting their lives, their homes, their future can be taken over their heads and without their knowledge, much less their consultation, by faceless men in distant corridors, on the basis of plans drawn up by remote experts, feel threatened and because threatened, feel resentful and aggressive.[121]

For him then, 'community development is the key to the alleviation of many social evils of today.'[122] When Daly spoke of community development, he was speaking of 'a process designed to create conditions of economic and social progress for the whole community with its active participation and fullest possible reliance upon the community's initiative.'[123] In the context of Northern Ireland, this meant urban regeneration and the creation of stable and well-thought through infrastructures that would alleviate the grinding and absolute poverty present in many areas. This supported his vision of the Peaceable Kingdom by encouraging solidarity amongst members of the community and enabling community development projects to emerge through the processes of subsidiarity. Daly thus placed a great deal of emphasis upon 'the creation of community where the sense of community does not yet exist, in country or urban areas; the avoidance of policies and the resisting of trends which break up existing communities, should be a first concern for all social planning. Planning is for people, for communities, rather than for production targets or progress report.'[124] Such ideas were extended to the middle classes, who in Daly's vision for the Peaceable Kingdom needed to move from a culture of blame[125] to one of understanding and mutual solidarity and support.[126] Such a vision of community was explained in the Acts of the Apostles thus: 'All the believers were together and had everything in common. They sold property and possessions to give to anyone who had need.'[127]

At the centre of this discourse lay a critique of social housing policy and its obliteration of communities in particular in West Belfast. In the late 1960s and 1970s, policy and security decisions 'ignored the deeply rooted and pernicious problems of segregation, sectarianism and social exclusion',[128] creating conditions which left communities vulnerable to both state and paramilitary violence as well as the myriad of problems associated with deprivation. Social housing was further decimated in the UK during the 1980s by the Thatcher government and led to the development of sub-standard living conditions that essentially violated human rights.[129] Such conditions were the result of decades of mis-planning worsened by cuts to local authority budgets which prevented even the most basic maintenance being carried out. The Divis Flats in West Belfast[130] were, for Daly, emblematic of this issue. Built in the modernist style as a solution to the slum conditions of much working-class housing in the area, these flats were seen as 'an expression of deeper social purpose, letting light and air into a dark and dusty world, creating healthier places for a new generation.'[131] But, these machines for living like their counterparts all over the United Kingdom[132] were 'a disaster. Like other new-builds, dampness and mould was severe. Lifts failed to function, and refuse chutes became blocked, causing rubbish to collect and attract rats. Furthermore asbestos was widely used not just as installation, but in tiles, window frames, and the very casting of the concrete.'[133] Indeed, the inappropriate use of concrete, an inefficient building material in the damp climate of Northern Ireland, demonstrated the lack of thought and planning that went into the design of these buildings. One resident described the living conditions thus:

> When we moved into Gilford Row, there was no dampness but they were new, but now there is a lot of damp. There was dampness in my own flat in the children's room on the ceiling, it was to do with the balconies, the water lying on the balconies then when there was heavy rain, the water used to come in through the ceiling. They were very damp and cold for children to sleep in. There was heating but it was more often off than on.[134]

Other residents reported being covered in fleabites, whilst a 1987 study found higher than average rates of asthma amongst the residents.[135] *Housing and Health in West Belfast* further found that 9% of children living in Divis were 'affected by depression or were weeping so much that they could not face school or mix with others,' and 14% were affected by a loss of appetite.[136] In addition, the panopticon-like design of the blocks, which allowed the British Army to monitor the front door of each flat from an observation point on the twentieth floor of the main tower, led to paranoia and a siege mentality developing amongst the residents.[137]

The 1980s saw concerted campaigning from Divis residents for the demolition of the flats, and only one block remains at the time of writing. Daly fully supported this campaign and railed against the living conditions present in the complex in 1985, stating that:

> The Divis complex should never have been built. No refurbishing will ever make it an acceptable human environment. It stands as a monument to a bad period of urban planning which, however well intentioned at the time, was disastrously misconceived, and has been demonstrated by experience to have been a source of immense human and community

misery. People should not be allowed to go on suffering indefinitely from
planning blunders of the past, for which they are in no way responsible.

. . .

> I regret to have to say that the worst of the flats are quite unfit for
> human habitation and are a disgrace to public housing, but this is due
> to structural defects and inadequate or failed maintenance programmes.
> Even the refurbished flats would still be a quite unacceptable environ-
> ment for decent community living.[138]

At the heart of this discourse was a concern for human rights: such housing
conditions meant that people were unable to flourish and were left without
even the most basic amenities, leaving those living in such areas trapped in a
cycle of poverty,[139] which led to social exclusion, preventing them from participating in the life of Northern Irish society. This neglect was, Daly argued,
the fault of the government, and in particular the Housing Executive.[140]

Such problems were exacerbated by the decimation of community life
that had been facilitated by the construction of the Divis complex both in
terms of inter-personal relationships and infrastructure. Pre-existing social
solidarities, similar to those described in *Family and Kinship in East London*,[141] were destroyed when 'slums' such as Sailortown to the north of the
city centre and Brown Square and the Lower Falls to the west were cleared
to facilitate the government's programme of regeneration. The construction
of Divis was viewed by those most affected thus:

> Divis was conceived without involving the people who would live there,
> against the wishes of some of the Loney community. As quick and
> thoughtless solution to "slum clearance". By replacing honest informa-
> tion with slick salesmanship, with no regard for the infrastructure of an
> established community, to suit the politicians and the profiteers.[142]

Once popular and safe neighbourhoods characterised by good cross-
community relations became stigmatised. Play areas for children were
situated in places where parents could not monitor their offspring easily,
continuous walkways exacerbated already persistent feelings of insecurity
caused by the conflict, and none of the social amenities needed to build community were provided. Consequently, 'serious problems with crime, vandalism, and drug abuse quickly emerged, as residents hid in the seclusion
of their anonymous flats, fearful of the vast open spaces below them. . . .
[They] became prisoners within their own complex.'[143] The physical infrastructure, initially designed as a new way of creating community, was one
of the main problems preventing the establishment of the Peaceable Kingdom. This housing infrastructure was facilitating social exclusion by iso-
lating people, stopping them from standing in solidarity with one another
through the creation of conditions of fear and hopelessness. As the architect,
Richard Rogers, puts it, 'In the urgency of housebuilding after the Second

World War, planners had lost sight of the way actual people lived, and had left them without any of their familiar social support structures. Combined with high unemployment and heavy-handed policing, the mix was toxic.'[144] Neither could solidarity's twin, subsidiarity, be achieved in such an environment as the social capital required for its establishment could not be built.

However, it was not just the immediate locality that was affected by this urban regeneration. The entire infrastructure of the city was reworked from the 1960s onwards in line with the recommendations of the Matthews Plan. These actions further divided an already fractured city. The flagship of this plan was the Westlink, or A12, which cut through West Belfast, joining the Ms1, 2, and 3 together to form the busiest road in Northern Ireland. Elizabeth DeYoung described the results of the Matthew's Plan thus:

> The urban landscape bears witness to years of deindustrialisation, poor planning and conflict. . . . The Westlink Motorway cleaves across Clifton Street, physically separating the area from the city centre through a series of intersections and high traffic junctions. Housing adjacent to the motorway thus suffers from noise and air pollution to a high degree. Vacant land and surface car parks dot the area, further reinforcing the "shutterzone" and further impeding foot traffic.[145]

The result has been what Brendan Murtagh calls a 'twin-speed city' where the social disadvantage and segregation which characterise the outskirts of the city excludes these neighbourhoods from the 'economic optimism' of the city centre, thereby marginalising them further.[146] A 'green zone' was effectively created in Belfast city centre during the 1980s as the commercial district separated itself from the working-class communities within its reach, with similar consequences of alienation and community resentment, to those seen in the regeneration of East London for the 2012 Olympics.[147] This process of regeneration meant that communities were effectively cut off from accessing work and leisure opportunities to be found in a city centre planned to attract inward investment.[148]

Daly approached this issue with his usual mix of reality and vision. He pointed out in strong terms that:

> West Belfast has been allowed to take on all the appearances of urban blight and industrial wasteland. It has fallen behind almost all comparable areas in terms of arterial roads and approach roads, road frontages, shop front refurbishment and general environmental renewal. This environmental neglect serves as a deterrent to potential investors and is depressing and demoralising for the inhabitants. The people of West Belfast deserve better.[149]

Offering the following (by this point, mainstream) solutions to planners: 'Housing plans must provide for shops, services and amenities, including recreational provision and children's play facilities which are needed for proper community development. Housing plans must also provide for workshop units and industrial outlets.'[150]

Peace and strong community relations could not develop without the government providing for the basic infrastructural needs of a local area and the removal of peace walls which acted as physical barriers to reinforce the completely understandable reluctance of Protestants and Catholics to interact with one another. Once such matters were addressed, or at the very least acknowledged, the form of community development described by the UN could begin to emerge. Here, solidarity and subsidiarity would combine as:

> The Catholic community in West Belfast have a vital role to play in any rehabilitation plan for the area. Communities at street level and at parish level must be concerned about improving the environment, doing all they can to discourage graffiti writing, and to clear up graffiti, in general keeping their neighbourhood a place of which they can be proud.[151]

This combined with the help of more socio-economically advantaged Catholics in different parts of the city and diocese would enable the spirit of the early church to be re-established.

Prisoners and human rights

Daly's teachings and writings on social justice were closely linked to one of the major issues of injustice in Northern Irish society: the treatment of prisoners. Daly was particularly interested in the plight of prisoners and linked their situation and conditions very closely to the creation of the Peaceable Kingdom. In 1988, he wrote the following which illustrates his identification of the connection between prisons and the Peaceable Kingdom: 'Imprisonment should properly have no place in a truly Christian society. In a community which really lived by the standards of Jesus, prisons would be redundant. If prisons are necessary, it can only be because society is not living by the standards proclaimed by Jesus'.[152] Thus, motivated by the Gospels of Matthew and Luke[153] which 'characteristically referred to [prisoners] as objects of divine piety,'[154] and the corporal works of mercy,[155] he sought to plead their case with the authorities; ensure that they received fair treatment[156]; and alert consciences to the assault upon justice that was occurring within the prison system both north and south of the border. Indeed, in a 1985 address to prison chaplains, he stated that a society could be judged by its treatment of prisoners and that only a society that 'lived up to St Paul's precepts'[157] would be worthy of the moniker of Peaceable Kingdom because 'prison reform is inseparable from reform of society itself.'[158]

The biases in the judicial system in Northern Ireland meant that one of the key principles of international human rights standards – the right to a fair trial – was being swept aside in the name of security in the region. But security forces, as Daly pointed out, 'precisely because they are society's resistance to violence, have all the greater obligation to respect justice and human rights.'[159] Here, Walzer's extra conditions for the Doctrine of Double Effect came into play,[160] as Daly argued that the British State needed to take the moral lead in its actions to eradicate violence. The justice of retribution, or of an 'eye for an eye'[161] was to be replaced with a New Testament vision of society in which prisoners were to experience the justice of rehabilitation, allowing them to move away from their previous affiliations to paramilitary organisations. However, Daly believed that the abuse of the judicial system in Northern Ireland began at the time of arrest, with the use of super-grasses,[162] epitomising the inherent corrosion of human rights:

> Yet the progress of democratic legal systems, particularly in the countries of common law tradition, has rested upon the principle that the accused is presumed innocent unless and until his guilt is established beyond all reasonable doubt. In supergrass trials, very severe strain is placed on this sacroscant principle. In the present climate of Northern Ireland, impartiality among juries would be impossible to attain. But the aim of a civilised society is to show that there is impeachable fairness and equality and manifest justice in its courts of law, and that there is neither need nor sense nor moral justification for having recourse to violence in order to secure justice. Any procedure which casts doubt on the integrity of the legal system plays ultimately into the hands of those who believe in violence.[163]

Such use of supergrasses when combined with frequent miscarriages of justice, such as the Birmingham Six and the Guildford Four, 'raised . . . serious questions about the impartiality of the British justice system.'[164] Issues with the justice system were further compounded by extra-judicial killings by the security forces who Daly argued 'precisely because they are society's resistance to violence, have all the greater obligation to respect justice and human rights.'[165] The fact that the security forces were immune to prosecution for human rights infringements reinforced the unjust nature of the British judicial system; something which Daly argued needed to be rectified:

> It seems to be feared, by none more than the security authorities themselves, that to make security personnel answerable to the courts in cases of alleged infringement of human rights in the course of security operations would undermine the credibility of the whole security operation and the morale of the security forces. On the contrary, it could go far towards strengthening the credibility and morale.[166]

Such behaviour on the part of the British government created a cycle of violence and created propaganda for the republican forces to exploit.

Once they were imprisoned, the British government sought to treat those convicted of terrorist offences in the same manner as 'ordinary' inmates, that is, as criminals rather than as politically motivated combatants. Whilst Daly agreed with this idea in principle, he argued that given the means through which some of these convictions were secured, 'there [was] still something of a special category'[167] in existence for paramilitaries. Furthermore, once imprisoned, the behaviour of politically motivated detainees was dominated by the ideals that had inspired their crime. The British government reacted to this in a way that Daly felt to be mistaken: 'They pose a special security problem, and their presence tilts the balance of prison policy towards security rather than towards the other objectives of a humane prison system.'[168] This balance, with its focus upon revenge and retribution rather than rehabilitation, lay at the heart of Daly's critique of British government policy both in terms of the prison system and wider society: 'Repressive measures indeed sometimes mirror the inherent injustices and inequalities existing in the society itself.'[169] The consequent degradation of human rights became his main concern, both when dealing with the issue of the H-Block protests, the use of torture during interrogation,[170] and the mistreatment of prisoners in general. When writing to the Secretary of State for Northern Ireland, Jim Prior, in 1984, he argued that 'measures taken in the name of security can be self-defeating. Unless there is a minimum of human relationship between prisoners and staff, life within the prison becomes intolerable for both, and the resulting tensions increase the security risks.'[171] He had previously emphasised the inhumane nature of the measures taken by prison authorities that provoked the hunger strikes when he commented:

> It could be argued that the counter-measures taken by the prison authorities were unnecessarily severe. Part of the present procedures are intimate body searches, which are performed in a manner which is degrading and brutalising for prisoners, . . . and which are conducted with a frequency which does not seem necessary or justified by strict needs of prison security.[172]

Such behaviour on the part of authorities was the antithesis of the human rights principles laid down by the United Nations to which the British government had signed up.[173] More pertinently for Daly though, the Catholic Church taught that 'Human rights are to be defended not only individually but also as a whole: protecting them only partially would imply a kind of failure to recognise them.'[174] He thus emphasised the communal impact of imprisonment:

> The large number of prisoners indicted for paramilitary offences, a majority of whom come from the kind of alienated and deprived communities which I have mentioned, were an important factor in sustaining the climate of political violence. For each person in jail, one could

count on average at least 30 people in the extended family or in the wider community who were closely affected by that person's imprisonment. Conditions for prisoners, prison discipline, the behaviour of prison officers, family and marital visits, granting or refusing of compassionate parole, all of these have had direct impact on the extended family outside, and often on whole communities. This was an obvious area calling for pastoral concern.[175]

This comment on the implications of imprisonment for communities was in keeping with Daly's vision for social justice and the Peaceable Kingdom. Every person was seen as belonging to a community with the complex web of relationships and solidarity that such membership entails. Thus, to impinge on the human rights of one is to impinge on the human rights of all.

Daly's writings on the plight of prisoners also related their situation to social deprivation with its inherent lack of justice:[176]

Visits to the wings of the Maze and Maghaberry and Crumlin Road prisons revealed again and again the close connection between social deprivation and law breaking. So far as republican prisoners are concerned, these visits have left no doubt but that very few indeed of those prisoners would have been involved in criminal activity or would even have seen the inside of a prison, had it not been for the circumstances in which they grew up. This does not condone their crimes, but it does point to the wrongness of calling them criminal types or thugs or people who choose mindless violence for violence's sake.[177]

The British government was therefore fuelling the conflict and preventing a peaceful settlement from being established by repressing the poor through the employment of excess security measures and by failing to tend to the needs of those residing in the most deprived areas, both republican and loyalist.[178] Catholic teaching on the issue of injustice and its relationship to deprivation was clear: for example, Paul VI had taught in *Populorum Progressio* that 'In certain regions a privileged minority enjoys the refinements of life, while the rest of the inhabitants, impoverished, disunited, "are deprived of almost all possibility of acting on their own initiative and responsibility, and often subsist in living and working conditions unworthy of the human person".'[179]

Daly therefore used Catholic social teaching on human rights to critique and offer a resolution to the issue of prisoners' rights. John XXIII had stipulated that people had a 'right to freedom from bodily harm as well as a right to those commodities necessary for an appropriate standard of living' *inter alia* a right to family life, clothing, a home, education, and health care.[180] Daly built upon these ideas and combined them with the Church's emphasis upon rehabilitation for prisoners which acted as the test of a civilised society. For example, when commenting on the H-Block issue he suggested 'a

general review of prison conditions could well remove entirely the anach-
ronistic and by now nearly superseded obligation to wear prison clothes.
It could devise ways of ensuring that even non-cooperative prisoners have
access to the excellent educational and recreational services which are nor-
mally available and which these prisoners need ever more than others.'[181]
In addition, he argued for the use of mercy by the British government in its
dealings with prisoners:[182] 'Prudent acts of clemency, conducted in a responsible and systematic manner, could be a recognition of society's collective
responsibility for what the whole community did and failed to do in allowing a political and social situation to develop in which young people were left
at the mercy of emotional and passional forces stronger than themselves.'[183]
A concern for human rights and the rehabilitation of prisoners was for Daly,
as stated earlier, the mark of a civilised society. Through his work on the
issue of prisoners, he demonstrated how a just society could be established
in Northern Ireland: everyone's human rights would be respected no matter how they themselves had behaved, and prisoners would be given access
to work and education as a means of rehabilitation. By engaging in such
policies the British would remove one of the main grievances of republicans
(and other paramilitary groups), thereby demonstrating the efficacy of a
non-violent approach and removing one justification for violence.

Conclusion

In his message for the 1981 World Day for Peace, Daly outlined the importance
of social justice to his vision for the Peaceable Kingdom; in it he stated that: 'a
plan to reduce and ultimately eliminate poverty in both [Protestant and Catho-
lic] areas should and could unite people from both communities in a movement
of joint Christian and human commitment to social justice.'[184] There can be no
doubt that social injustice and the human degradation that followed on from
it was one of, if not the, cause of the conflict in Northern Ireland. It therefore
had to be resolutely tackled if the Peaceable Kingdom were to be created in the
region. However, this area provided the most resistance within communities,
as many, especially during the hedonistic days of Thatcherism, did not understand the difference between charity and justice and did not acknowledge that
justice was a universal right. Daly responded to this problematic thus:

   To overcome this, three conditions are necessary:

1   We must admit that there are injustices in our society;
2   We must not make distinctions in our thought between Protestant and
     Catholic;
3   Our Christian convictions must not be confined to our times spent in
     church and to periods of worship and prayer: concern for justice must
     influence everything.[185]

The lived Christianity espoused by Daly was an integrated existence, one full of tension and difficulty which demanded a reformation of society along the lines of Catholic social teaching. Through his work on social and economic justice, Daly was very much involved in consciousness raising as a means of motivating the laity to use their talents to build the Peaceable Kingdom. However, Daly was also aware that, without a reform of the political structures in Northern Ireland, peace was impossible.

Notes

1 Jürgen Moltman cited in Cahal Daly, 'Justice and Law: The Birmingham Six and the Stalker-Sampson Report' *The Furrow*, 1988, vol. 39, no. 3, pp. 165–171, 171.
2 Cahal Daly, *Steps on My Pilgrim Journey: Memories and Reflections* (Dublin: Veritas, 1988), p. 514.
3 *Irish Independent*, 27 December 1997, cited by Daly in 'From the Justice of Each Comes Peace for All', World Day of Peace, Corpus Christi Church, Drumcondra, Dublin', 1 January 1998 in *Addresses on Peace in Northern Ireland, 1997–2001*.
4 Cited in Power, *From Ecumenism to Community Relations* p. 137.
5 'Industry and Society', Address to the Institute of Directors, Conway Hotel, Belfast', 11 January 1991 in *Addresses on Peace in Northern Ireland, 1991–1992*, Emphasis added.
6 Daly, *Steps on My Pilgrim Journey*, p. 93.
7 Daly, *Steps on My Pilgrim Journey*, p. 93.
8 Cahal Daly, 'Christus Rex Society: The Origins and Purposes of a Catholic Diocesan Sociological Association in Ireland, 1941–1946', *Sociological Origins*, 2006, vol. 5, no. 1, pp. 38–42.
9 Daly, *Steps on My Pilgrim Journey*, p. 95.
10 'Ecumenical Service in the Octagon of the University of Ulster at Coleraine', Address for Week of Prayer for Christian Unity, 22 January 1986 in *Addresses on Peace in Northern Ireland, 1984–1986*.
11 'The Role and Responsibility of the Churches in the Northern Crisis', Address to the Dublin University History Society, 8 May 1975, *Addresses on Peace in Northern Ireland, 1968–1975*.
12 'Third Conference of Catholic Prison Chaplains', Domantine, Newry, 19 October 1988 in Northern Ireland Political Collection, Linen Hall Library, Belfast, *Addresses on Peace in Northern Ireland, 1987–1988*, vol. 4, P13581.
13 'Third Conference of Catholic Prison Chaplains'.
14 For an analysis and exposition of this concept, see John Loughlin, *Human Dignity in the Judaeo-Christian Tradition: Catholic, Orthodox, Anglican, and Protestant Perspectives* (London: Bloomsbury, 2019).
15 J Bryan Hehir, 'Religious Activism for Human Rights: A Christian Case Study', in John Witte and Johan van der Vyver (eds.), *Religious Human Rights in Global Perspective*, vol. 1 (Leiden: Brill, 1996), pp. 97–120, 105. For a fuller discussion of the historical development of Catholic human rights discourses, see Zachary R Calo, 'Catholic Social Thought and Human Rights', *American Journal of Economics and Sociology*, 2015, vol. 74, no. 1, pp. 93–112, 95–103; Kenneth R Himes, *Christianity and the Political Order: Conflict, Cooptation, and Cooperation* (New York: Orbis, 2013), pp. 306–310; and Thomas Hoppe, 'Human Rights', in Judith A Dwyer (ed.), *The New Dictionary of Catholic Social Thought* (Collegeville: Liturgical Press, 1994), pp. 454–470.

16   Himes, *Christianity and the Political Order*, p. 306.
17   Gal 3:28.
18   *Coming Back Home: Pastoral Letter from Bishop Cahal B Daly to His People in Down and Connor, Lent 1983*, Northern Ireland Political Collection, Linen Hall Library, Belfast, P2125, p. 19.
19   1 Cor 1:26–28 and Rom 12:16–19.
20   'Northern Ireland Prison Chaplains' Association', Address at AGM, Stormont, 1 May 1985 in Northern Ireland Political Collection, Linen Hall Library, Belfast, *Addresses on Peace in Northern Ireland, 1984–1986*.
21   Lk 1:46–56. This is the first great manifesto in the New Testament, the other being the cleansing of the Temple, Mk 11:15–19.
22   Daly, except for the World Day for Peace Messages and some Vatican II documents, rarely quotes papal teachings on social justice, preferring instead to ground his vision in the New Testament, with particular reference to the Gospels.
23   Cardinal Joseph Ratzinger, *Libertatis Conscientia*, 22 March 1986, §50, cf. §§ 66, 67, & 68, www.vatican.va/roman_curia/congregations/cfaith/documents/rc_con_cfaith_doc_19860322_freedom-liberation_en.html (accessed 21 August 2019).
24   *Libertatis Conscientia*, §64. Cf. *Evangelii Gaudium*: 'To evangelise is to make the kingdom of God present in our world.' §176.
25   Donal Dorr, *Option for the Poor and for the Earth: From Leo XIII to Pope Francis* (Maryknoll, NY: Orbis, 2016), p. 148.
26   Elaine Graham, *Between a Rock and a Hard Place: Public Theology in a Post-Secular Age* (London: SCM, 2013), p. xxvi.
27   For a guide to the documents which constitute the social teaching of the church, see: Kenneth R Himes (ed.), and Lisa Sowle Cahill, Charles E Curran, David Hollenbach and Thomas Shannon (associate eds.), *Modern Catholic Social Teaching: Commentaries and Interpretations* (Washington, DC: Georgetown University Press, 2005).
28   Marie-Dominique Chenu, *La "doctrine social" de l'Église comme idéologie* (Paris: Cerf, 1979), p. 72.
29   Pius XI, *Quadragesimo Anno*, 15 May 1931, §142, http://w2.vatican.va/content/pius-xi/en/encyclicals/documents/hf_p-xi_enc_19310515_quadragesimo-anno.html (accessed 21 August 2019); and Pius XI, *Divini Redemptoris*, 19 March 1937, §53 https://w2.vatican.va/content/pius-xi/en/encyclicals/documents/hf_p-xi_enc_19370319_divini-redemptoris.html (accessed 21 August 2019).
30   Paul VI, *Populorum Progressio*, 26 March 1967, http://w2.vatican.va/content/paul-vi/en/encyclicals/documents/hf_p-vi_enc_26031967_populorum.html, §§ 29, 30, & 32 (accessed 12 August 2019).
31   Calo, 'Catholic Social Thought and Human Rights', p. 107.
32   'Identifying and Facing the Challenges in the Local Situation', Corrymeela Community and the Irish School of Ecumenics, 10 May 1989 in *Addresses on Peace in Northern Ireland, 1989–1990*. Emphasis added.
33   David Hollenbach, '*Pacem in Terris* and Human Rights', *Journal of Catholic Social Thought*, 2013, vol. 10, no. 1, pp. 5–15, 10.
34   Paul VI, *Dignitatis Humanae*, 7 December 1965, §4, www.vatican.va/archive/hist_councils/ii_vatican_council/documents/vat-ii_decl_19651207_dignitatis-humanae_en.html (accessed 21 August 2019).
35   'Mass for Peace and Justice', St Comgall's Parish, Antrim, 6 February 1987, *Addresses on Peace in Northern Ireland, 1987–1988*.
36   SJ Roger Haight, 'Praxis', Judith A Dwyer (ed.), *The New Dictionary of Catholic Social Thought* (Collegeville: Liturgical Press, 1994), pp. 776–777.
37   Quoted in Graham, *Between a Rock and a Hard Place*, p. 10.

38 Gutiérrez, 'The Option for the Poor Arises from Faith in Christ', p. 320.
39 *Populorum Progressio*, §43.
40 Paul VI, *Octogesima Adveniens*, 14 May 1971, §24–25, http://w2.vatican.va/content/paul-vi/en/apost_letters/documents/hf_p-vi_apl_19710514_octogesima-adveniens.html, §37 (accessed 13 August 2019).
41 Paul Teague, *Northern Ireland: The Political Economy of Peace*, The Senator George J Mitchell Institute for Global Peace, Security and Justice Working Paper Series, IGPSJ WP 01–16, October 2016, www.qub.ac.uk/Research/GRI/mitchell-institute/FileStore/Filetoupload,727473,en.pdf (accessed 21 August 2019).
42 'Christian Peace: The Challenge to the Individual', Social Study Conference, Falcarragh, 11 August 1972 in *Addresses on Peace in Northern Ireland, 1968–1975*.
43 'West Belfast: Time for a New Deal', St Luke's Church, Twinbrook, Belfast, 24 April 1988 in *Addresses on Peace in Northern Ireland, 1987–1988*.
44 *Catholic Herald*, 14 January 1977.
45 'Christian Peace: The Challenge to the Individual'.
46 'Christian Peace: The Challenge to the Individual'.
47 'The Lower Falls Road: A Wronged But Forgiving People', St Peter's Pro-Cathedral, 31 March 1985 in *Addresses on Peace in Northern Ireland 1984–1986*.
48 'The Lower Falls Road'.
49 'Identifying and Facing the Challenges in the Local Situation'.
50 'The Lower Falls Road'.
51 'West Belfast: Time for a New Deal'.
52 Cited in 'The Lower Falls Road'.
53 'The Lower Falls Road'.
54 'West Belfast: Time for a New Deal'.
55 'West Belfast: Time for a New Deal'.
56 Author's Interview with Kenneth Bloomfield, Belfast, 23 June 2011.
57 'Christian Peace: The Challenge to the Individual'.
58 'Industry and Society'.
59 'Christian Peace: The Challenge to the Individual'.
60 Anthony M Gallagher, *Majority Minority Review 2: Employment, Unemployment and Religion in Northern Ireland* (Coleraine: Centre for the Study of Conflict, University of Ulster, 1991), http://cain.ulst.ac.uk/csc/reports/majmin2.htm#contents (accessed 21 August 2019). Daly himself discounted all of these arguments; see 'Identifying and Facing the Challenges in the Local Situation'.
61 Gallagher, *Employment, Unemployment and Religion in Northern Ireland*.
62 Richard Rose, *Governing Without Consensus* (London: Faber, 1991). Indeed, this was a publication that Daly relied heavily upon when determining his early analysis of the conflict in Northern Ireland.
63 John Curtice and Tony Gallagher, 'The Northern Ireland Dimension', in R Jowell, S Witherspoon and L Brook (eds.), *British Social Attitudes: The 7th Report* (Aldershot: Gower, 1990), pp. 183–216, 209.
64 Sarah Nelson, 'Protestant "Ideology" Considered: The Case of "discrimination"', in Ivor Crewe (ed.), *The Politics of Race* (London: Croom Helm, 1975), pp. 155–187, 178.
65 HMSO, Fair Employment (Northern Ireland) Act 1976, http://cain.ulst.ac.uk/hmso/fea1976.htm (accessed 21 August 2019).
66 Cited in AM Gallagher, 'Employment, Unemployment and Religion in Northern Ireland', *Majority Minority Review*, vol. 2, https://cain.ulster.ac.uk/csc/reports/mm210.htm (accessed 21 August 2019).
67 Raymond T Russell, 'Fair Employment in Northern Ireland: The Decades of Change (1990–2010)', Northern Ireland Assembly Research and Information Service Research Paper, 10 August 2012, www.niassembly.gov.uk/globalassets/

documents/raise/publications/2012/general/12112.pdf (accessed 21 August 2019).

68 Kevin McNamara, Interview with Cardinal Cahal Daly, 7 February 2002, Dr Kevin McNamara Private Papers. Emphasis added.

69 'White House Conference on Trade and Investment', Washington DC, USA, 24–26 May 1995 in *Addresses on Peace in Northern Ireland 1993–1996*.

70 'Identifying and Facing the Challenges in the Local Situation'.

71 Power, *From Ecumenism to Community Relations*, pp. 83–100 for Daly's comments on this.

72 See Fr Seán McManus, *The MacBride Principles*, University of Minnesota Human Rights Library, December 1997, http://hrlibrary.umn.edu/links/mac bride.html#principles (accessed 21 August 2019).

73 Kevin McNamara, Account of conversation with Cardinal Daly, 7 February 2002, Dr Kevin McNamara, Private Papers.

74 Kevin McNamara, Meeting with Rt Hon Kevin McNamara MP, RE: The Mac-Bride Principles, 6 February 2002. Dr Kevin McNamara Private Papers. For further details of the churches and MacBride, see Kevin McNamara, *The MacBride Principles Irish America Strikes Back* (Liverpool: Liverpool University Press, 2009), pp. 38–39.

75 Statistics taken from Gallagher, *Employment, Unemployment and Religion in Northern Ireland*.

76 Cahal Daly, 'Peace Through Social Justice', in *The Price of Peace* (Belfast: The Blackstaff Press, 1991), pp. 111–136, 115.

77 Cahal Daly, *Dialogue for Peace* (Dublin: Irish Messenger Publications, 1983), p. 17.

78 'Freedom to Trust: Fourteenth World Day of Peace, Longford', 1 January 1981, *Addresses on Peace in Northern Ireland, 1976–1983*, vol. 2.

79 'Young People in Crisis: the Youth Service Role', Seminar to Youth Committee for Northern Ireland, Cultra, 18 June 1984 in *Addresses on Peace in Northern Ireland 1984–1986*.

80 'Identifying and Facing the Challenges in the Local Situation'.

81 'Solemn First Evensong of St Bartholomew', 125th Anniversary of the Parish, 23 August 1992, *Addresses on Peace in Northern Ireland 1991–1992*.

82 'Solemn First Evensong of St Bartholomew'.

83 Leo XIII, *Rerum Novarum*, 15 May 1891, §1, http://w2.vatican.va/content/leo-xiii/en/encyclicals/documents/hf_l-xiii_enc_15051891_rerum-novarum.html (accessed 25 March 2019).

84 'Address given at the Longford Chamber of Commerce', 12 November 1975, *Addresses on Peace in Northern Ireland, 1968–1975*.

85 'Conformity and Conscience', 24th Annual Summer School of the Social Study Conference, St Kieran's College, Kilkenny, 4 August 1976 in *Addresses on Peace in Northern Ireland 1976–1983*.

86 For its relationship to peace, see 'Identifying and Facing the Challenges in the Local Situation'.

87 'Conformity and Conscience'.

88 *Rerum Novarum*, §8.

89 John XXIII, *Mater et Magistra*, 15 May 1961, §119, http://w2.vatican.va/con tent/john-xxiii/en/encyclicals/documents/hf_j-xxiii_enc_15051961_mater.html (accessed 13 August 2019).

90 *Populorum Progressio*, §23.

91 *Sollicitudo Rei Socialis*, 30 December 1987, §42, http://w2.vatican.va/content/john-paul-ii/en/encyclicals/documents/hf_jp-ii_enc_30121987_sollicitudo-rei-socialis.html, accessed 13 August 2019).

92 Quoted Edward J O'Boyle, 'Blessed John Paul II on Social Mortgage: Origins, Questions, and Norms', *Logos: A Journal of Catholic Thought and Culture*, 2014, vol. 17, no. 2, pp. 119–135, 129.

93 Abraham Maslow, *Motivation and Personality* (New York: Harper and Brothers, 1954).

94 'Conformity and Conscience'.

95 'Industry and Society'.

96 'Industry and Society.'

97 O'Boyle, 'Blessed John Paul II on Social Mortgage', pp. 128–129.

98 'Industry and Society'.

99 'Mass for Peace and Justice'.

100 'Mass for Peace and Justice'.

101 'Conformity and Conscience'.

102 'Solemn First Evensong of St Bartholomew'.

103 See Philip Booth (ed.), *Catholic Social Teaching and the Market Economy* (London: Institute of Economic Affairs, 2007). For an example of how such ideas have been mainstreamed in thinking on development, see Oxfam International, *An Economy for the 99%: It's Time to Build a HUMAN Economy That Benefits Everyone, Not Just the Privileged Few,* January 2017, www.oxfam. org/sites/www.oxfam.org/files/file_attachments/bp-economy-for-99-percent-160117-en.pdf (accessed 21 August 2019).

104 In his 2013 Apostolic Exhortation, *Evangelii Gaudium*, Pope Francis stated that 'One cause of this situation is found in our relationship with money, since we calmly accept its dominion over ourselves and our societies. The current financial crisis can make us overlook the fact that it originated in a profound human crisis: the denial of the primacy of the human person! We have created new idols. The worship of the ancient golden calf (cf. Ex 32:1–35) has returned in a new and ruthless guise in the idolatry of money and the dictatorship of an impersonal economy lacking a truly human purpose. The worldwide crisis affecting finance and the economy lays bare their imbalances and, above all, their lack of real concern for human beings; man is reduced to one of his needs alone: consumption.' §55.

105 'Solemn First Evensong of St Bartholomew'.

106 'Industry and Society'.

107 Holy See, *Compendium of the Social Doctrine of the Church* (Vatican City: 2004), §304, www.vatican.va/roman_curia/pontifical_councils/justpeace/documents/rc_pc_justpeace_doc_20060526_compendio-dott-soc_en.html (accessed 13 August 2019).

108 Holy See, *Catechism of the Catholic Church*, §2435, www.vatican.va/archive/ENG0015/_INDEX.HTM (accessed 21 August 2019).

109 John Paul II, *Laborem Exercens*, 14 September 1981, §20, http://w2.vatican. va/content/john-paul-ii/en/encyclicals/documents/hf_jp-ii_enc_14091981_laborem-exercens.html (accessed 21 August 2019).

110 *Laborem Exercens*, §20.

111 *Laborem Exercens*, §20.

112 Cahal Daly, *Mass and the World of Work* (Dublin: Irish Messenger Publications, 1981), p. 15.

113 Daly, *Mass and the World of Work*, p. 14.

114 'Mass for Peace and Justice', and 'Identifying and Facing the Challenges in the Local Situation.'

115 Irish Catholic Bishops' Conference, *The Work of Justice*, September 1977, §89, shortened version available at www.catholicbishops.ie/wp-content/uploads/images/docs/pastoral%20letter%20-%20the%20work%20of%20justice.pdf (accessed 21 August 2019).

116 *The Work of Justice*, §§114–118.

117 'Mass for Peace and Justice'.

118 Identifying and Facing the Challenges in the Local Situation'; cf. *Rerum Novarum*, §22.

119 *Rerum Novarum*, §22.

120 Rumy Hasan, 'Riots and Urban Unrest in Britain in the 1980s and 1990s: A Critique of Dominant Explanations', in Michael Lavalette and Gerry Mooney (eds.), *Class Struggle and Social Welfare* (London: Routledge, 2000), pp. 173–198.

121 'The Role and Responsibility of the Churches in the Northern Crisis'.

122 'Mass for Peace and Justice'.

123 United Nations definition cited in Wilson A Head, 'Community Development in Post-Industrial Society', in Dan A Chekki (ed.), *Community Development* (New Delhi: Vikas Publishing, 1979), pp. 101–115, 101.

124 'Mass for Peace and Justice'.

125 'It is sad that the living conditions of the poor are known to few in the more prosperous sectors of the public. It is chiefly when certain areas are thought to be associated with street violence and vandalism and juvenile crime, that the existence of these areas and the living and housing conditions in them capture public attention. But the public interest is often limited to the demand that the violence and vandalism be curbed, for example by measure such as increased police presence, firmer legal action, more severe penalties etc; or that juvenile crime be cleared up by the detention of young offenders.' 'Mass for Peace and Justice'.

126 'The Catholic community in the rest of the city and the diocese, especially in the more advantaged parishes, will also lend their support and help. In the spirit of the early church as described in the Acts of the Apostles, we shall try to share the gifts God has given us with others, "according to what each one needs" (Acts 2:45). It was in that spirit that Catholics Caring was set up. It has accomplished much, but it has yet to achieve its full potential. It is not a question just of giving to them but of receiving and learning from them, for they too have much to teach and much to give.' 'West Belfast: Time for a New Deal'.

127 Acts 2:44–45.

128 Elizabeth DeYoung, 'Girwood Barracks: Power, Politics and Planning in the Post-Ceasefire City', PhD Thesis, University of Liverpool, 2018. Cf. 'Identifying and Facing the Challenges in the Local Situation'.

129 Peter Somerville, 'Conservative Housing Policy', in Hugh M Bochel (ed.), *The Conservative Party and Social Policy* (Bristol: Policy Press, 2011), pp. 119–149.

130 The Divis Complex consisted of 12 eight-story blocks of terraces and flats and the 20-story Divis Tower. Built in 1966, it housed 2400 residents in 850 flats, 100% of whom were Catholic. During the conflict, the tower was the scene of paramilitary activity and had an army observation point on its top two floors which, during the most intense periods of fighting, could only be reached by helicopter.

131 Richard Rogers, *A Place for All People: Life, Architecture and the Fair Society* (Edinburgh: Canongate, 2017), p. 22.

132 Think, for example, of Ernö Goldfinger's Trellick Tower in North Kensington, London, which acted as the inspiration for JG Ballard's 1975 novel, *High Rise*.

133 Jennifer Curtis, ' "Community" and the Re-Making of 1970s Belfast', *Ethnos*, 2008, vol. 73, no. 3, pp. 399–426, 418.

134 Divis Study Group, *Balconies, Brits and Bin Lids: An Oral History of Divis Flats* (Belfast: Divis Study Group, 1998), Northern Ireland Political Collection, Linen Hall Library, Belfast, P9137.

135 Tim Blackman, Eileen Evason, Martin Melaugh and Roberta Woods, *Housing and Health in West Belfast: A Case Study of Divis Flats and the Twinbrook Estate* (Belfast: Divis Joint Development Committee, 1987), Northern Ireland Political Collection, Linen Hall Library, Belfast, P7768.
136 Blackman, et al., *Housing and Health in West Belfast*, p. 11.
137 Megan Deirdre Roy, 'Divis Flats: The Social and Political Implications of a Modern Housing Project in Belfast, Northern Ireland, 1968–1998', *Iowa Historical Journal*, 2007, vol. 1, no. 1, pp. 1–44, 2.
138 'The Lower Falls Road'.
139 'Reach Out to the Poor, World Day of Peace', St Malachy's Church, Armagh, 1 January 1993 in *Addresses on Peace in Northern Ireland, 1993–1996*.
140 'Identifying and Facing the Challenges in the Local Situation'.
141 Michael Young and Peter Wilmott, *Family and Kinship in East London* (London: Penguin, 1957).
142 Divis Flats, *The Dreadful Enclosure* (Belfast: Art and Research Exchange, 1985), Northern Ireland Political Collection, Linen Hall Library, Belfast, P2484.
143 Roy, 'Divis Flats', pp. 19–20.
144 Rogers, *A Place for All People*, p. 156.
145 Elizabeth DeYoung, 'The New Lodge and the "New Belfast"? A Case for Community-Led Development', Report Prepared for Aston Community Trust, July 2016.
146 Brendan Murtagh, 'New Spaces and Old in "Post-Conflict" Belfast', Divided Cities/Contested States Working Papers, no. 5, p. 4, www.conflictincities.org/PDFs/WorkingPaper5_10.9.08.pdf (accessed 21 August 2019).
147 Similar consequences were seen with the regeneration of East London in preparation for the 2012 London Olympics. See Paul Watt, ' "It's Not for Us": Regeneration, the 2012 Olympics, and the Gentrification of East London', *City: Analysis of Urban Trends, Culture, Theory, Policy and Action*, 2013, vol. 17, no. 1, pp. 99–119.
148 William JV Neill, Diana S Fitzsimons and Brendan Murtagh, *Reimagining the Pariah City: Urban Development in Belfast and Detroit* (London: Avebury, 1995).
149 'West Belfast: Time for a New Deal'.
150 'Christmas and the Cry of the Poor'.
151 'West Belfast: Time for a New Deal'.
152 'I was in prison and you never visited me', "Broken Nails" Programme Brochure, 9–18 December 1988, *Addresses on Peace in Northern Ireland, 1987–1988*.
153 Mt 25:36 and Lk 4:18.
154 Cahal Daly, *The Price of Peace* (Belfast: The Blackstaff Press, 1991), p. 92. In his autobiography, Daly states that 'work for the needs and rights of prisoners and for the welfare of prisoners' families is also a clear command of the Lord in the Gospels.' Daly, *Steps on My Pilgrim Journey*, p. 252.
155 See *Catechism of the Catholic Church*, §2447. These corporal works of mercy are a number of charitable actions for the common good which reflect the Church's teachings on social justice. These are feeding the hungry, sheltering the homeless, clothing the naked, visiting the sick and imprisoned, and burying the dead. As well as carrying out such actions, advocating for such groups is seen as a central element of the Catholic faith.
156 Whilst his central aim was the promotion of justice for a marginalised group, thus securing peace as Paul VI asked by working for justice, one of the side effects of this would be the removal of a propaganda tool for the IRA, further promoting peace: 'I am firmly convinced that this would make a significant

contribution to the prospects for peace, and would, at the same time, deliver a blow to IRA propaganda.' Cahal Daly, 'Violence Destroys the Work of Justice', *The Furrow*, 1980, vol. 31, no. 2, pp. 71–87, 78.

157 'Northern Ireland Prison Chaplain's Association'.
158 'Third Conference of Catholic Prison Chaplains'.
159 'The Politics of Peace'.
160 Michael Walzer, *Just and Unjust Wars: A Moral Argument with Historical Illustrations* (New York: Basic Books, 1977), p. 153.
161 Ex 21:24.
162 The term 'supergrass' is British slang for an informant who turns Queen's evidence in return for immunity from prosecution. The use of supergrasses in Northern Ireland began in 1981 and was discontinued in 1985. Many supergrass convictions were subsequently overturned. For further discussion of this, see Angela Duffy, *Informers in 20th Century Ireland* (Jefferson, NC: McFarland, 2018), in particular Chapter 5.
163 'Peace: A Moral Imperative', World Day of Peace Address, St Anne's Church, Derriaghy, 1 January 1986, *Addresses on Peace in Northern Ireland 1984–1986*.
164 Ministry and Witness in a Time of Political Conflict', Ypres, Belgium, 19 April 1997 in *Addresses on Peace in Northern Ireland 1997–2001*.
165 'The Politics of Peace'.
166 'The Politics of Peace'.
167 Daly, 'Violence Destroys the Work of Justice', p. 78.
168 Daly, *The Price of Peace*, p. 98.
169 'The Politics of Peace'.
170 'Further harm was done by the rigorous methods of interrogation used. Reports of 'torture methods' shocked members at Westminster and the former ombudsman, Sir Edward Compton, was asked to conduct an enquiry . . . documented evidence was published on brutality of Army methods which has never been categorically denied.' *Violence in Ireland and the Christian Conscience* (Dublin: Veritas, 1973), p. 33.
171 Letter to Jim Prior, Secretary of State for Northern Ireland, 24 July 1984, Public Record Office of Northern Ireland, Belfast, NIO/12/530a.
172 Daly, 'Violence Destroys the Work of Justice', p. 79.
173 United Nations, *Universal Declaration of Human Rights*, 10 December 1948, www.un.org/en/documents/udhr/ (accessed 21 August 2019).
174 See *Compendium of the Social Doctrine of the Church*, §154.
175 'Ministry and Witness in a Time of Political Conflict'.
176 See for example Daly, *The Price of Peace*, pp. 99, 101.
177 'Ministry and Witness in a Time of Political Conflict'.
178 Daly, *The Price of Peace*, p. 114.
179 *Populorum Progressio*, §9.
180 Hoppe, 'Human Rights', p. 460.
181 Daly, 'Violence Destroys the Work of Justice', pp. 79–80.
182 For a practical example of this, see Teresa Malcolm, 'Cardinal Calls for Prisoner Transfer', *National Catholic Reporter*, 26 April 1996.
183 Daly, *The Price of Peace*, p. 108.
184 'Freedom to Trust'.
185 'Third Conference of Catholic Prison Chaplains'.

4   Political justice

For Daly, the search for the Peaceable Kingdom in Northern Ireland was based upon contemporary realities. These were the social and economic injustices that were preventing a positive peace emerging by perpetuating inequality and provoking both paramilitaries and the state into acts of violence. The alterative possible future presented by him was focused upon God's relationship to, and desires for, the world, whereby institutions would choose to reform themselves rather than being overthrown and replaced by equally flawed models leading to further repression and discontent. It was through such a method that Daly prevented his work from becoming utopian.

Much of his discourse centred upon the nature of political justice, and in particular the steps that the British and Irish states needed to take to create the Peaceable Kingdom. British policy, focusing as it did on the containment of violence in the hope that a mutually hurting stalemate[1] would eventually lead to a cessation of paramilitary activity, was fundamentally flawed. This point was made by Daly in 1978 when he argued that 'even if the violence were eliminated, Northern Ireland would remain chronically politically unstable and a violence prone society unless the root causes of the violence were firmly tackled and unless the political structures of a just society, recognised as such by both communities were established.'[2] Daly argued that the British state was abdicating its responsibilities to the people of Northern Ireland by failing to create a society 'in which the pursuit of the good, the true, the beautiful, and the just will be made less difficult for more and more people, and obstacles to the attainment of these moral ends will be as far as possible reduced or removed.'[3] Thus, in an era of religious freedom ushered in by the Second Vatican Council, the state, instead of being subservient to a dominant church which viewed itself as a political power, was now being critiqued instead of courted and asked to ensure that justice transcended political ideologies.

Daly's analysis was not just confined to the structures of the state but also included participation in the democratic process by both unionists and nationalists. For a state to work, it has to operate as a community. The Catholic Church's teachings on the nature of democracy and Daly's interpretation of them for the Northern Irish context demanded that people take justice and the need to ensure human flourishing into account in their political decision-making. For Daly,

> politics is a morality for living. It is [the] patient unwearying effort to achieve the obtainable good for living people now. It is open to any dialogue, ready for any discussion with any person or group whose views are relevant or whose consent is necessary, in order that people may have peace.[4]

Both nationalists and unionists had to behave in a way that would make peace possible, and Daly spent a good deal of time, in addition to critiquing the behaviours of the British and Irish governments, outlining how this was possible and its relationship to seeking the Peaceable Kingdom.

Daly offered his critique of the British and Irish states using the non-violent method of protest and persuasion through formal statements and communications with wider society.[5] He sought to hold the British and Irish governments to account, sometimes quite forcefully reminding them of the needed to take responsibility in the search for an equitable solution to the conflict rather than relying upon the suppression of violence as a means of conflict management. Daly's engagement in what can be broadly termed a redefinition of the Catholic Church's relationship to the state, and therefore direct political participation in Ireland, should be viewed very much in terms of the emergent political peace process and the need for more equitable structures of governance to be established. Daly's methods and the vision presented for such structures were grounded in the Gospel and the Magisterium. His method centred upon a rational and empirically based interpretation of the Northern Irish context and was communicated through non-violent means. Additionally, he saw the pursuit of political justice as a means of achieving the binary of personal and social salvation and conversion that was so crucial to his ministry to the people of Northern Ireland. But before considering this, we must briefly explore the nature of Catholic teachings on church and state.

Church-state relations in a Roman Catholic context

From the 1960s onwards, the Catholic Church sought to influence society through the adoption of what Eric O Hanson has termed 'a cultural pastoral approach.'[6] Globally, it developed a more ethical stance on evangelisation than it had previously employed. Failings, such as forced conversions, were acknowledged: 'In the life of the people of God in its pilgrimage, through the vicissitudes of human history, there have at times appeared patterns of behaviour which was not in keeping with the spirit of the Gospel and were even opposed to it.'[7] The Second Vatican Council brought the Catholic Church into partnership with the world and placed it firmly within civil society. There can be no doubt that within an Irish context prior to this the Catholic Church was firmly embedded within the state: in the Republic as a result of its special relationship with government and in Northern Ireland as a consequence of its provision of a 'state within a state' for the minority community. Vatican II changed 'the structural location of the church in relation to state and society.'[8] Somewhat ironically, in its demands for universal religious freedom, the Catholic Church freed itself from the shackles of authoritarianism and placed itself at the service of society. Consequently, it provided firmer ground upon which to base its critiques of injustice. The Church's main mission was now to proclaim the Gospel in accordance with the teachings of Christ, who communicated by example rather than by force. Such an 'approach was not one of coercion or condemnation. The only force at their disposal was the persuasion of an authentic witness.'[9] The rights and beliefs of other religions were to be acknowledged and respected. However, as Emile Perreau-Saussine has argued, 'in recognising the freedom of religion, the church certainly didn't stop hoping that society might become as Christian as possible.'[10] The Church provided a vision of the world based upon the concept of the Peaceable Kingdom which placed the onus on local bishops to discern their own role within their contexts. In Latin America, this led to liberation theology. In Northern Ireland, Daly undertook the 'culture-forming task of constructing a religiously-informed public philosophy.'[11] It was a task he enthusiastically embraced. Consequently, religious freedom did not lead to the privatisation of religion but rather constructed a new paradigm for a Catholic dialogue with state and society.

The Catholic Church thus redefined and reimagined itself as a 'voice for the voiceless' whilst at the same time seeking to create conditions through which the poor, marginalised, and vulnerable were able to advocate for themselves. This was achieved by the translation of the Catholic social teaching tenets of solidarity and subsidiarity into practical action primarily undertaken by the laity. The Church's role was now focused on the promotion of the dignity and flourishing of the human person, transforming society from within using the prototype provided by Jesus's ministry through its dialectical presence in the world. As *Gaudium et Spes* taught: 'This Council can provide no more eloquent proof of its solidarity with the entire human family with which it is bound up, as well as its respect and love for that family, than by engaging with it in conversation about these various problems.'[12] After the Second Vatican Council, therefore, the Catholic Church found itself once more in step with the world; it was no longer a reactionary institution seeking control. Rather, as this quotation from Daly illustrates:

> The Catholic Church in Ireland totally rejects the concept of a confessional state. We have not sought and we do not seek a Catholic State for a Catholic people. We believe that the alliance of the Church and State is harmful for the State. We rejoiced when the ambiguous formula regarding the special position of the Catholic Church was struck out of

the Constitution by the electorate of the Republic. The Catholic Church in Ireland *has no power and seeks no power except the power of the gospel it preaches* and the consciences and convictions of those who freely accept that teaching.[13]

Daly's verbal submission to the New Ireland Form tells us much of changing attitudes to church and state in the post-conciliar era. Whilst he is speaking of changes to the Republic's constitution,[14] there is a universality to his words. Before this, the church's attitude towards the state had been defensive and intense, seeking to protect and consolidate its own power and exercise an authority over states and their citizens that was defined by a triumphalist belief in the truth of its teachings.[15] In redefining this relationship, Vatican II freed the Church to preach the Gospel. The Church now placed itself firmly at the service of the world in order to transform it. 'The council struck a new balance between the needs of the political order and the transcendent status of the faith, recovering a sense of tradition as something that combined the acceptance of revelation with its reinterpretation.'[16] That 'sense of tradition' was the Gospel, and the Catholic Church sought to align itself more closely with the ministry of Jesus.[17] To bring about the Peaceable Kingdom, the church had to become proactive. As Yves Congar argues:

> The Church is the direct preparation for the kingdom, having within itself the strength of the Holy Spirit, and she cannot but strive to transform the world to the utmost. Of necessity she seeks as much as possible to reduce evil in the world, to rebuild it in good order, to make operative the healing, uplifting, transforming force of . . . the gifts of grace.[18]

It stood back from the state, adopting the view that 'the status quo can never be sacralised and placed beyond scrutiny or considered immune from the necessity of ongoing reform.'[19] The Catholic Church therefore sought to become a moral influencer rather than an equal partner within the political sphere.

Such thinking transformed the Church into a servant of the world and provided it with greater freedom to dialogue with and critique society. The theme of human dignity and flourishing was recurrent in Daly's writings, and this chapter explains his discourse on the nature of the state and a citizen's participation in it, and its relationship to the Peaceable Kingdom that he sought to proclaim as the message of the Gospel for the earthly city. *Gaudium et Spes* therefore provided a theological rationale for this form of political engagement by the Church. The Church now became a pastoral guide for the laity, and politicians aimed at helping them to make choices informed by their faith in their political action. As one would expect in the Northern Irish context, Daly's discourse on the nature of democracy and political participation by the laity was dominated by the nature of the two communities and the pressing need to build meaningful relationships between them.

The nature of democracy in Northern Ireland

Although any consideration of 'the best form of government constitutes philosophically a negligible part in Catholic political thought,'[20] it is clear as R Scott Appleby argues that the Second Vatican Council aligned the church with democracy,[21] seeing this as the best means to secure the common good.[22] Indeed, Daly supported and advocated for the creation of democratic structures within the context of Northern Ireland throughout his bishopric, arguing that the democratic deficit was one of the main drivers and causes of the conflict there. Democracy is

> in keeping with Christian affirmations of human dignity, freedom, and participation. People want to exercise their God-given ability to reason and seek out the good that beckons to them; they require an appropriate sphere of liberty in which to act on the life plans they develop and pursue; and they want to exercise self-governance through participation in the decision-making processes of the institutions that direct and order their lives.[23]

Such thinking was fully supported by *Gaudium et Spes* which acknowledged the diversity of forms of government but implicitly promoted democracy as the most suitable political system for the common good. It did so by stating that 'of course it is the role of political authority to organise and direct citizens in promoting the common good, but this authority must dispose the energies of the whole citizenry toward the common good, not mechanically or despotically, but primarily as a moral force which depends on freedom.'[24]

The polis as the pursuit of the common good

Having rediscovered a degree of confidence in human nature during the twentieth century, the Church now taught that it was an active community of the people of God with a mission in the world as well as a realm beyond it. The need to protect human dignity lay at the heart of the Church's mission, and 'since the person is both sacred and social a common life must be established that preserves and promotes well being.'[25] The Church's aim therefore was to perfect and free the individual through the teachings of the Gospel and in doing so work towards a more ideal society in which peace in the fullest sense of the term was the norm. Each person's life, dignity, and destiny was thus bound up with the good of the community. As Himes argues:

> Life in various communities enlarges and perfects the individual. To develop as a person, participation in the community is necessary, for communal life provides the opportunity to give oneself away to another and by doing so the person becomes more fully realised. Giving of

oneself, in relationships of mutuality, permits both parties to grow toward their full humanity. Participation in the dynamic of giving and receiving within the community leads both to the person's well-being and the good of others.[26]

Such communities can only be genuine where the dignity of the human person is recognised and secured, and where the conditions allow everyone to flourish. As *Gaudium et Spes* taught, the first community an individual encounters is the family.[27] However, the good of the person can only be attained when they are 'able to participate in a rich diversity of communal relationships, ranging from those as small as family to those as large as the national and global societies.'[28] The political system therefore holds an important role in Catholic teachings on the community. Although the Catholic church did not bind itself to any political system or community, it did stand opposed to the extremes of both individualism and collectivism.[29] Consequently a vision of the state emerged from Catholic teaching which emphasised the importance of the common good or human flourishing and supported democracy.

Catholic social teaching suggests that the state should work in partnership with society, supporting the twin concepts of solidarity and subsidiarity that underpin Catholic definitions of community. It cannot dominate the lives of its citizens but instead should work in concert with civil society in order to protect human rights and dignity, and enable each person to contribute according to their 'abilities and in the light of the needs of others.'[30] The Catholic Church teaches that the 'highest purpose of the political community is [therefore] to promote the common good.'[31] Although the concept of the common good has been present in the vocabulary of the Catholic Church from the Pontificate of Leo XIII,[32] it was not until the Pontificate of John XXIII that a definition was provided. In both *Mater et Magistra* and *Pacem in Terris*, he described the common good as 'the sum total of conditions of social life, by which people may reach their perfection more fully and easily.'[33] This definition was subsequently used in Vatican II's *Gaudium et Spes*[34] and has remained the basis for the Church's understanding of the term since.[35] Once more the binary of the two kingdoms can be seen:

> The common good of the 'earthly city' is of central concern to all who seek to love their neighbour. But this 'terrestrial common good' is not of absolute value; only God has that status. Therefore respect for the transcendent dignity of the person is a precondition for the attainment of that earthly and political good that recognises its own limitations.[36]

People must be free to achieve their ultimate transcendent perfection in a way which recognises their dignity and that of others, whilst seeking the realisation of the kingdom on earth; thus the creation of a political system focused upon the common good is instrumental to this.

The concept of the common good provided the state with limited but clearly defined responsibilities through which it could protect and promote human dignity. *Dignitatis Humanae* provides a clear definition of this. The government is not entirely responsible for the operation of society, as this would restrict rather than promote freedom, instead 'government is responsible for the achievement of that part of the common good that enables society to function as a community of fellow citizens.'[37] This is realised through the maintenance of public order which is defined as:

1   Justice: which secures for people what is due to them, that is, human rights;
2   Public peace: which will only be genuine peace when founded on justice; and
3   Public morality: the standards of public behaviour on which consensus exists in society.[38]

A reciprocal relationship consequently emerges amongst the individual, community, and state: the state should place itself at the service of the individual and community in the manner outlined in *Dignitatis Humanae*, and individuals and communities should work together to 'restrain evildoers and remedy unjust situations, and to promote the practice of virtue . . . while preserving or establishing good mores and institutions.'[39] The state above all provides individuals and communities with the means to achieve both perfection within themselves and society. The state in Northern Ireland (in the form of the British government) singularly failed to provide such conditions, and as a result was the subject of a sustained and sometimes searing critique from Daly, in which he accused it of abdicating its responsibilities to the citizens of Northern Ireland.

The Second Vatican Council presented the Catholic Church with a new model of self- understanding and mission. It had redefined itself as a servant-church dedicated to the realisation of the Peaceable Kingdom, both spiritually and temporally. The Church adopted a different style of public role through which it was necessary to engage with politics. Bishops, such as Daly, were now undertaking a religious mission with political implications. Bishops were now expected to translate Catholic teachings, especially regarding social and political questions, for the context in which the Church found itself. This was part of their teaching responsibility, and the Church argued that this provided them with the legitimacy and authority to speak on social and political matters. Daly sought to engage in this process in Northern Ireland, especially in relation to politics, and church-state relations. In his work, he tried to provide pastoral and moral guidance which was based both on the Gospel and Catholic social teaching. However, issues of authority within the Church meant that such a role demanded sensitivity. *All* members of the Church were now believed to be equal, and bishops now needed to provide guidance rather than acting as a moral and sometimes draconian authority over the lives of the faithful. Such tensions were particularly obvious when it came to issues relating to lay activity in politics, an area which was one of concern for Daly. He sought to redefine the relationship of church to state in Northern Ireland, changing the Church's style of leadership by moving it away from a focus upon the needs of its own community and taking it towards one in which *all* of society was under his pastoral care and guidance.

The laity and attitudes to the 'other'

As well as seeking to diagnose the malady afflicting Northern Irish society, Daly also sought cures. Once more, these were rooted firmly within the Gospel and the social teachings of the Catholic Church. The solution to the issue of the double minority, which Daly argued was one of the key causes of the conflict, was mutual understanding and acceptance. This would be achieved by the use of the methods of ecumenical dialogue discussed in Chapter 2. Daly defined the initial terms of such mutual acceptance and understanding quite forcefully in 1972:

> Nationalists and republicans simply must stop pretending that Unionists are lapsed United Irishmen, merely requiring a push from Britain or a pamphlet from republican headquarters to bring them back to the Tone tradition. Unionists must simply stop claiming that nationalists are secret unionists, prevented by republican intimidation or Catholic educational indoctrination from avowing their attachment to the British connection.[40]

Initially, Daly placed the onus on nationalists to make a 'sustained effort to understand [unionist] thinking'[41] but by 1975, he was suggesting that 'each community must come to accept each other on the others' terms'.[42] Daly felt that there was a deliberate misunderstanding between unionists and nationalists: 'The opportunities for consensus are threatened by [unionists'] refusal to distinguish constitutional nationalism and republicanism.'[43] Such endeavours would, he hoped, lead to the creation of mutual trust between the two communities, a crucial element in the process of building the Peaceable Kingdom.

In 1987, Daly framed this is terms of solidarity, a vital component of the Catholic Church's vision of democracy. Daly's employment of solidarity as a means of ameliorating the conflict in Northern Ireland enables us to see clearly the missionary nature of the Catholic Church during the conflict. Once more the binary nature of this endeavour can be seen: not only was the individual being transformed, but through such a development, Daly was also enabling a more Christocentric vision to emerge that would reshape the structures of society. The concept of solidarity sought to change the ways in which human relationships were viewed and enacted. Steering a path between the individualism espoused by liberalism and the authoritarian collectivism demanded by communism and fascism, solidarity placed human dignity at the heart of relationships. In doing so, all people were called upon to reclaim responsibility for themselves and play a more active role in transforming the shape of society into that espoused by the Gospels. Solidarity was particularly important to John Paul II's papacy, and in *Sollicitudo rei Socialis* he defined it as 'a firm and persevering determination to commit oneself to the common good; that is to say to the good of all and of each individual because we are all really responsible for all.'[44] The need to overcome division was central to this concept,[45] and it therefore had a great deal of resonance for Northern Irish society. As Daly's analysis of the causes of the conflict had shown, the common good had been ignored in Northern Ireland. Solidarity – a core element, alongside development of peace[46] – was non-existent in Northern Ireland, a situation which was perpetuated by the failure of the two communities to even attempt to understand each other: 'Human solidarity breaks down the cycles of violence, as one grievance evokes another, as one war is followed by another.'[47] The clash between unionism and nationalism was an ideological conflict which was preventing peace in Northern Ireland – a factor which was highlighted by Daly when he quoted Pope John Paul II:

> Can there be a lasting peace in a world ruled by relations – social, economic and political – that favour one group or nation at the expense of another? Can a genuine peace be established without an effective recognition of that wonderful truth that we are all equal in dignity, equal because we have been formed in the image of God, who is our Father?[48]

Daly's understanding of peace and conflict was sophisticated enough to understand that harmony and the common good were not going to be achieved just by a bland conversation during which participants essentially talked at one another without really seeking to understanding the other's viewpoint.[49] Rather, he called for a profound change of mind-set within the context of Northern Ireland: 'We must be concerned for the rights of the other community as well as for our own.'[50] This was because:

> Democracy is dialogue. It is negated when we impose the silence of the grave on those who disagree; or when we drive out of our society or community or street those "of the other kind". Democracy is reasonable discussion, persuasion, conviction. It dies when we replace persuasion by force and treat others as objects to be bombed into unwilling submission, not persons to be persuaded into free consent.[51]

These were radical statements for a Catholic bishop and shows how he sought to transform Northern Irish society. Christians (both Catholic *and*

Protestant) needed to become determined 'to overcome sources of division within themselves and in society.'[52] Daly espoused this clearly when he said:

> It is natural and it is good and even obligatory to be concerned about the fundamental and inalienable rights of our own community. What is more difficult, but in our situation imperative, is that . . . we take to ourselves the warning of the Pope against "ideologies that breed hatred or distrust".[53]

Such a process would lead to the development of meaningful dialogue through which the two communities would acknowledge and understand their interdependence and become dedicated to working for the common good of all and the creation of a stable democracy in Northern Ireland.

Daly therefore saw the causes of the conflict in Northern Ireland as individual and communal as well as structural: ' "structures of sin" and personal sins, in which the sinful structures are rooted, cause disorder in the soul and disunity in society.'[54] Thus, the solutions put forward were structural based upon a meaningful political dialogue and on the role of the laity in creating new political mind-sets within and across communal boundaries.

The laity and attitudes to the state

As new understandings of mission in the post-conciliar era mandated, the laity was now expected to become politically conscious and active. *Gaudium et Spes* taught: 'Let all Christians appreciate their special and personal vocation in the political community. This vocation requires that they give conspicuous example of devotion to the sense of duty and of service to the advancement of the common good.'[55] Speaking in 1973 and addressing *all* Christians (both Catholic and Protestant), Daly had argued that 'the Vatican Council . . . summons to a real renewal of our politics.'[56] In the context of Northern Ireland, this was an urgent task, and Daly sought, in particular, to help Christians redefine their attitude to the state itself. His teaching on this matter was based upon Jesus's command to 'Give to the emperor the things that are the emperor's, and to God the things that are God's.'[57] Daly's use of this particular passage to illustrate and explain his teachings on the proper relationship of the Christian to the state, instead of for example Romans 13,[58] is telling and demonstrates his desire to contextualise and translate the teachings of the Catholic Church for Northern Ireland. The relationship of religion to the state, and in particular the obligation to pay taxes, was one of the burning issues of Jesus's time. The Zealots, who were dedicated to resisting and overthrowing the Roman regime and replacing it with a Jewish government, were refusing to pay tax. Thus, the question put to Jesus by the Pharisees and Herodians, 'is it lawful to pay taxes to the emperor, or not?'[59] was loaded. It demonstrated an allegiance to group and identity that placed ideology above fidelity to God. Daly states that in his reply 'Jesus . . . transcends the whole discussion, raising it to a higher plane.'[60] Although there has been some debate as to Jesus's revolutionary intentions, in his reply He did not seek to replace one government with another; rather He 'wanted a change that would affect every department of life and that would reach down to the most basic assumptions of Jew and Roman.'[61] Here, the particular relevance of this Gospel passage for Northern Ireland becomes evident. Unionists and nationalists in Northern Ireland had been guilty of the same fault as Zealots, Pharisees, and Herodians: they had put their allegiance to the group above God, allowing their lives to be ordered by nationalistic ideologies rather than the Gospels: 'The Nation and the Cause become self-justifying sources of moral value, superseding the ten commandments.'[62] In doing so, they had contributed to the creation of the conflict. Instead, Daly told them that they should: 'Let God be God not the party nor the nation, not the race or the class, not the system or the slogan, not the Revolution nor the Constitution.'[63] In re-developing their relationship to the state, Daly was asking the laity to regain control of their political ideology and seek to employ it to realise the Peaceable Kingdom because 'it is in the Lord that we find our strength and not in any political tradition.'[64] A new Christian attitude to politics had to emerge; one which was imbued with compassion and love for everyone rather than just the in-group.

In a conflict dominated by language and its use as a social identifier,[65] Daly used the abuse of language as an example of the lack of compassion and love in Northern Irish politics. By tackling this issue, all Christians could become politically aware and involved. In doing so, the laity could move towards the new forms of actions and changes in lifestyle required to fully realise the new role as missionaries of the Kingdom handed to them at the Second Vatican Council. Slogans such as 'get the British out!', 'Ulster is British', 'Never trust the British', and 'No surrender', were commonplace in Northern Ireland during the conflict. In Daly's view, such language was paralysing politics in Northern Ireland and creating an atmosphere in which progress was unlikely to be made and most importantly, preventing the establishment of democracy. Much of this language was used 'unthinkingly'[66] and as 'Christians were to be exemplary citizens of the society in which they lived',[67] they should make a conscious attempt to avoid its use as 'to rid the language of each community of disparaging and offensive terms . . . would be a contribution to building bridges of understanding and mutual acceptance between our communities.'[68]

Political consciousness and activity were core elements of the Church's mission in society. Once more the binaries of individual and community, and the two kingdoms were evident in Daly's thought. To seek the transformation of society that Daly argued was the key to the creation of the Peaceable Kingdom; people had to renew themselves: 'No revolution in society will produce a new man without the conversion of heart which turns our hard hearts into hearts with the universal tenderness of Christ.'[69] As the Second Vatican Council had 'rediscovered a degree of confidence in human nature,'[70] the political mission gave Christians the chance to 'attain their own perfection'[71] through their transformation of society.

Political participation by the laity

The political vocation was a recurring theme in Daly's writings and once more the primacy of the laity in the temporal realm was at the centre of his argument: 'No society can ultimately be better than its politics. This is why all Christians must now learn that an absolutely primary field for Christian action and concern is precisely politics. . . . It is forty years since Maritain called for saints of politics.'[72] Here, Daly was returning the church to its early Christian roots during which Christians were expected to 'battle' together for a 'common cause',[73] namely Christ's Gospel with all its political implications for the transformation of society. Daly's initial emphasis lay upon the regeneration of politics, citing the renewal of the church at Vatican II as an inspiration for this:

> I suggest that the post-conciliar experience of the Church can indeed be the van-guard for the renewal of political life and institutions. Never, perhaps in her history has the Church been so resolutely committed to radical renewal and to risk-taking change than in these years since the close of the Second Vatican Council.[74]

He thus called for a similar *aggiornamento* to take place within Northern Irish politics. Daly's initial writings on the matter in the early 1970s were framed as 'an appeal to the Christian conscience of every single politician.'[75] Thus, the individual as well as society was to be perfected by this renewal of the political sphere. The individual politician needed to be shaped by his Christian faith and become 'endowed with both the Christian passion for justice, charity and truth, and the indispensable technical and cultural competence required for modern government.'[76] Christianity was therefore public and not private. It could not be compartmentalised within the politician's life: 'A politician's Christianity is proved by the nature of his politics as much as by the frequency of his prayer.'[77] The Christian political vocation therefore involved a commitment to the truth in which the individual engaged in an ongoing critique of society based upon the Gospel which promoted peace rather than violence. This issue of violence was to recur strongly in Daly's writings in the 1980s, and which was linked to his ongoing critique of paramilitary organisations, when he censured politicians for failing to show leadership in Northern Ireland. Although he had acknowledged the powerlessness of politicians in the late 1970s which was being caused by the lack of democracy in Northern Ireland,[78] Daly believed that a dearth of political leadership was creating a vacuum which was being filled by paramilitaries. Despite the lack of official structures through which politicians could speak, he stated that: 'Brave voices on both sides have been raised calling for . . . respect for differences between communities; but more such voices must be raised and be raised more loudly and more clearly. Such spokesmen must make still more vigorous efforts to promote their reconciling influence.'[79] Such ideas were, by the 1990s, being framed in terms of the social contract of Christianity which built upon those expressed in the 1970s and 1980s. Here, Daly was arguing that the political vocation required Christians to opt-in to politics.[80] Indeed, there was a moral obligation to do so.

Daly was thus arguing for a change of heart by the people of Northern Ireland. Such change would not only prepare them individually for salvation but would also challenge and ultimately transform the unjust structures of society. He understood that the conflict was not just caused by the socio-economic deprivation discussed in Chapter 3 but that attitudes and relationships also had to be converted in order to build the Peaceable Kingdom. Despite the democratic deficit that was crippling Northern Ireland's formal political representation, Christians still had a political role to play. They could do this by overcoming communal boundaries through dialogue, decompartmentalising their faith and putting it at the centre of their political decision-making, and reflecting upon the attitudes and actions towards the other that were fuelling the conflict. However, structural change of the sort that could only be brought about at a governmental level was also needed to create the Peaceable Kingdom. It was for this reason that Daly also sought to critique the states involved.

The British government and the peace process

Daly was in constant dialogue with the British government, whose behaviour he argued represented a 'serious abdication of political responsibility'.[81] On matters ranging from security policy and its inherent human rights abuses, the economy, and development and justice, he continually provided moral guidance to the state to ensure that society became more grounded in the ideals of the Peaceable Kingdom. He argued that 'the problem in Northern Ireland is a fundamentally political one.'[82] Consequently, whilst his discourse with the laity, and politicians in particular, was focused on the salvation of both individual and society, in his dialogue with the British government, he concentrated upon the political, particularly constitutional, support and structures that the British needed to put in place to bring peace to Northern Ireland. This would be the bedrock of a society upon which justice and peace could be built. It also held the British firmly to account for their role in creating the conflict in the first place. Three major themes emerge in Daly's discourse with the British: first, he critiqued their lack of leadership and management of the situation; second, he criticised the democratic deficit that was emerging as a result of the government's abdication of its responsibilities; finally from the 1990s onwards, he supported and evaluated the emerging peace process. In each of these areas, Daly remained committed to the teachings of the Gospel and the social teachings of the Catholic Church, and contextualised them with increasing diplomacy as the political situation in Northern Ireland evolved.

The British government's lack of leadership

To say that Daly was disappointed with the British government's record in Northern Ireland would be an understatement. In 1973, he wrote:

> History will undoubtedly show that a major factor in the slow decline into anarchy which Northern Ireland has witnessed in the past four years was the failure of successive governments of the United Kingdom to take sufficient interest in the affairs of Northern Ireland, even to maintain a desk or an adequate dossier about the political and community problems of an area which it nonetheless claimed to be an integral part of Her Majesty's Government.[83]

Indeed, his anger at them is evident throughout the 1970s when he argued that their failure to govern was *the* fundamental problem facing the region. It was only in the aftermath of the 1981 hunger strikes that his tone became more emollient. In 1972, during the aftermath of Bloody Sunday, he stated:

> Many of us has hoped that Britain might, in this post-colonial age, at last attempt to atone for centuries of harm and hurt in her relations with Ireland by providing the firm and decisive leadership needed to guarantee justice in the North, and build a future for the whole of Ireland. These hopes have been cruelly disappointed. This time of Ireland's need has been also the time of Britain's most miserable desertion. The British government has failed in the most elementary responsibility of a government – it has not governed.[84]

Although we must temper this analysis by the fact that it was written just after Bloody Sunday, which saw the British army open fire on unarmed civilians taking part in a peaceful civil rights march in Derry, it is correct. The British government had been caught unaware by the start of the conflict in Northern Ireland, despite the fact that

> Britain's leaders were warned again and again of the gravity of the situation existing in the North and of the increasingly dangerous state of emotion and feeling in the rest of Ireland. They were warned of the grave and urgent need of resolute political action, for radical and structural reforms. They did not listen.[85]

Indeed, during the period in question Britain's leaders wanted nothing more than to return as quickly as possible to the convention of 'non-interference' by Westminster in Stormont's affairs.[86] This policy preference was exacerbated by the fact that the British government had little expertise on the area, fundamentally misunderstanding the problem as something akin to the social difficulties it was facing at home. As Bill Roulston suggests, 'British politicians saw nothing wrong with Northern Ireland that could not be cured by a good strong dose of the same social-democratic reform that had emerged in post-war Britain.'[87] This was to a certain extent true. Northern Ireland was indeed in need of social reform as Daly had suggested in his writings on social and economic justice. But it was also in desperate need of political reform – a fact that the British government initially failed to understand. As a consequence, Daly argued 'opportunity after opportunity has been missed'[88] to solve the Northern Irish question.

The first meaningful attempt to do so came with the October 1972 Green Paper: *The Future of Northern Ireland.*[89] Daly quite rightly pointed out the 'radical' and 'historic' nature of this paper: Britain was, for the first time, recognising the existence of the two communities in Northern Ireland and the need for the Republic of Ireland to be involved in any solution.[90] The proposals were the subject of a referendum, known as the Border Poll, on 8 March 1973. The poll asked the electorate whether it should remain in the UK or reunify with Ireland. The nationalist community boycotted the referendum. It was followed by the publication of a White Paper, *Northern Ireland Constitutional Proposals*, later that same month.[91] These papers, according to Daly, represented a 'significant shift in British government attitudes and policies towards Northern Ireland.'[92] For Daly they were, until the Good Friday Agreement of 1998, the highpoint of British policy regarding the constitutional question. Indeed, in a 1993 analysis of British government policy, he stated that 'my enumeration of these policy principles is based on the 1972 British Government Paper, and my quotations are all taken directly from that document.'[93] It is thus worth exploring some of their policy proposals in more detail.

The British government's strategy in the early 1970s was 'to construct a "moderate" power-sharing executive of nationalists and unionists which could devolve power back to Northern Ireland.'[94] This was based upon a belief that the vast majority of people in Northern Ireland were peaceful moderates who could be persuaded to embrace power sharing. Indeed, it was frequently argued that 'people who had looked into the abyss of ethnic violence . . . would surely not vote for those extremists who stood in the way of fair compromise.'[95] The documents that led to the 1973 Sunningdale Agreement[96] and subsequent (unsuccessful) constitutional arrangements were all a reflection of this analysis.

The Future of Northern Ireland provided the British government's minimum requirements for the political development of Northern Ireland. It contained two key elements: first that there should be a revised form of assembly in Northern Ireland and that it must

> be capable of involving all its members constructively in ways which satisfy them and those they represent that the whole community has

a part to, play in the government of the Province. As a minimum this would involve assuring minority groups of an effective voice and a real influence; but there are strong arguments that the objective of real participation should be achieved by giving minority interests a share in the exercise of executive power if this can be achieved by means which are not unduly complex or artificial, and which do not represent an obstacle to effective government.[97]

Second, the paper argued for an Irish dimension in the governance of the region:

> Whatever arrangements are made for the future administration of Northern Ireland must take account of the Province's relationship with the Republic of Ireland: and to the extent that this is done, there is an obligation upon the Republic to reciprocate. . . . It remains the view of the United Kingdom Government that it is for the people of Northern Ireland to decide what should be their relationship to the United Kingdom and to the Republic of Ireland: and that it should not be impossible to devise measures which will meet the best interests of all three. Such measures would seek to secure the acceptance, in both Northern Ireland and in the Republic, of the present status of Northern Ireland, and of the possibility which would have to be compatible with the principle of consent-of subsequent change in that status; to make possible effective consultation and co-operation in Ireland for the benefit of North and South alike; and to provide a firm basis for concerted governmental and community action against those terrorist organisations which represent a threat to free democratic institutions in Ireland as a whole.[98]

Although its wording on this matter was vague as Cunningham points out: 'This recognition was significant because it was the clearest indication since the abortive Council of Ireland of the early 1920s settlement that the British government did not see Northern Ireland as a solely "internal" matter.'[99] The subsequent White Paper outlined five areas in which it was hoped that advances could be made to settle the political future of Northern Ireland. These were: the development of some form of devolved institution; a unicameral legislative assembly of between 80 and 100 members; an important role for a committee structure within the executive; a codification of human rights and freedoms; and institutional arrangements for co-operation and consultation on an all-Ireland basis. The assembly's principle areas of responsibility would be education, housing, social services, industrial development, agriculture, and the environment.[100] These structures were, according to Daly, the 'inherent principles'[101] upon which the governance of Northern Ireland should be based and were the central elements of his vision for a socially and economically just society.

Additionally, the sections on historical background and causes of the conflict held significance for Daly. *The Future of Northern Ireland* acknowledged the failings of the Stormont Parliament[102] and in particular the 'deliberate policies of discrimination, particularly in relation to housing and public employment by some though not all of the local authorities in Northern Ireland, and of a toleration of local government electoral boundaries in some areas which produced wholly artificial results,'[103] an analysis which wholly resonated with Daly's own.

In his 1973 response to the government's proposals, Daly stated that 'It is to be hoped that the lesson [of British failings in Northern Ireland] has at last been learnt and that the utmost practicable urgency will be given now to the implementation of the new Constitutional proposals, and the holding of elections preparatory to setting in place the new structures.'[104] Daly argued that these lessons had not been learnt and that the British government continually failed to live up to its moral responsibilities to the people of Northern Ireland. The first of these was its failure to develop an appropriate analysis of the situation. There was a very strong need for an internal solution to be developed within the region which Daly urged the laity to take responsibility for. But Britain still needed to provide a political framework through which such a solution could be reached.[105] Speaking in 1977, Daly stated: 'The last sign that Britain gave of serious thinking about the Irish question was in the Green Paper of 1972, and the ensuing Constitutional Proposals of 1973. To have allowed that policy to fall in ruins and to have done nothing since to rebuild on the ruins, is a lamentable desertion from responsibility.'[106] The resulting structures collapsed with the Ulster Workers Strike in May 1974. This meant that, despite its efforts to find a 'quick fix' solution[107] to the Northern Irish question, the British government still retained responsibility for the region through direct rule. This had been introduced on 24 March 1972[108] as a temporary measure to provide a space in which 'to mediate a more equitable constitutional arrangement amongst political parties from both sides of the sectarian divide.'[109] It came to an end 26 years later under the terms of the 1998 Good Friday Agreement, although it has been temporarily re-imposed in the years since.

The democratic deficit

This lack of 'serious thinking' and failure of the British government to take full responsibility for Northern Ireland allowed a political vacuum to emerge.[110] This, Daly argued, enabled paramilitarism to flourish, creating a cycle of violence that was hindering the nascent peace process, thereby preventing the people of Northern Ireland from exercising their democratic rights. The Peaceable Kingdom could not be established without a functioning democratic system.[111] Full and uninhibited democratic participation was the foundation stone of the Catholic Church's vision of the structures of governance. Democracy depended upon modes of participation which allowed for *all* citizens to contribute to the common good, either directly as politicians or indirectly by exercising their right to vote in a fashion mindful of the Church's teachings on human dignity, and to be subsequently represented in fully functioning institutions where 'all proposals are freely discussed and examined.'[112] It was through the creation of such structures that a long-term peace based upon human dignity and flourishing could be secured. Indeed, as I have argued elsewhere, human rights and dignity were *the* lens through which the Catholic Church measured the democratic effectiveness of a society,[113] as it was central to the institution's teaching that:

> When political activity comes up against moral principles that do not admit of exception, compromise or derogation, the Catholic commitment becomes more evident and laden with responsibility. In the face of *fundamental and inalienable ethical demands*, Christians must recognize that what is at stake is the essence of the moral law, which concerns the integral good of the human person.[114]

Christians, in other words, should have the freedom to vote according to their consciences and to be represented as such.[115]

Thus, from 1921 onwards, Northern Ireland was not, by the Catholic Church's measure, a peaceful society, something that Daly frequently pointed out. Instead, it was one in which economic, social, and political injustices combined to prevent the Catholic/nationalist minority from exercising their agency. Structural violence defined access to the most basic elements contained within the Catholic definition of human rights – a fundamental component of which was the meaningful form of political participation described earlier. The state, according to the earliest instances Catholic social teaching, beyond the provision of democratic processes, should not define or seek to control the manner in which citizens should participate:

> The teaching of Leo XIII on the form of political government, namely, that men are free to choose whatever form they please, provided that proper regard is had for the requirements of justice and of the common good, is equally applicable in due proportion, it is hardly necessary to say, to the guilds of the various industries and professions.[116]

The state should not be feared; rather it should be a vehicle for the promotion of the common good.[117] Yet, according to Daly's line of reasoning, the British government and subsequently the unionist ruling elite created a democratic deficit which effectively excluded the Catholic/nationalist minority from engaging with the political structures established in 1921.

Daly's analysis of the structural violence inherent in the Stormont regime blames the British government for imposing inappropriate structures of power and political participation (i.e. voting systems) upon the newly devolved government. He agrees with the analysis provided by the 1973 White Paper which

> penetratingly diagnoses the inherent defect of the Northern Ireland political institutions of fifty years. This defect is traced by the paper to the adoption of United Kingdom conventions regarding parliamentary democracy, and in particular that of a majority rule, in a territory where these conventions had consequences entirely different from those entailed in the neighbouring island.[118]

Paul Bew, Peter Gibbon, and Henry Patterson best express such consequences when they argue:

> From its creation in 1921 until its destruction in 1972, the Northern Ireland state was ruled by a single party, the Ulster Unionists. This party was supported for all purposes exclusively by Protestants, who comprised two-thirds of the local population. In the course of its rule it departed in a number of notable ways from the normal forms of parliamentary democracy.[119]

In terms of Catholic social teaching, therefore, the creation of what was effectively a one-party state was profoundly damaging. It produced a situation in which the absence of government by informed consent fuelled alienation and resentment. Furthermore, Catholics were unable to advocate in any meaningful sense of the term for social, economic, and political justice. Such a situation that left them vulnerable to exploitation and discrimination and injustice was almost inevitable.[120] Daly argued, sectarianism consequently became embedded within the political system. The result was a vicious circle of injustice and inequality, and alienation, which was aggravated by the behaviour of the devolved government.[121] Indeed, 'The outcome could have arguably been different had the ruling unionist majority treated the nationalist minority with scrupulous fairness and justice and tried to reconcile them to the new regime. This, unfortunately, was not the case.'[122]

In Daly's analysis, the British government compounded this marginalisation and alienation and extended it to the unionist/Protestant communities by allowing regional politics to become paralysed. In doing so, it further prevented the proper democratic channels for the discussion and representation of the region's needs, leaving its citizens vulnerable to violence. Speaking in the aftermath of the violent collapse of the 1973 Sunningdale Agreement, he argued that:

> Its most immediate result is of course that the elected representatives of the people are deprived of all influence, of all audience, and of all initiative. There is no assembly at which they can speak, where they can present their point of view. There is no importance attached to

their remarks, because normal political life is suspended in all its forms. There's a complete absence of normal political exchange, a normal political dialogue.[123]

Here, we can see Daly creating a specific element of the preferential option for the poor, marginalised, and vulnerable in relation to the political classes in Northern Ireland. Politicians were being prevented access to official spaces of dialogue through which injustices could be voiced and solutions debated and implemented. The consequence of this situation were voids of hopelessness which were filled by those who 'spoke' for their communities through violence, and who threatened those who preferred nonviolent political methods, and the civil servants who supported them, with assassination.[124]

Above all therefore, Daly's vision of peace was a society in which justice should transcend politics,[125] with political allegiances being put aside to ensure fair and appropriate political representation to be established which would allow for divergent political opinions to be heard. Nationalists 'could not hope to share in government unless they exchanged their nationalist convictions for unionist ones. It is a basic injustice in a constitution that it requires a citizen to change his political party before he can share in the government of the state in which he is a citizen.'[126] Daly commented again on this in 1993 when the political peace process was starting to become public, saying that 'It is a peculiarity of the Northern Ireland constitution, in its present form, that such an unqualified commitment in effect entails being no longer a nationalist but a unionist.'[127] He therefore offered the following solution:

In the concrete Northern Ireland situation, I am convinced that justice between the two historic communities requires that representatives of the two minority communities be given proportionate but real access to the levels where political decisions are taken which determine the distribution of power, wealth, and opportunity, the allocation of industries, resources and jobs. It is a matter for political discussion and negotiation how this can be brought about.[128]

The peace process

Like most politically aware people in Northern Ireland, Daly understood that the principles of the Sunningdale Agreement were the best hope for political stability and peace in the region.[129] These structures would create the preconditions, such as the absence of violence and political representation, necessary for a permanent, positive peace to emerge. However, it was not until the 1990s that relationships between the key protagonists (i.e. the British and Irish governments, and the Northern Irish political parties) had developed sufficiently for a political settlement to emerge. Daly summed up the conditions thus:

> This is a time of unprecedented opportunities. We have constitutional nationalist committed to an agreed Ireland, which by definition cannot come into being without unionist consent. We have an Irish government pledged to a democratic settlement reached by agreement between the nationalists and unionists and ratified by the votes of the people of Northern Ireland and of the republic of Ireland respectively. We have a British prime minister sincerely committed to achieving by agreement a permanent settlement in Northern Ireland.[130]

Here, Daly sums up his roadmap for a successful political process which would allow a permanent peace to emerge. First, the full and willing participation of the British and Irish governments in driving the process forward; second, the centrality of the principle of consent; third, the moral responsibility of Northern Ireland's politicians to take the will of the people for peace seriously; and finally, the means through which preconditions for peace must be balanced with the need for progress.

Although Daly had advocated that any solution to the conflict in Northern Ireland needed to be primarily internal, the involvement of the British and Irish governments in the talks was key, involving moral as well as political elements. Only the British prime minister and the Irish Taoiseach had the political capital and authority necessary to the process in terms of setting frameworks and providing the discipline to effect change. That this was a moral responsibility was apparent when he stated:

> It might be rightly said that neither the British and Irish government would be pardoned for not making the achievement of peace in Northern Ireland a priority objective. Neither government dare, even in its own interest, shirk the responsibility or opportunity. Any political advantage thought to be obtained would be dearly bought and short lived.[131]

Daly constantly encouraged the British and Irish governments to remain involved in the process, particularly when events such as the ceasefires could lead to the idea that peace had already been won: 'I do hope that [peace] doesn't lead to complacency either on the part of the governments – particularly the British government – or the political parties. The climate is now right for the political process. We mustn't let the opportunity slip and pressure must be kept on.'[132] However, his main focus, as is to be expected, was on the politicians representing the various traditions of Northern Ireland, with his discourse seeking to provide a moral stimulus for those involved.

Most of Daly's writings in the period leading up to the 1998 Good Friday Agreement on the matter concentrated on the principle of consent: consent for a united Ireland from within the unionist/loyalist tradition, and recognition of the territorial integrity of Northern Ireland by the nationalist/republican community.[133] Daly was continuing a theme that had been in place in his other writings on political justice, namely the importance of mutual understanding and respect for the creation of the Peaceable Kingdom. Without recognition of the rights of the other, peace was impossible. Given the fundamental nature of sovereignty to the conflict in Northern Ireland, nothing could be achieved unless each community stopped seeing the rights of the other as diametrically opposed to their own and therefore a threat:

> Neither community can forge a new future without the co-operation of the other; an agreed future must be one in which each community sees its own identity and rights protected, but also recognises and welcomes recognition and protection for the identity and rights of the other community. The way to peace cannot be through victory for one community or defeat of the other. Northern Ireland must become a place where both communities can feel equally at home.[134]

In line with his advocacy of nonviolence, Daly was particularly admiring of parties such as the Ulster Unionist Party and the nationalist SDLP who favoured a constitutional approach and were prepared to take risks to achieve peace. For example, he said of the Ulster Unionists that their flexibility and openness was: 'all the more deserving of admiration because of the understandable uncertainty and sense of isolation being experienced inside the unionist community at this time. No one should underestimate unionist apprehensions. Nationalists however, would, I believe, wish to reassure them.'[135] Whilst the SDLP had led nationalists

> from sterile abstentionalism and negative and mainly rhetorical anti-partitionalism, accompanied by a degree of anti-British and anti-unionist emotion and polemic, to a position of de facto acceptance of the Northern Ireland state and willingness to work within its institutions for the betterment of the total community; all this, with no abandonment of the aspiration towards eventual Irish unity, without which the very concept of Irish nationalism would become meaningless.[136]

Daly placed more emphasis upon the role of nationalists in this element of the process. This is unsurprising given the insecurity caused within the unionist community by the Republic of Ireland's involvement in the process, and the nationalist community's historic policy of abstentionalism and separation from the state. Politicians were asked to bear the moral responsibility for overcoming such issues: 'Participants in the coming talks should pay attention to the people and their desire for peace, and not let themselves be paralysed by political ideologies.'[137] Whilst, 'people out in both communities could help by letting their political representatives know of their support for the talks.'[138]

He was further vexed by the issue of participation in the talks that centred around the decommissioning of weapons in the aftermath of the 1994 and 1996 ceasefires. For him, right intention rather than right action was the key: 'Commitment to exclusively peaceful means and to the democratic peace process rather than actual physical decommissioning should be the ultimate precondition for talks.'[139] Despite his focus of the role of nationalist politicians in securing a political settlement, he was also obliquely critical of elements within unionism/loyalism which were slowing progress: 'All preconditions should be laid down. The "not an inch" philosophy has no place in the situation facing us today. It belongs to the past from which we are trying to move forward. It cannot be part of the future which we now wish to build together.[140]

Daly, like most in Northern Ireland, had reached the conclusion that Irish reunification could only happen by consent, and was not the key to the more just society necessary for the creation of the Peaceable Kingdom. In fact, the converse was true: by insisting on reunification the political rights of 60% of the population would be denied, further perpetuating injustice. In line with the role of the bishop in the post-Vatican era, Daly did not offer concrete solutions (this was the role of the informed laity). However, his attitude on the matter can be discerned from this comment on the political evolution of Sinn Fein made in 1993:

> Even more significant is the evidence that Sinn Fein has come to speak of agreement and consent and respect for the diversity of traditions as part of their 'peace process', and of the need for work for the agreement of the people of Northern Ireland through a process of reconciliation, aimed at winning the allegiance of the unionist, as well as of the nationalist, tradition within the island of Ireland. All of these concepts are obviously not diametrically opposite to the broad principles of British policy, nor are they radically incapable of being reconciled with those principles.[141]

Through the mention of concepts such as reconciliation and respect for the diversity of traditions, Daly is pointing to the potential contribution of the Catholic Church to the peace process and the heart of his public theology of peace. Thus, whilst as an institution the church and Daly could not contribute directly to the negotiations leading to a political settlement, it could help to create the relationships necessary within society to ensure its longevity. It was the grassroots rather than political peace process which was the main focus of Daly's writings. However, as well as critiquing the British government, Daly also sought to stimulate the moral imagination of politicians in the Republic of Ireland, seeing them as a key constituency in the creation of the Peaceable Kingdom.

The role of the Republic of Ireland

As the uproar surrounding the Anglo-Irish Agreement so patently demon-strated, the question of the Republic of Ireland's role in the Northern state was crucial to the successful achievement of a peaceful settlement on the island. Although the Catholic Church had sought to develop a new church-state hypothesis after Vatican II, this did not mean that it accepted secular norms and values. The Church sought to transform rather than control the state and in doing so guide it towards the adoption of the values of the Peaceable Kingdom as outlined in the Beatitudes. In Irish terms, this meant that in theory it now became an institution amongst others speaking in the public square rather than one which had the previously cosy relationship with the state outlined in Article 44 before its revision in 1973.[142] Daly fully engaged with this new dispensation in his relationship with politicians and the state in the Republic in relation to the conflict in Northern Ireland. He outlined and urged for the adoption of attitudes and policies that would facilitate peace and social justice through the creation of mutual under-standing and acceptance of democratic rights between the communities in Northern Ireland. He guided politicians towards a politics of consensus. At the heart of Daly's contextualisation lay a new dispensation based upon mutual understanding and most importantly a respect for, rather than fear or suspicion of, difference.

As a nationalist, Daly hoped for the reunification of Ireland, describing it in 1973 as 'an irreversible aim in Irish political life.'[143] However, this was to be reunification by consent rather than by force. Unionists should be persuaded that life in the Republic would be respectful of their dignity, values, and principles. He believed that the government of the Republic of Ireland should have an active role in determining the future of the Northern state. Three themes emerged, each of which echoed Daly's earlier writings on the responsibility of the individual and the state towards the establish-ment of the Peaceable Kingdom and the common good – which in this con-text would emerge with the cessation of armed conflict and the subsequent creation of a state (hopefully a reunified Ireland) which accepted, under-stood, and respected diversity. Daly placed the responsibility for such aims on the laity, framing his writings on the issues involved as pastoral guidance designed to assist and guide them in their decision-making. This concept of responsibility was always to the fore. As *Gaudium et Spes* had taught,[144] Christians (i.e. Catholics *and* Protestants) were accountable to each other as a result of their humanity and creation in God's image.[145] They were there-fore expected to ensure that they promoted mutual understanding (a phrase which Daly used *ad infinitum*) and to behave in a manner which reflected church teachings on human dignity.

Given Daly's analysis of the causes of the conflict and the need to trans-form relationships between the communities in Northern Ireland, the main focus of his discourse on the role of the Republic of Ireland was the need to reassure unionists that their rights, especially their right to political self-determination, would be maintained under any political settlement. The first issue that he tackled in this regard was nationalist attitudes to unionists. For nationalists, of both the constitutional and physical-force varieties, the involvement of the government of the Republic of Ireland in any peace negotiations or structures was an imperative, given their desire for reunification – a desire that Daly shared. But for unionists, any involvement by this 'foreign state' was anathema, the start of a process that would see the dissolution of the Union for which they had fought so hard to maintain. Ignoring unionism was not an option for nationalists and republicans as 'there is no magic whereby this massive fact can be just made to go away.'[146] Daly was nothing, if not a realist. He argued that the reality of partition had to be accepted by nationalists and republicans as it 'gave governmental embodiment to that composite of convictions, loyalties, values, emotions, prejudices and fears which is Northern Unionism.'[147] Here, his vision for a Peaceable Kingdom is clear: peace cannot be achieved through coercion or force; it has to be achieved by mutual consent and facilitated by a robust and honest dialogue between the conflicting parties.

The government also had a part to play in the creation of a society in which unionists would feel welcome:

> It is also important that the Irish government and the Republic's political parties see themselves not solely concerned about the nationalist community and its rights, but also as concerned about the Unionist community; for unionists too are part of the people of Ireland and unionists' rights and their welfare, their sensitivities and their fears must be a matter of concern to anyone who claims to speak for and to serve the Irish people.[148]

Much could be done, according to Daly, by changing the irredentist wording of articles 2 and 3 of the 1937 Constitution. Until 1998, the Irish Constitution stated that:

Article 2

The national territory consists of the whole island of Ireland, its islands and the territorial seas.

Article 3

Pending the re-integration of the national territory, and without prejudice to the right of the Parliament and Government established by this Constitution to exercise jurisdiction over the whole of that territory, the laws enacted by that Parliament shall have the like area and extent of application as the laws of Saorstát Éireann and the like extra-territorial effect.[149]

This wording was one of the key elements of unionist discontent. For example, in the 1973 election called after the Sunningdale Agreement, the Ulster Unionist Party stated in its manifesto that:

> There **must** be acceptance by the Republic of the right of the people of Northern Ireland to self-determination. This means asking the government and politicians of the Republic to translate their verbal commitment to the idea that force will not be allowed to bring about a United Ireland into political and constitutional action. We propose that this declaration be in the form of a solemn and binding agreement between the three governments concerned.
>
> . . .
>
> **We totally reject any attempts by the Dublin Government to interfere in the internal affairs of Northern Ireland, nor will we allow any Council of Ireland to become a stage on the road to Irish Unity.**[150]

This was a topic frequently explored by Daly, especially during his time as Bishop of Ardagh and Clonmacnois, the boundaries of which were entirely within the Republic. Daly's focus in this regard was on advocating changes to the Irish Constitution, and his rhetoric centered upon what he called the 'almost incurable romanticism, sentimentalism and naiveté'[151] surrounding Southern thinking on the North. He therefore called for the Constitution to be reworded:

> There does seem to me to be something the political parties in the Republic could do, which would have a hope of making a real, as distinct from a verbal contribution to the situation. I refer to a revision of the wording of Articles 2 and 3 of the Constitution, so as to remove from them any appearance of territorial claim or of coercive intent by the Parliament and people of the Republic in respect of the Six counties of Northern Ireland.[152]

Despite Daly's desire to see the Irish Constitution reworded, the significance of his attitude lies in its relationship to his reorientation of church-state relationships which in terms of the politics of the relationship between the Republic and Northern Ireland was expressed through the concept of mutual understanding.

To that end, Daly initially focused on southern politicians, reminding them in 1972 that they needed 'to act wisely as servants of Christian justice and love.'[153] Daly argued that politicians had a special vocation, which required that they reflected upon their own actions and determined their impact upon wider society. He therefore viewed them as individuals with a serious responsibility towards society,[154] who needed to acquire a 'close, accurate knowledge of the realities of the Northern situation, an intimate understanding of the Northern traditions and the Northern mind, both Protestant and Catholic,'[155] and stop making 'political capital' from the situation.[156] Here, the concentration upon mutual understanding between north and south as a solution to the conflict in Northern Ireland is clear. Such understanding could only be achieved through 'continuous contact'[157] and dialogue. This would allow two key elements to emerge: first, it would enable Irish politicians and the state in the south to develop a deeper analysis of the causes of the conflict and the steps needed to ameliorate it. To Daly, it was clear that southern politicians had not taken this step and that this was preventing the development of the second component: the creation of a new inclusive vision for a reunified Ireland. The development of mutual understanding would allow the Republic to 'offer the North a viable alternative which will be acceptable to them,'[158] thereby creating a path to reunification. This would benefit society exponentially as it would force the Republic to 'raise our living standards and improve our social welfare code, thereby making more of a reality the idea of a just society.'[159] Through these teachings the binary of the individual and the collective in Daly's work is clear: by developing 'sincerity and courage'[160] in relation to the Northern question, politicians would be shaping better selves whilst at the same time moving Ireland towards the creation of society based upon Gospel values – which was the ultimate aim of church-state engagement post-Vatican II.

Conclusion

The Second Vatican Council effectively separated church from state, declaring that no one should be 'forced to act in a manner contrary to his own beliefs, whether privately or publicly, whether alone or in association with others, within due limits.'[161] In adopting such a position, the Catholic Church now placed itself firmly within society in order to more effectively critique it, a task which was at the heart of Daly's ministry. Whilst his work on social and economic justice was based upon much-needed consciousness building, his teaching on political justice took a different tone. Most people within Northern Ireland were aware of, and agreed with, the need for political change, if only to break the democratic deadlock that paralysed society throughout the Troubles. Daly here was urging people to live a different form of political life. Once he had pointed out the political issues which mainly concentrated on inappropriate relationships with the state and attitudes towards nationalist ideologies, Daly was able to envisage an alternative possible future. This was not a utopian future but one that had already been set out in British government documents and had started to be realised with the 1973 Sunningdale Agreement. Daly, however, understood that none of this could work without a much-needed change of heart by everyone in Northern Ireland, something he urged the laity to do by removing their support from politicians that acted inappropriately, instead supporting those that argued for equitable solutions that took the common good and human flourishing into account. The main problem that needed to be overcome in this regard was the direct violence being perpetrated by both paramilitaries and the state, and it is to Daly's teachings on this we now turn.

Notes

1 The United States Institute of Peace defines a mutually hurting stalemate as a 'situation in which neither party thinks it can win a given conflict without incurring excessive loss, and in which both are suffering from a continuation of fighting. The conflict is judged to have entered a period of ripeness, a propitious moment for third party mediation.' USIP, Glossary, www.usip.org/glossary/mutually-hurting-stalemate (accessed 5 November 2017).
2 'Northern Ireland: A Shared Responsibility', Address to Members of Pax Christi in London, 14 April 1978, *Addresses on Peace in Northern Ireland, 1976–1983*.
3 'Conformity and Conscience', 24th Annual Summer School of the Social Study Conference, St Kieran's College, Kilkenny, 4 August 1976 in *Addresses on Peace in Northern Ireland 1976–1983*.
4 'Christian Peace: The Challenge to the Individual', Social Study Conference, Falcarragh, 11 August 1972 in *Addresses on Peace in Northern Ireland, 1968–1975*.
5 Gene Sharp, *From Dictatorship to Democracy* (London: Serpent's Tail, 2012), pp. 124–125.
6 Eric O Hanson, *The Catholic Church in World Politics* (Princeton: Princeton University Press, 1987), p. 76.
7 Paul VI, *Dignitatis Humanae*, 7 December 1965 §12, www.vatican.va/archive/hist_councils/ii_vatican_council/documents/vat-ii_decl_19651207_dignitatis-humanae_en.html (accessed 21 August 2019).
8 Jose Casanova, *Public Religions in the Modern World* (Chicago: Chicago University Press, 1994), p. 70.
9 Richard R Gaillardetz and Catherine E Clifford, *Keys to the Council: Unlocking the Teaching of Vatican II* (Collegeville: Liturgical Press, 2012), p. 145.
10 Emile Perreau-Saussine, *Catholicism and Democracy: An Essay in the History of Political Thought*, trans. Richard Rex (Princeton: Princeton University Press, 2001), p. 131.
11 Richard John Neuhaus, *The Catholic Moment: The Paradox of the Church in the Postmodern World* (San Francisco, CA: Harper and Row, 1987), p. 283.
12 *Gaudium et Spes*, §3.
13 Cited in Karen Andersen, 'Ireland in the Twenty-First Century: Secularization or Religious Vitality?' in Detlet Pollack, Olaf Müller and Gert Pickell (eds.), *The Social Significance of Religion in the Enlarged Europe: Secularization, Individualization and Pillarization* (Abingdon: Routledge, 2012), pp. 51–76, 54. Emphasis added.
14 Article 44 of the original 1937 Constitution states: 'The State acknowledges that the homage of public worship is due to Almighty God. It shall hold His Name in reverence, and shall respect and honour religion. The State recognises the special position of the Holy Catholic Apostolic and Roman Church as the guardian of the Faith professed by the great majority of the citizens. . . . The State shall not impose any disabilities or make any discrimination on the ground of religious profession, belief or status.' Irish Stationery Office, *Bunreacht Na hÉireann – Constitution of Ireland* (Dublin: Irish Stationery Office, 1942). The Fifth Amendment of the Irish Constitution was signed into law on 5 January 1973,

and Article 44 now states: 'The State recognises the special position of the Holy Catholic Apostolic and Roman Church as the guardian of the Faith professed by the great majority of the citizens. The State also recognises the Church of Ireland, the Presbyterian Church in Ireland, the Methodist Church in Ireland, the Religious Society of Friends in Ireland, as well as the Jewish Congregations and the other religious denominations existing in Ireland at the date of the coming into operation of this Constitution.' Irish Stationery Office, *Bunreacht Na hÉireann – Constitution of Ireland* (Dublin: Irish Stationery Office, 2015), www.irishstatutebook.ie/eli/1972/ca/5/enacted/en/html (accessed 22 August 2019).

15 See John H Whyte, *Church and State in Modern Ireland 1923–1979*, 2nd Edition (Dublin: Gill and Macmillan, 1980).
16 Perreau- Saussine, *Catholicism and Democracy*, p. 115.
17 *Gaudium et Spes*, §3.
18 Yves Congar, *Lay People in the Church: A Study for a Theology of the Laity* (Westminster: Newman Press, 1957), p. 91.
19 Kenneth R Himes, *Christianity and the Political Order: Conflict, Cooptation, and Cooperation* (New York: Orbis, 2013), p. 235.
20 Henri Rommen, *The State in Catholic Social Teaching* (St Louis: Herder, 1945), p. 479.
21 R Scott Appleby, 'From State to Civil Society and Back Again: The Catholic Church as a Transnational Actor, 1965–2005', in Abigail Green and Vincent Viaene (eds.), *Religious Internationals in the Modern World: Globalization and Faith Communities Since 1750* (New York: Palgrave, 2012), pp. 319–342, 321.
22 For a discussion of the historical development of this, see Himes, *Christianity and the Political Order*, pp. 216–220.
23 Himes, *Christianity and the Political Order*, p. 225.
24 *Gaudium et Spes*, §74; Himes, *Christianity and the Political Order*, p. 223.
25 Himes, *Christianity and the Political Order*, p. 240.
26 Himes, *Christianity and the Political Order*, p. 199.
27 *Gaudium et Spes*, §26. Indeed, the family is often referred to as a site of peace-making, see for example, John Paul II, 'The Family creates the peace of the human family', World Day of Peace Message 1994, 8 December 1993, https://w2.vatican.va/content/john-paul-ii/en/messages/peace/documents/hf_jp-ii_mes_08121993_xxvii-world-day-for-peace.html (accessed 22 August 2019).
28 David Hollenbach SJ, 'Common Good', in Judith A Dwyer (ed.), *The New Dictionary of Catholic Social Thought* (Collegeville: Liturgical Press, 1994), pp. 192–197, 195.
29 Hollenbach, 'Common Good', p. 193; Rodger Charles SJ, *Christian Social Witness and Teaching: The Catholic Tradition from Genesis to Centesimus Annus*, vol. 2 (Leominster: Gracewing, 1998), p. 228.
30 *Gaudium et Spes*, §30.
31 J Brian Benestad, *Church, State and Society: An Introduction to Catholic Social Doctrine* (Washington, DC: The Catholic University of America Press, 2011), p. 81.
32 *Rerum Novarum* which stated that 'Now a State chiefly prospers and thrives through moral rule, well-regulated family life, respect for religion and justice, the moderation and fair imposing of public taxes, the progress of the arts and of trade, the abundant yield of the land-through everything, in fact, which makes the citizens better and happier. Hereby, then, it lies in the power of a ruler to benefit every class in the State, and amongst the rest to promote to the utmost the interests of the poor; and this in virtue of his office, and without being open to suspicion of undue interference – since it is the province of the commonwealth to serve the common good.' §32.

33 John XXIII, *Mater et Magistra*, 15 May 1961, §65, http://w2.vatican.va/con
    tent/john-xxiii/en/encyclicals/documents/hf_j-xxiii_enc_15051961_mater.html
    (accessed 13 August 2019); John XXIII, *Pacem in Terris*, 11 April 1963, §58,
    http://w2.vatican.va/content/john-xxiii/en/encyclicals/documents/hf_j-xxiii_
    enc_11041963_pacem.html (accessed 27 January 2020).
34 *Gaudium et Spes*, §26.
35 Holy See, *Catechism of the Catholic Church*, §§1924–1927, www.vatican.
    va/archive/ENG0015/_INDEX.HTM (accessed 21 August 2019); Holy See,
    The Compendium of the Social Doctrine of the Church (Vatican City: 2004),
    §164, www.vatican.va/roman_curia/pontifical_councils/justpeace/documents/
    rc_pc_justpeace_doc_20060526_compendio-dott-soc_en.html (accessed   13
    August 2019).
36 Hollenbach, 'Common Good', p. 194.
37 Hollenbach, 'Common Good', p. 196.
38 *Dignitatis Humanae*, §7.
39 Benestad, *Church, State and Society*, p. 83.
40 'Response to the Auditor's Paper at Trinity College Theological Society'.
41 'Christian Peace: The Challenge to the Individual'.
42 'Reconciliation: The Path to Peace', Address to Mark the World Day of Peace, 1
    January 1975, *Addresses on Peace in Northern Ireland, 1968–1975*.
43 'Building Bridges in a Divided Community', St Anne's Cathedral and Servite
    Priory, Benburb, 22 and 23 March 1983 in *Addresses on Peace in Northern
    Ireland, 1976–1983*.
44 *Sollicitudo Rei Socialis*, 30 December 1987, §38, http://w2.vatican.va/content/
    john-paul-ii/en/encyclicals/documents/hf_jp-ii_enc_30121987_sollicitudo-rei-
    socialis.html, accessed 13 August 2019).
45 See for example §49: 'By sharing the good things you give us, may we secure
    justice and equality for every human being, an end to all division and a human
    society built on love and peace.'
46 'Building Peace Day after Day' Address for World Day of Peace, 1 January 1987,
    Addresses on Peace in Northern Ireland, vol. 4, 1987–1988.
47 Matthew L Lamb, 'Solidarity', in Judith A Dwyer (ed.), *The New Dictionary
    of Catholic Social Thought* (Collegeville: Liturgical Press, 1994), pp. 908–912,
    912.
48 'Building Peace Day After Day', World Day of Peace Address, 1 January 1987
    in *Addresses on Peace in Northern Ireland, 1987–1988*. Quotation taken from
    John Paul II, 'Development and Solidarity: Two Keys to Peace', World Day of
    Peace Message 1987, 8 December 1986, http://w2.vatican.va/content/john-paul-
    ii/en/messages/peace/documents/hf_jp-ii_mes_19861208_xx-world-day-for-
    peace.html (accessed 22 August 2019).
49 Maria Power, 'Getting to Know the Other: Inter-church Groups in Belfast
    and the Peace Process', in Marianne Elliott (ed.), *The Long Road to Peace in
    Northern Ireland*, 2nd Edition (Liverpool: Liverpool University Press, 2007),
    pp. 192–206.
50 'Building Peace Day After Day'.
51 'Power for Peace', Sermon for Peace Day in St Mel's Cathedral, 1 January 1976
    in *Address on Peace in Northern Ireland, 1976–1983*.
52 Benestad, *Church, State and Society*, p. 103.
53 'Building Peace Day after Day'.
54 Benestad, *Church, State and Society*, p. 103.
55 *Gaudium et Spes*, §74.
56 Cahal B Daly, 'The Christian in Politics', Speaker's Club, Clonmel, 26 May 1973,
    Addresses on Peace in Northern Ireland, 1968–1975.

57 Mk 12:17.
58 'Let every person be subject to the governing authorities, for there is no authority except from God, and those authorities that exist have been instituted by God. . . . For the same reason you also pay taxes, for the authorities are God's servants, who busy with this very thing. Pay to all what is due to them – taxes to whom taxes are due, revenue to whom revenue is due, respect to whom respect is due, honour to whom honour is due.' Romans 13:1, 6–7.
59 Mk, 12:14.
60 'Christ and Revolution', June 1972 in *Addresses on Peace in Northern Ireland, 1968–1975*.
61 Albert Nolan OP, *Jesus Before Christianity* (Maryknoll, NY: Orbis Books, 1992), p. 95.
62 Cahal Daly, *Dialogue for Peace* (Dublin: Irish Messenger Publications, 1983).
63 'Christ and Revolution'.
64 'Northern Ireland: Risk and Opportunity for the Churches'.
65 See for example Seán Byrne and Neal Carter, 'Social Cubism: Six Social Forces of Ethnoterritorial Politics in Northern Ireland and Quebec', *Peace and Conflict Studies*, 1996, vol. 3, no. 2, article 5, http://nsuworks.nova.edu/pcs/vol3/iss2/5/ (accessed 22 August 2019).
66 'Northern Ireland: Is There a Way Forward?' Address to "Challenge 90" Course for Business Leaders, Training Centre, Millisle, 21 September1988 in *Addresses on Peace in Northern Ireland, 1987–1988*.
67 'The Christian in Politics'.
68 'Northern Ireland: Is There a Way Forward?'
69 'Christ and Revolution'.
70 Perreau-Saussine, *Catholicism and Democracy*, p. 129. See also Andrew Greeley, *No Bigger Than Necessary* (New York: Meridian Books, 1977).
71 *Gaudium et Spes*, §74.
72 'Sermon at Mass for Derry Victims', St Mel's Cathedral, 2 February 1972 in *Addresses on Peace in Northern Ireland, 1968–1975*.
73 Phil 1:27
74 'The Christian in Politics'.
75 'The Christian in Politics'.
76 'The Christian in Politics'.
77 'The Christian in Politics'.
78 *Catholic Herald*, 14 January 1977.
79 Daly, *Dialogue for Peace*'.
80 'Industry and Society', Address to the Institute of Directors, Conway Hotel, Belfast', 11 January 1991 in *Addresses on Peace in Northern Ireland, 1991–1992*.
81 'Northern Ireland: From Impasse to Initiative', Address at Conference on "Action for Justice: The Christian Vision" – Commission for International Justice and Peace – St Mary's College, London, 1 September 1979 in *Addresses on Peace in Northern Ireland 1976–1983*.
82 Daly, *Dialogue for Peace*, p. 9.
83 'From Whitepaper to a New Beginning: Christian and Violence', 23 March 1973 in *Addresses on Peace in Northern Ireland, 1968–1975*.
84 'Sermon at the Funeral Mass for Derry Victims'.
85 'Sermon at the Funeral Mass for Derry Victims'.
86 'The cardinal aim of our policy must be to influence Northern Ireland to solve its own problems.' James Callaghan, *Time and Chance* (London: Politico's Publishing Ltd, 1987), p. 500. See also James Callaghan, *A House Divided: The Dilemma of Northern Ireland* (London: William Collins & Sons, 1973); Joe Haines, *The Politics of Power* (London: Jonathan Cape Ltd, 1977), pp. 112–139.

87 Bill Rolston, 'Reformism and Sectarianism', in John Darby (ed.), *Northern Ireland: The Background to the Conflict* (Belfast: Blackstaff, 1983), pp. 198–199.
88 'From Whitepaper to a New Beginning'.
89 HMSO, *The Future of Northern Ireland*, 1972, http://cain.ulst.ac.uk/hmso/nio1972.htm (accessed 22 August 2019).
90 'Response to the Auditor's Paper at Trinity College Theological Society'.
91 HMSO, *Northern Ireland Constitutional Proposals*, March 1973, https://cain.ulster.ac.uk/hmso/cmd5259.htm (accessed 22 August 2019).
92 'From Whitepaper to a New Beginning'.
93 Cahal Daly, *Peace: Now Is the Time* (Dublin: Veritas, 1993), p. 24.
94 Paul Dixon, 'Paths to Peace in Northern Ireland (II): The Peace Processes 1973–74 and 1994–1996', *Democratization*, 1997, no. 4, vol. 3, pp. 1–25, 1.
95 Dixon, 'Paths to Peace in Northern Ireland (II)', p. 4.
96 HMSO, The Sunningdale Agreement, 9 December 1973, http://cain.ulst.ac.uk/events/sunningdale/agreement.htm (accessed 22 August 2019).
97 *The Future of Northern Ireland*, §79(f).
98 *The Future of Northern Ireland*, §78.
99 Michael Cunningham, *British Government Policy in Northern Ireland 1969–2000*, 2nd Edition (Manchester: Manchester University Press, 2001), p. 13.
100 Cunningham, *British Government Policy in Northern Ireland*, p. 14.
101 Daly, *Peace: Now Is the Time*, p. 20.
102 *The Future of Northern Ireland*, §14.
103 *The Future of Northern Ireland*, §17.
104 'From Whitepaper to a New Beginning'.
105 Joint Statement by Catholic Bishops, 21 November 1971 in Irish Catholic Bishops' Conference, *Justice, Love and Peace: Pastoral Letters of the Irish Bishops, 1969–1979* (Dublin: Veritas, 1979), p. 42.
106 'Peace and the Sacredness of Human Life'.
107 Peter R Neumann, *Britain's Long War: British Strategy in the Northern Ireland Conflict, 1969–1998* (London: Palgrave Macmillan, 2003), p. 70.
108 Cunningham, *British Government Policy in Northern Ireland*, p. 12.
109 Neumann, *Britain's Long War*, p. 70.
110 'The Situation in Northern Ireland' Interview on Radio Vaticana, 2 December 1976 in *Addresses on Peace in Northern Ireland, 1976–1983*.
111 Democracy was the Catholic Church's political system of choice. See *Gaudium et Spes*, §25.
112 Congregation for the Doctrine of the Faith, *A Doctrinal Note on Some Questions Regarding the Participation of Catholics in Public Life*, 24 November 2002, §6, www.vatican.va/roman_curia/congregations/cfaith/documents/rc_con_cfaith_doc_20021124_politica_en.html (accessed 22 August 2019).
113 Maria Power, 'A Serious Moral Question to be Properly Understood: The Catholic Church and Human Rights in the 1980s', in Tim White (ed.), *Northern Ireland and International Relations* (Manchester: Manchester University Press, 2017), pp. 131–143.
114 *A Doctrinal Note on Some Questions Regarding the Participation of Catholics in Public Life*, §4.
115 See for example the *Compendium* which states, 'The Church values the democratic system inasmuch as it ensures the participation of citizens in making political choices, guarantees to the governed the possibility both of electing and holding accountable those who govern them, and of replacing them through peaceful means when appropriate. Thus she cannot encourage the formation of narrow ruling groups which usurp the power of the State for individual interests or for ideological ends.' §406.

116 *Quadragessimo Anno*, §86.
117 *Quadragessimo Anno*, §95.
118 'Response to the Auditor's Paper at the Trinity College Theological Society', see also 'Reconciliation: the Path to Peace'.
119 Paul Bew, Peter Gibbon and Henry Paterson, *Northern Ireland: 1921–2001: Political Power and Social Classes* (New York: Serif Press: 2002), preface.
120 'Response to the Auditor's Paper at the Trinity College Theological Society'.
121 The initial reaction of the Catholic Nationalist community to this was nonviolent protest.
122 'Living with Difference: How Much Consensus?' Seminar in Fontborne Academy, Milton, Mass, USA, 13 February 1993 in *Addresses on Peace in Northern Ireland 1993–1996*.
123 'The Situation in Northern Ireland'.
124 For example, the Nationalist leader, John Hume, and the senior civil servant Kenneth Bloomfield both survived assassination attempts.
125 'Northern Ireland: A Shared Responsibility'.
126 'Renewed Heart for Peace', Address for World Day of Peace 1 January 1984 in *Address on Peace in Northern Ireland, 1984–1986*.
127 'Living with Difference: How Much Consensus?'
128 'Northern Ireland: A Shared Responsibility'.
129 'Meeting of the Parliamentary Catholic Community' House of Commons, Westminster, 1 December 1993 in *Addresses on Peace in Northern Ireland 1993–1996*.
130 'From Peace Process to Peace'.
131 'Day of Prayer for Peace in Ireland' St Patrick's Cathedral, Armagh, 21 November 1993 in *Addresses on Peace in Northern Ireland 1993–1996*.
132 'Mass for Peace' St Mark's Church, Massachusetts, USA, 3 November 1994 in *Addresses on Peace in Northern Ireland 1993–1996*.
133 He also noted that this was a key concern of the British and Irish governments: 'The British government has in fact committed itself to foster agreement and reconciliation, leading to a new political framework founded on consent, and to encourage, facilitate, and enable the achievement of such agreement of a period through a process of dialogue and cooperation, based on full respect for the rights and identities of both traditions of Northern Ireland.' 'Day of Prayer for Peace in Bosnia and Ireland'.
134 'From Peace Process to Peace'.
135 'Day of Prayer for Peace in Ireland'.
136 'Meeting of the Parliamentary Catholic Community'.
137 'Northern Ireland: Peace or Disaster?'
138 'Believers United in Building Peace' World Day of Peace Message, St Malachy's Church, Armagh, 1 January 1992 in *Addresses on Peace in Northern Ireland 1991–1992*.
139 'Let Us Give Children a Future of Peace' Message for World Day of Peace, 1 January 1996 in *Addresses on Peace in Northern Ireland 1993–1996*.
140 'The Urgency of Building Peace' Visit of President Clinton, 29 November 1995 in *Addresses on Peace in Northern Ireland 1993–1996*.
141 'Meeting of the Parliamentary Catholic Community'.
142 It is not the author's intention to offer an assessment of the efficacy of this change; see Gary Carville, 'Ireland and Vatican II: Aspects of episcopal engagement with and receipt of a Church Council, 1959–1977', PhD Thesis, Dublin City University, 2018.
143 'Statement on the Sunningdale Agreement', 10 December 1973 in *Addresses on Peace in Northern Ireland, 1968–1975*.

144 *Gaudium et Spes*, §§30, 31, 39, and 42.
145 Gen 1:26 'God said, Let us make [human beings] in our own image, in the likeness of ourselves.'
146 Daly, 'Towards the New Ireland', Offered to *The Cross*, September 1972 in *Addresses on Peace in Northern Ireland, 1968–1975*.
147 'Towards the New Ireland'.
148 'Building Peace Day After Day'.
149 *Bunreacht Na hÉireann – Constitution of Ireland*.
150 Ulster Unionist Party, *Peace. Order and Good Govt* (1973), Northern Ireland Political Collection, Linen Hall Library, Belfast, P1218. Emphasis in original.
151 'Changes in the Constitution and Irish Catholics', 9 February 1973 in *Addresses on Peace in Northern Ireland, 1968–1975*.
152 'The Role and Responsibility of the Churches in the Northern Crisis'.
153 'Sermon for World Day of Peace', St Mel's Cathedral, 1 January 1972 in *Addresses on Peace in Northern Ireland, 1968–1975*.
154 'Address for World Peace Day 1974', St Mel's Cathedral, 1 January 1974 in *Addresses on Peace in Northern Ireland, 1968–1975*.
155 'Sermon for World Day of Peace'.
156 'Building Peace Day after Day'.
157 'Sermon for World Day of Peace'.
158 'Changes in the Constitution and Irish Catholics'.
159 'Changes in the Constitution and Irish Catholics'.
160 'Address for World Peace Day'.
161 *Dignitatis Humanae*, §2.

5   Direct violence

Although the Catholic Church's teaching on just war became increasingly restricted throughout the twentieth century, as J Brian Benestad has pointed out, 'one of the most urgent tasks of Catholic social teaching is to keep the principles of the just war doctrine before the eyes of government leaders and citizens.'[1] The institutional church has continuously achieved this: for example, John Paul II fulfilled this role in the months before the 2003 invasion of Iraq when he stated, for example:

> "*NO TO WAR*"! War is not always inevitable. It is always a defeat for humanity. International law, honest dialogue, solidarity between States, the noble exercise of diplomacy: these are methods worthy of individuals and nations in resolving their differences. I say this as I think of those who still place their trust in nuclear weapons and of the all-too-numerous conflicts which continue to hold hostage our brothers and sisters in humanity.[2]

War therefore may be necessary for justice, but the Church argued that war needed to be held up to continuous moral scrutiny, and that measured, controlled force was the only force that could be justified. The Catholic position therefore 'establishes a strong presumption against war which is binding on all; it then examines whether this presumption maybe overridden, precisely in the name of preserving the kind of peace which protects human dignity and human rights.'[3] Peace should always be preferred wherever possible, and the benefits of any armed combat must significantly outweigh the risks. Two elements were central to this reasoning: the common good and human dignity, in particular the role of individual conscience both in the civil and religious realms. Sowle-Cahill sums the importance of such ideas to reasoning on the use of force thus:

> Far from Reinhold Nieburh's paradoxical mingling of sin and responsibility in seeking beneficent political outcomes; far from Ramsey's effort to make rules for resolving conflicts part of the love mandate itself; the Roman Catholic pontiffs and their interpreters take a more Thomistic

path by rooting a national right to self-defence in a reason-discerned natural order and in the mutual rights and duties that make for the common good.[4]

In terms of the common good, the changing nature of international politics meant that the increasing interrelatedness of nation-states was now an important element of the Church's teaching on the use of force. 'Just as individuals must regulate their activity so as to support and contribute to the common good of their society, so, too, nation-states must regulate themselves so as not to violate the requirements of the universal common good.'[5] Compassion joined justice as a key element in decision-making. This has meant that at times self-defence could be prohibited because the risks of war would outweigh the benefits. The role of individual conscience further served to highlight Catholicism's changing understandings of the world order. By emphasising such an issue, it no longer expected citizens to show deference to political authority. Instead, it encouraged them to question it and hold it up to moral scrutiny. This demonstrates the sea-change that was occurring within Catholicism; gone were medieval attitudes to the state and ruling elites which handed power and decision-making to a central authority. In its place can be seen an emphasis upon the individual who was now expected to use his or her conscience to assess the validity of the state's decision-making regarding the use of force. In such a manner, the social order based upon the common good and human flourishing could be preserved.

The provisional IRA's campaign as a just war

Within the Northern Irish context, however, just war doctrine was not being used by the state, but by the Provisional IRA, who framed their armed campaign against the British as a 'just war' and presented themselves as a legitimate authority representing the nationalist community.[6] The Provisional IRA argued that it was the moral and legal heir of the government of the all-Ireland Republic, with the website of Sinn Féin, the political leaders of republicanism, questioning the legitimacy of both political entities on the island and making its case for leadership of the nationalist community thus:

> Throughout history, the island of Ireland has been regarded as a single national unit. Prior to the Norman invasion from England in 1169, the Irish people had their own system of law, culture and language and their own political and social structures. Following this invasion the island continued to be governed as a single political unity, as a colony of Britain, until 1921.[7]

For Daly, such rhetoric represented an abuse of history[8]: 'The historic republican cause is being morally contaminated by the deeds now being perpetrated by order of the leaders now claiming to represent it.'[9] In the rhetoric of republicanism there was a wilful misrepresentation of the context of the Northern Irish conflict: 'They forget that the real British presence which is the heart of the whole Irish problem here is the presence here in the North East of the island of close to a million Irish people of unionist political persuasion and almost all of protestant religious faith, who identify themselves as also British and yet claim this island as their home by virtue of nearly 400 years of residence and toil and industry by their forbears.'[10]

In the spring of 1970, a series of articles appeared in *An Phoblacht*,[11] the main newspaper of the Republican movement, discussing the nature of the conflict in Northern Ireland and in particular its relationship to justice. The articles which were written by Deasún Breatnach, an Irish journalist and editor of *An Phoblacht* from 1973–1974 and 1977–1979, considered issues such as justice, non-violent resistance and self-defence, and human dignity from a republican perspective. The demands of the Second Vatican Council for the laity were the focus of these articles, with for example the first stating that:

> One of the judgements that came from Vatican II was that Christians must care, as individuals and as members of groups; that the Christian reaction must be positive for all our waking hours; and that we must see in everyone regardless of religion, colour, language, class – Christ our neighbour. That the only antidote for a sick society is active love.
>
> A society becoming more callous and less tolerant and with abuses by authority against minority groups becoming more common, is developing in this Ireland of ours, north and south. Now is the time to examine our consciences and to react positively.[12]

As the series developed, it began to consider the issues of violence and non-violence which had been key elements of the discussion and conclusions of the Second Vatican Council concerning the use of force. Invoking the language of human dignity, the second article argued that protest against injustice was a legitimate element of Christianity: 'The refusal to participate against the call of logic and conscience, and the violent opposition to peaceful protest, may very well be the equivalent of denying Christ as the cock crowed once, twice . . . for we are all our brothers' keepers.'[13] The final article provides what is in essence a theological justification for the use of violence which seems to be loosely based upon a selective reading of the teachings of *Populorum Progressio*:[14]

> In fact, there is a clear theology of violence in the teaching of the Church. The obligation to seek for peace at all times. . . . But one may defend oneself; one may kill in self-defence; one may take part in a just war or

revolution . . . from the moral as well as tactical viewpoint, there comes a time when the people must stand their ground, even if the result is violence.[15]

Here, Breatnach is speaking of just war which since the twentieth century has been one of the twin pillars, alongside nonviolence, of Catholic social teaching on the use of force. The Irish have often used the theory of just war to justify their actions against the British State, and despite later denials that they framed their activities in these terms, the Provisional IRA were no exception to this. Until the mid-1980s then, Daly carried out a 'dialogue' with the IRA and Sinn Féin regarding this, the highpoint of which was John Paul II's sermon at Drogheda, written by Daly, which ardently condemned violence as a form of liberation from oppression.

But as Daly argued in 1973, 'it is characteristic of ideologies to transfer religious feelings and fervours to non-religious causes; to place political programmes in the category of supra-rational truth, which belongs properly to religious dogma.'[16] Daly is perhaps best known for his denunciation of the IRA's argument in favour of their just war position. He held that Republicans were not engaged in a just war but instead were destroying the very communities that it arguably defended.[17]

Daly's rejection of the IRA's argument centred upon the fourth condition of a just war that 'the use of arms must not produce evils and disorders graver than the evil to be eliminated.'[18] As far as Daly was concerned, those using just-war doctrine did not understand it and were consequently misapplying it. In 1976, he contended that:

> A common misunderstanding of the just war theology is that its aim is to justify war or violence. This is not so. Its central affirmation is to declare that war, violence, killing are immoral- except in certain extreme conditions. Indeed for this theology, the killing of the innocent is intrinsically evil, and there are no exceptions.[19]

Although Daly was adamant that such 'extreme conditions' did not exist, as 'peaceful and political action' *did* have the potential to bring about the required reform of society,[20] the IRA argued that its armed campaign was a last resort which sought to bring justice to the people of Northern Ireland. This justice had been denied them by the presence of the British government in the region and the lack of self-determination for 40% of the population. All other routes to justice had been tried and failed.[21] In 1988, Gerry Adams, leader of Sinn Féin, explained the rationale behind the use of violence thus:

> Armed struggle is forced upon the IRA. Neither the IRA nor Sinn Féin want this war but the ineffectualness of all other forms of struggle, the conditions of repression that we have experienced and British attitudes, have made armed struggle inevitable. The deaths and injuries caused by

the war are all tragedies, which have been forced upon the people by the British presence.[22]

In his 1979 sermon at Drogheda, John Paul II adamantly refuted such reasoning, stating that:

> Christianity does not command us to close our eyes to difficult human problems. It does not permit us to neglect and refuse to see unjust social or international situations. What Christianity does forbid is to seek solutions to these situations by the ways of hatred, by the murdering of defenceless people, by the methods of terrorism. Let me say more: Christianity understands and recognizes the noble and just struggle for justice; but Christianity is decisively opposed to fomenting hatred and to promoting or provoking violence or struggle for the sake of "struggle". The command, "Thou shalt not kill", must be binding on the conscience of humanity, if the terrible tragedy and destiny of Cain is not to be repeated.[23]

This provoked republicans to respond: 'In all conscience we believe that force is by far the only means of removing the evil of the British presence in Ireland . . . physical resistance to British terror was in keeping with traditional Christian teaching on the right to resist oppression.'[24] However, for Daly, the use of just war, or indeed any meaningful conversation about its employment, was a diversion from the real issue at hand which was the impact that the violence was having on communities. Daly argued that the IRA was damaging the common good by denying the human rights of the very community it argued it defended. He thus changed the terms of the debate, focusing instead upon the juxtaposition of revolution versus reform. It was through this discourse that his vision of the Peaceable Kingdom can be seen, and that the binary of the 'already but not yet' emerges.

The Provisional IRA as revolutionary leaders

The focus of Daly's writings and sermons on direct violence was its impact upon human rights and dignity, and the development of the common good. Given the Provisional IRA's focus on the liberation of the nationalist community from the oppression of British rule, it was natural that Daly would turn to the wealth of teaching offered by the Catholic Church on the validity and consequences of revolutionary violence. Some Latin American liberation theologians, for instance, had presented 'certain kinds of revolutionary violence as defensive in character, a response to prior violations of human rights'[25]; a case certainly put forward by the Provisional IRA for its position, retaining 'its right to engage in warfare . . . based on . . . the right to revolt against tyranny and oppression.'[26] However, the Catholic Church argued that such actions would hinder the development of human rights in a region.[27] He demonstrated some understanding regarding the frustration of those who resorted to violence, suggesting that 'it was almost as though they felt they had to engage in destruction before we could be brought to realise they were there at all.'[28] But in response to this, he made a strong case for the use of nonviolent methods to overcome such grievances, demonstrating the futility of violence and its inability to give birth to a peaceful and just society, stating in 1972 that nonviolence 'has done more for human progress than violence has ever done.'[29] Indeed, as a direct consequence of the context which he was reimagining, Daly went further in his consideration of the legitimate use of revolutionary violence, suggesting that the consequences for society were the same as those emanating from the misuse of just war doctrine. In Northern Ireland he believed that:

> We are witnessing the emergence of a philosophy and methodology of total revolutionary violence, which corresponds exactly to the evil philosophy of total war and is equally intrinsically immoral. There is a spiralling rhythm of viciousness as between revolution and repression, which irresistibly impels towards the most brutal excesses and the most indiscriminate destruction.[30]

The supposed use of revolutionary violence by the IRA to free people from the oppression of the British government was therefore futile and self-defeating: as well as the destruction of society, 'quite simply, it is letting the British Government off the moral hook and providing it with a plausible moral alibi for refusal of constitutional or political change.'[31]

Daly regularly suggested that denunciations of violence by church leaders were 'utterly futile'[32] because they did not address the heart of the matter which was the impact of violence upon justice. In making such an argument, Daly is showing the value of his work and the importance of the moral imagination in the creation of a positive peace within Northern Irish society. Thus, through his writings on the use of direct violence and its impact on communities, Daly was engaged in the process of consciousness-raising which was a vital element in preparing individuals to work for the creation of the Peaceable Kingdom. Such consciousness-raising was engaged in a mutually enhancing tension alongside the teaching of active nonviolence. This was primarily intended to interrupt the cycle of both governmental and paramilitary oppression because those advocating it 'seek first to raise the consciousness of individuals, to awaken their human dignity, and to break down the alienation that helps to keep them oppressed.'[33] This, Daly hoped, would leave people open to creating and working towards the alternative possible future in Northern Ireland based upon Christ's Peaceable Kingdom as described in the Gospels.

Peace and justice could not be achieved through violence; on this Daly was clear.[34] As Paul VI had taught in 1967, violence was one of the major causes of oppression and injustice: 'Everyone knows . . . that revolutionary uprisings . . . engender new injustices, introduce new inequalities and bring new disasters. The evil situation that exists, and it surely is evil, may not be dealt with in such a way that an even worse situation results.'[35] Although the Church's and Daly's answer to such an issue was consistent advocacy of nonviolence, people first had to be conscientised regarding the effects of violence upon the community and the individual. This, alongside the challenge he posed to the British government on its human rights abuses during the Troubles, was the principal way in which Daly confronted the IRA and others engaged in direct violence within the region. The following quotation, taken from an article written for the *Catholic Herald* in 1976, provides a summation of Daly's attitude to revolutionary violence:

> The past seven years of violence in the North of Ireland provide a laboratory demonstration of the evils of revolutionary violence in modern conditions. These tragic years provide conclusive demonstration of the truth of Pope Paul's recent warning that violence creates greater evils and greater injustices than those which it set out to eradicate. The ends desired by the revolutionaries have long ago been pre-empted by the means they have used.[36]

The 'greater evils' alluded to were both communal and personal, and affected both the victims and perpetrators of violence.

On a day-to-day level, the impact of violence upon communities was clear: 'violence destroys the work of justice.'[37] Most paramilitary violence was centred upon deprived areas, and that which wasn't, was carried out on the whole by those from working-class districts. Thus, although those perpetrating the violence claimed to be liberating people from the injustice of British rule and the failure of the social and political reforms sought by the Civil Rights movement,[38] as Daly pointed out in a sermon to the people of West Belfast: 'All our social problems in Divis and in West Belfast are compounded by paramilitary violence.'[39] Places of employment, leisure, and means of transport were frequently bombed.[40] As a consequence people were prevented from achieving their potential as they became trapped in areas ignored by both government and business. Thus the cycle of deprivation and violence, which gave rise to the conflict in the first place, was compounded and continued. The IRA through their use of violence became oppressors themselves.[41] This was the lynchpin of Daly's argument against the use of violence in Northern Ireland. Although he was a nationalist, who also sought the reunification of the island, his belief in human rights, the common good, and the ability of justice and peace to bring these to fruition meant that he completely refuted the idea that violence could achieve this political aim. His understanding of the interrelatedness of the structures of society and the nature of post-revolutionary reform supported this logic. The reunification of Ireland would not automatically bring about a just and peaceful society; rather as the example of the post-partition south demonstrated would be the site of yet more violence and hardship.[42] In his 1987 World Day for Peace Message, he addressed this issue directly, stating:

> Some speak of radical overthrow of the whole existing order, a revolutionary reconstruction of society. Revolutionaries have only contempt for reforms which they dismiss scornfully as "bourgeois reformism". They regard normality as danger and "normalisation" as a threat to their revolution.
>
> But revolution itself is inevitably to be followed by a prolonged series of reforms, designed gradually to bring about a more just and equal society. Armed revolution however, only makes these reforms more difficult, more fragile and especially more costly in terms of human suffering and damage to human rights and human dignity.[43]

The Peaceable Kingdom, that is, a society governed by fairness and equality, could not be achieved quickly. Violence, seen by many as the quick way to achieve an organisation's aims, could not lay the foundation for desperately needed infrastructural reforms. The problems in Northern Ireland were not only political, but also social and economic. Instead of hastening reform, paramilitary violence was delaying it. It was providing the British government with the necessary excuses needed to ignore some of the most deprived areas of the United Kingdom and facilitating the completion of the project of segregation commenced by Stormont: 'The violence alleged to be for their liberation brought about for Catholics something very like the containment which Stormont tried to achieve but could never fully succeed in bringing about.'[44] Daly wanted revolution too, but one based upon peaceful and non-violent reform. It was a revolution which would facilitate a just outcome for all based upon a process or negotiation and dialogue rather than force and built by the whole community.[45]

However, Daly in his concentration on the social implications of violence, did not forget the individual or, more importantly for a Catholic bishop, their salvation. He was acutely aware of the terror that acts of violence wrought on victims, witnesses, and those living in everyday anticipation of it: 'The immediate effects of the present violence in the North represent an already crushing burden of human tragedy. One has only to think of the wrecked and ravaged little homes, the nerve-racked mothers, the hysterical children, the terrified old and ill, the worried wives and families of internees.'[46] He also showed concern for perpetrators, taking care to brand their acts but not the person as 'evil', commenting in 1972 that 'Even to say that methods are immoral is not necessarily to say that those who use them are evil.'[47] Further, he prompted them to contemplate the nature of salvation and the purpose of life, which is ultimately to prepare one's self to encounter God in the afterlife. He did so by reminding them of the personal consequence of their acts: The primary and most awesome responsibility rests on the militants and especially with the leadership both militarily and political of the Provisional IRA. They bear a frightening responsibility before God in their decision whether to extend the truce or resume hostilities on 3rd January.'[48] Such comments alluded to the nature of conscience and the impact of violence and terror upon the conscience of both perpetrators and witnesses, which was Daly's main concern when writing and speaking of the consequences of direct violence. This discourse centred upon one of the most fundamental teachings of the Catholic Church without which the Peaceable Kingdom cannot be realised: respect for human life.

Conscience

The economic costs of the violence and sectarian division in Northern Ireland have been well documented, with for example, manufacturing and unemployment declining by 40% throughout the course of the conflict because of a cessation of foreign investment. It has also been estimated that without the public subventions of the British government to the region (which for example, in 1992/3 totalled £3.3 billion), the living standards of the population would have approached those of Mexico or Argentina.[49] Daly was alive to these issues related as they were to the creation of the Peaceable Kingdom. However, he was also concerned with the moral development of the population, and in particular with the hardening of people's attitudes towards violence and the impact that this would have on their spiritual and ultimately social development. To that end, in his 1979 World Day for Peace Message, Daly provided the following assessment of the impact of violence upon the people of Northern Ireland: 'The worst consequences of violence, however, have been moral and spiritual, rather than material. The foundation of all moral principle and the source of all human rights is absolute respect from the sacredness of human life. Human life is now cheaper and more expendable than an armalite rifle.'[50] Without a proper understanding of the dignity of human life and the consequences of its degradation for the community, the dual mission of the church (i.e. the salvation of souls and the realisation of the values of the Peaceable Kingdom) would be impossible. Thus, the maintenance of what would perhaps now be called a moral compass around issues of violence was crucial. Each person, be they lay or clergy, Protestant or Catholic, British or Irish, had a role to play; one which hinged upon living in right relationship with God guided by a morally sound conscience which was defined by the Second Vatican Council as:

> In the depths of his conscience, man detects a law which he does not impose upon himself, but which holds him to obedience. Always summoning him to love good and avoid evil, the voice of conscience when necessary speaks to his heart: do this, shun that. For man has in his heart a law written by God; to obey it is the very dignity of man; according to it he will be judged. Conscience is the most secret core and sanctuary of a man. There he is alone with God, Whose voice echoes in his depths. In a wonderful manner conscience reveals that law which is fulfilled by love of

God and neighbour. In fidelity to conscience, Christians are joined with the rest of men in the search for truth, and for the genuine solution to the numerous problems which arise in the life of individuals from social relationships. Hence the more right conscience holds sway, the more persons and groups turn aside from blind choice and strive to be guided by the objective norms of morality. Conscience frequently errs from invincible ignorance without losing its dignity. The same cannot be said for a man who cares but little for truth and goodness, or for a conscience which by degrees grows practically sightless as a result of habitual sin.[51]

In line with such teaching, when writing and preaching about violence, Daly's primary concern was not discrediting the IRA's use of just war, but rather it was focussed upon the (d)evolution or 'perversion'[52] of conscience that was occurring, not just amongst the perpetrators of violence but within the community as a whole, whereby human life, the most sacred of God's gifts, was being cheapened to the point where people spoke in terms of 'an acceptable level of violence.'[53]

At the heart of all Catholic teaching lies the concept of human dignity, which is framed in terms of a person's desire for God, and the restlessness and spiritual deprivation caused by the rejection of this instinct. *Gaudium et Spes*, a document influential in Daly's thought, argues:

> The dignity of man rests above all on the fact that he is called to communion with God. This invitation to converse with God is addressed to man as soon as he comes into being. For if man exists it is because God has created him through love, and through love continues to hold him in existence. He cannot love fully according to the truth unless he freely acknowledges that love and entrusts himself to his creator.[54]

The true purpose of living then is 'to know and love God.'[55] Personal salvation can only be achieved through a right and full relationship with God, and the Peaceable Kingdom can only be attained when everyone begins 'to look upon his neighbour (without exception) as another self, above all bearing in mind his life and the means necessary for living it with dignity.'[56] Only then can the conditions leading to the Peaceable Kingdom be achieved.

The 'means necessary' to 'know and love God' and to live in unity with one's conscience are found in the Gospels and in the Ten Commandments, the fifth of which in Catholic teaching, 'you shall not kill,'[57] formed the basis of Daly's teachings on the impact of violence on Northern Irish society. Commenting on the death of Private John Randall, a 19-year-old solider shot dead by a sniper whilst on patrol in South Armagh, Daly pointed out that 'The ten commandments are the first casualty of the armed struggle.'[58] By such a comment, Daly meant that:

> The essential evil of deeds such as these is that they violate one of the most sacred and fundamental principles of the divine commandment

and moral conscience, namely that human life is inviolable, and that any attack on it is an offence against the majesty of God whose image is reflected in the human person and who is divine Lordship is the guarantor of sacredness of every human life.[59]

Killing damaged an individual's relationship with God and ran contrary to the principles of the Peaceable Kingdom in which every life was sacred and in which *every* person could flourish and attain their share in the common good. This dual emphasis in Daly's thinking and teaching is poignantly reflected in this 1976 World Day for Peace Message in which he stated that 'to end a life is to leave a man with no more time to pray, no time to make his soul, no time to repent, no time to begin again his real life's work which is to love and know God.'[60]

Daly was, however, equally concerned with the spiritual growth of the perpetrators of violence as well as the victims. Thus, although their actions were 'indefensible',[61] the perpetrators were themselves being 'brutalised' and 'injured'[62] through involvement in acts that ran contrary to the law of God. The ideology of republicanism demanded the disassociation of agent from action.[63] In their devaluation of the victim into a 'legitimate target', the perpetrators where dehumanising themselves by their 'passive submission' to a higher authority and the transference of responsibility for their actions onto others, for example 'the Brits'.[64]

Most important of all in terms of the impact of violence upon the perpetrators was the challenge that killing posed to one's existential beliefs and the subsequent psychic damage imposed through the moral injuries[65] sustained during the acts of violence. In addition to the feelings of guilt, depression, suicide, and shame commonly associated with the trauma of combat,[66] Daly, in his role as bishop, was directly concerned with the perpetrator's ability to know God, which was after all a person's *raison d'être*: 'To kill a man is to kill, in so far as it is in our power to do so, something of God. It is to kill in ourselves, some of our capacity for knowing God.'[67] This damage to a person's prospects of salvation was compounded by a corruption of a person's ability to form relationships not just with others but also ultimately with God. The implications of this for Daly's dual mission were profound. The faith needed for salvation and the work of creating the Peaceable Kingdom requires a transformation that can only be achieved through love; this love can only come from God. Killing destroys the capacity for love within the perpetrator:

> Awareness that God is God and awareness that man is man are both involved in the sense of the sacredness of human life. When this sense is damaged, all the resources of faith and of grace as well as of reason and love and the experience of being loved are needed for its repair.[68]

By turning away from God through the act of killing or violence, the perpetrator is diminishing his or her own sense of self-worth or esteem, as well as passing judgement of the worthiness of the victim: 'Those who kill scarcely see themselves as killing human beings; they are only hitting legitimate targets, paying back the Brits, deterring sectarian killers or else they are exterminating terrorists, restoring law and order, teaching loyalists a needed lesson.'[69]

Such attitudes also permeated the consciousness of the majority of the population not directly involved in paramilitary violence, and Daly was concerned that 'it may take generations before the terrible moral and spiritual price for these years of violence is paid.'[70] This blunting of conscience and the sense of the sacredness of human life allowed the population's thought processes and attitudes to be dominated by evil and hate rather than love. As Daly argued in 1976, 'to find killings acceptable might mean to find their evil acceptable; and this would be to begin to be contaminated by that evil, to begin to be made evil by it.'[71]

The actions of the paramilitaries and consequent impacts are preventing not just a negative but also a positive peace from being established because 'the fundamental principle of peace is a belief that each person is important.'[72] Diminishing one's own sense of self-worth as well as that of others creates an atmosphere of fear and distrust which prevents the interaction required for reconciliation. Consequently, barriers, both physical and psychological, are created which become seemingly impossible to cross. However, as John tells us in his first letter:

> There is no fear in love, but perfect love casts out fear; for fear has to do with punishment and whoever fears has not reached perfection in love. We love because he first loved us. Those who say "I love God", and hate their brothers or sisters, are liars; for those who do not love a brother or sister whom they have seen, cannot love a God whom they have not seen.[73]

The empowering and transformative faith and grace born of such love can only come from God, as Pope Francis taught in his first encyclical, *Lumen Fidei*:

> Faith is born of an encounter with the living God who calls us and reveals his love, a love which precedes us and upon which we can lean for security and for building our lives. Transformed by this love, we gain fresh vision, new eyes to see; we realize that it contains a great promise of fulfilment, and that a vision of the future opens up before us. Faith, received from God as a supernatural gift, becomes a light for our way, guiding our journey through time.[74]

It is through such faith that the moral imagination necessary for the establishment of the Peaceable Kingdom can emerge. Those engaged in the struggle for social justice and the reunification of Ireland, as well as those opposing them using violent means, are preventing the creation of the *very* structures which would alleviate their grievances and allow the long process of reform to begin.

At the same time, they are causing themselves moral and psychic damage which can, according to Daly, only be repaired through the love of God. This reconciling of conscience can only be achieved through a renunciation of the violence which is preventing God's love from acting in the lives of the perpetrators.[75]

> Political solutions are not the only need nor the greatest need of those committed to violence. Far more than this, they need a deep spiritual and moral conversion. A radical conversion of heart is what God is asking of them. He is offering them the grace they need to make this conversion possible.[76]

The grace found in this conversion will then enable them to hold the twin goals of personal salvation and societal transformation in a mutually enhancing tension and guide the moral imagination in the direction of long-term reform rather than damaging and violent revolution.

The British government

The atmosphere of fear and mistrust created by the paramilitary organisations was compounded by the British governments[77] who through their security policies also attacked the dignity of the human person. Thus, if the reform of society necessary for the Peaceable Kingdom to be established was to happen, Daly also needed to challenge the behaviour of the British governments, whose actions demonstrated little sense or any understanding of, or inclination towards acknowledging, the dignity of the human person.[78] Whilst the vision of an alternative possible future could come from any one sector of society, other institutions had to be convinced of its efficacy if it was to move forward. This element of Daly's work, therefore, was fundamentally about consciousness-raising, showing people how things are, rather than how they could or should be in order to galvanise them into action. In his writings on the British governments, there is little to be found regarding the personal salvation of ministers of state, soldiers, or police personnel. Instead, Daly sought to hold a mirror up to their actions in order to arouse their consciences, leading them to consider the process of long-term reform needed for the Peaceable Kingdom to emerge rather than remaining wedded to the paradigm of short-termism which characterised British efforts at resolving the crisis in Northern Ireland.

British counter-insurgency as a failure of politics

From the summer of 1969 onwards, the British governments' security policy in Northern Ireland was one of conflict containment[79] followed by management[80] through a series of unsuccessful political initiatives, such as the

1973 Sunningdale Agreement until the 1985 Anglo-Irish Agreement signalled the start of the Peace Process. The need to maintain 'an acceptable level of violence,'[81] however, led to short-termism characterising security policies, with counter-insurgency being 'limited to military, police, legal and punitive measures alone.'[82] Such policies were, according to Daly, providing propaganda for republican terrorist organisations, leading him to argue that 'it would be a strange kind of counter-subversion which would give the precisely subversives what they want. Government should deny them that satisfaction. . . . Clemency is a greater threat to the IRA then harsh repression.'[83] Before Tony Blair came to power in 1997, the British governments generally presented themselves as reluctant actors in Northern Ireland, seeking to stabilise, rather than resolve, the situation and return the region to devolved rule as quickly as possible. Feargal Cochrane sums up the attitude of the British governments thus: 'they resemble benevolent visitors to their schizophrenic relatives in a mental home. Whilst they love them, they can never quite relax, and feel unnerved by the inexplicable mood swings of their next of kin from overwhelming charm to violent rejection.'[84] Northern Ireland was a place apart or as Reginald Maudling put it, after his first visit in 1970, 'a bloody awful country.'[85] Initially then, British administrations did little to try and understand the underlying causes of the Troubles, which were socio-economic, as well as political in nature. Indeed, their confusion was such that they sought to comprehend the issues involved through the prism of British race relations policy, basing the 1969 Community Relations Act (Northern Ireland) almost word-for-word on the 1968 Race Relations Act,[86] analysing the causes of the conflict as a result of religious intolerance. If the issues being raised by the Civil Rights Movement had been seriously addressed, the conflict in Northern Ireland would not have escalated to the levels that it did. Indeed, even once the violence had been ignited there was still a strong case to be made for the nonviolent resolution of the conflict in Northern Ireland. Such a resolution could, according to Daly, be achieved through the establishment of the social and economic, and political justice discussed in Chapters 3; in other words, through the creation of a society characterised by the hallmarks of the Peaceable Kingdom.

Daly's assessment of the British governments' security policy was based upon the doctrine of double effect, initially developed by Thomas Aquinas to assess justifications for self-defence. Simply put, this doctrine 'is directed at well-intentioned agents who ask whether they may cause a serious harm in order to bring about a good end of overriding moral importance, when it is impossible to bring about the good end without the harm.'[87] Michael Walzer in his 1977 study *Just and Unjust Wars* adds the following to this definition: 'Double effect is a way of reconciling the absolute prohibition against attacking non-combatants with the legitimate conduct of military activity.'[88] Thus, counter-insurgency can sometimes be presented as a virtuous act, one that, for example, attempts to alleviate suffering and save lives in the long-term despite the collateral damage. However, Walzer believes that the reconciliation between the constituent elements of the Doctrine of Double Effect occurs too easily and places an additional layer of responsibility on decision-makers in such situations. He thus determines that the Doctrine of Double Effect can only be legitimately deployed if the intended good is achieved, and the foreseeable evil is reduced as far as possible so that: 'The intention of the actor is good, that is, he aims narrowly at the acceptable effect, the evil effect is not one of his ends; nor is it a means to his ends, and, aware of the evil involved, he seeks to minimise it, *accepting costs to himself*.'[89] Daly's persistent calls for clemency both towards communities and prisoners demonstrated clearly that his understanding of the Doctrine of Double Effect was aligned with Walzer's. Indeed, the violence being deployed by the British State was not even bringing about a 'good end': 'The Northern Ireland experience proves conclusively, if proof were needed, that counter-violence is not a virtuous remedy for an evil thing; but it is fatally infected by the evil which it purports to eliminate. It motivates and feeds the violence which it claims to supress.'[90]

In direct contrast to this, the British government argued that the high levels of violence, especially those experienced during the insurgency phase of the conflict,[91] justified robust forms of intervention, such as internment[92] and torture.[93] In 1972, the Heath government devised, but never implemented, Operation Folklore, which allowed soldiers to open fire 'without warning on persons merely carrying firearms (i.e. without having to be satisfied that they were about to use them etc.)'.[94] That such a scheme was developed shows a willingness on the part of the British to escalate the use of force well beyond what could be reasonably defined as 'minimum force'. Short-termism, aimed at returning power to the Stormont government as quickly as possible, dominated decision-making processes surrounding security policy in Northern Ireland. This behaviour was, according to Daly, preventing nonviolent processes (still in evidence at both an institutional and grassroots level in the region) from working: 'In Northern Ireland in particular military thinking has produced limited short run and narrow range results; but those are counter-balanced by long-term and wide-ranging negative results which, if the policies are continued, will work in the opposite sense to Sunningdale.'[95] Such an attitude was the direct consequence of a misunderstanding of the causes of the conflict in Northern Ireland, and a belief that a negative peace (i.e. a cessation of violence without a plan for post-conflict reconstruction) would be enough to provide a British victory in the region.

> To assume that security successes amount to a solution of the Northern Ireland problem would be to confuse the symptom with the disease. Violence in Northern Ireland is a symptom of a complex of underlying problems, and until those are resolutely and radically tackled, Northern Ireland will remain a chronically violence prone society.[96]

Therefore, the one consistent element of the British governments' record, both Labour and Conservative, in Northern Ireland since 1968 was its inability to understand the fundamentals of the problems fuelling violence and distrust or, as Daly put it, 'the confusion of symptom with disease.'[97] Not only did it fail to eradicate the social and economic grievances that had motivated the formation of the non-violent civil rights movement but also its response contributed to a cycle of violence that was to last nearly 30 years and claim the lives of 3637 people. However, for the British governments, despite pleas from churchmen and evidence from academics to the contrary, the maintenance of security took precedence over all other policy concerns.

A more appropriate response was therefore required which took into account the causes as well as the consequences of the conflict:

> The British government has not yet fully grasped that the only way forward out of our stalemate of destruction in Northern Ireland lies through a systematic policy for establishing conditions of credibility of the political and legal and judicial institutions under which we are governed, together with a patient and planned and methodical policy of building up public confidence that the security forces are non-partisan, politically impartial and fully answerable to the rule of law.[98]

Once more, Daly's moral imagination is brought into play as he offers a plan, based upon the principles of nonviolence and dialogue which would positively resolve the conflict by integrating much-needed elements of justice (economic and social, as well as political) into the process. The fundamental problem facing the people of Northern Ireland, both Catholic *and* Protestant, was a lack of agency. This created a vacuum[99] which was filled by violence: 'the present policy of indefinitely prolonging direct rule is creating a climate conducive to the indefinite prolongation of violence, and it must be replaced urgently by new political thinking.'[100] The only solution, according to Daly, was to create political institutions which would allow for the nonviolent change leading to the social and economic justice which was the key to the Peaceable Kingdom. To do so would end the culture of short-termism dominating political thought and fuelling the cycle of violence. The voices of those, such as the SDLP's John Hume, calling for constitutional change, needed to be placed at the centre of Whitehall's thinking on Northern Ireland, with security policies being subordinated, in a manner that implemented Walzer's thinking on the Doctrine of Double Effect to the pursuit of a nonviolent and just resolution to the conflict.

The behaviour of the security forces

The implementation of counter-insurgency and counter-terrorism policies in Northern Ireland overrode any of the 'normal' security concerns, such as protection from crime, the investigation of offences such as burglary, muggings, joyriding, and day-to-day visible community policing of the sort that those of us living in the rest of the UK, at least until the 1990s, expected, if not quite enjoyed, from the local or regional constabulary. Both the army and the police were seen as military forces and were equipped as such, with for instance the RUC (which became the Police Service of Northern Ireland in 2001) patrolling in armoured cars and routinely carrying weapons when their counterparts in the rest of the United Kingdom did not. Because Daly argued that 'security policies should be subordinated to and should be put at the service of clearly defined and resolutely pursued political aims',[101] he did not focus his attention too closely on the security services, preferring instead to direct his case towards those that governed them. According to Daly, there were three issues that needed to be addressed if the security forces were going to be able to contribute to the creation of the Peaceable Kingdom. First was the behaviour of the British Army, second the necessity of normalising policing, and finally the need to constantly monitor and reappraise security policies in the light of political developments. Each of these arguments was underlined by the Catholic Church's teaching on human dignity and justice, states which could only be achieved through non-violent approaches to governance.

Daly was dismissive of the British Army and its presence in Northern Ireland. He consistently argued that it provided the Provisional IRA with propaganda and recruitment opportunities. Speaking in 1973, he commented:

> One could draw a revealing graph plotting the rise and fall of IRA credibility and of popular support for the IRA, and showing their direct correlation with the escalation and de-escalation of British Army repression. On every occasion since 1969, whenever there seemed to be a genuine and effective commitment to replace military repression by political reform, republican activists have been rapidly discredited.[102]

His anger in the aftermath of Bloody Sunday was palpable,[103] and whilst he tried to be fair in his assessment of the role of the British Army in Northern Ireland, he saw its role as one of degradation and humiliation of the populous, which built resentment and fuelled the conflict. The British Army, in his analysis, had no role to play in the region: 'generals,' he commented, 'are not only irrelevant but dangerous.'[104] In 1992, in the aftermath of the Coalisland Riots[105]:

> Recent events in Nationalist areas like Coalisland show clearly that some British Army Regiments (notably the Parachute Regiment) are not suitable to street-side duties in Northern Ireland and show in general that the British Army must display great sensitivity and tact in the interface with the civilian population, especially in nationalist areas, if their counter-terrorist operations are not to become counter-productive. Events like those in Coalisland serve only the interests of IRA propaganda.[106]

The key here was the impediment that the British Army was creating for the safeguarding of human dignity and justice in Northern Ireland. The army added another layer of authority and repression for many in working-class communities, and the threat of the type of violence described earlier fuelled and confirmed pre-existing resentments towards the British government.

The presence of the British Army in the region was thwarting the nature of policing there and preventing the Peaceable Kingdom from being established. Daly argued that the police's overriding concern with counter-terrorism meant that ordinary people were suffering when crimes such as joyriding and burglary were not investigated:

> Policing which is fully answerable to the law, which is impartial, professional, efficient, and caring is an essential condition of justice in any society. When policing breaks down, it is the weakest and innocent who suffer, the aged, the housebound, the children and young people. In many areas, particularly in cities and towns, and particularly in what we used to call working-class areas, which sadly now are too often pools of unemployment, ordinary policing has broken down to a disturbing extent. The result is that the quality of life has been seriously damaged, through the almost uncontrolled social epidemic of car-stealing, mugging, robbery and burglary, vandalism and general misbehaviour on the part of a lawless minority. These communities have a right in justice to normal policing.[107]

This, he argued, was a failure on the part of the government who oversaw security policy, and did not reflect upon its impact on the everyday lives of people.

The British governments were to a large extent at fault, and the short-termism which characterised their attitude to Northern Ireland needed to be addressed in order to make any progress towards a negative, let alone positive, peace:

> The methods used for the repression of violence need constant scrutiny and appraisal. This matter cannot be left solely to the security authorities. These are naturally trained and predisposed to think in military terms, in terms of statistics of incidents and of causalities . . . they are relevant to short term pacification, and leave completely untouched the long-term reform of the society which is breeding the violence. What is worse, some measures of repression can actually increase the alienation and resentment of certain groups, can generate the kind of hopelessness which leads to fanaticism and can embitter a new generation and deliver them as ready made recruits to the revolutionary movements. Repressive measures indeed sometimes mirror the inherent injustices and inequalities existing in society itself.[108]

The entire security structure in Northern Ireland needed to be reformed to allow those living in the areas most affected to flourish:

> If violence were called off, the streets could be cleared of the oppressive army and security forces presence, and there could be a return to normal policing, so greatly needed if people are to walk the streets without fear. If they are to be freed from imprisonment in their own homes and allowed to sleep in their beds secure. If violence were called off, the rehabilitation of this whole area as a flagship of Irish culture and for pride in Irish identity could be greatly accelerated.[109]

This would allow normal life to begin for many.

Conclusion

Normal life for Daly would begin with the establishment of the Peaceable Kingdom. However, this was being prevented by the normalisation of direct violence in the region which had formed a vicious circle with the structural and cultural violence of sectarianism, the democratic deficit, and socio-economic inequality creating a perfect storm of injustice. Daly was fair minded in his approach to this issue and understood and taught that the violence was not one sided. The British government and paramilitary or terrorist organisations were equally to blame. Direct violence affected *everyone* involved, perpetrator as well as victim. It destroyed consciences and distorted understandings of human dignity and the right to life. Through his work on direct violence, Daly returned his attention to the individual and the need for personal salvation to be joined with communal transformation to allow the translation from imagination to praxis to occur. This focus demonstrated the complexity of the task undertaken by Daly, and the determination with which members of the Catholic Church, indeed the Christian churches, needed to work. All areas of life from prayer to voting were to be undertaken with the creation of the Peaceable Kingdom in mind and demonstrated the urgent need for a contextual theology within the region.

Notes

1 J Brian Benestad, *Church, State and Society: An Introduction to Catholic Social Doctrine* (Washington, DC: The Catholic University of America Press, 2011), p. 403.
2 John Paul II, 'Address of His Holiness Pope John Paul II to the Diplomatic Corps', 13 January 2003, http://w2.vatican.va/content/john-paul-ii/en/speeches/2003/january/documents/hf_jp-ii_spe_20030113_diplomatic-corps.html (accessed 22 August 2019).
3 United States National Conference of Catholic Bishops, 'The Challenge of Peace: God's Promise and Our Response. A Pastoral Letter on War and Peace',

3 May 1983, §70, www.usccb.org/upload/challenge-peace-gods-promise-our-response-1983.pdf (accessed 22 August 2019).

4 Lisa Sowle Cahill, *Love Your Enemies: Discipleship, Pacifism, and Just War Theory* (Minneapolis, Fortress Press, 1994), p. 205.

5 Kenneth R Himes, 'Pacifism and the Just War Tradition in Roman Catholic Social Teaching', in John A Coleman (ed.), *One Hundred Years of Catholic Social Thought: Celebration and Challenge* (New York: Orbis, 1991), p. 332.

6 Sissel Rosland, 'Narratives of Legitimacy: Political Discourse in the Early Phase of the Troubles in Northern Ireland', *Peace and Conflict Studies*, 2008, vol. 15, no. 1, article 2, https://nsuworks.nova.edu/pcs/vol15/iss1/2/ (accessed 22 August 2019).

7 Sinn Féin Education Department, *Freedom* (Dublin: Sinn Féin Education Department, 1991), Northern Ireland Political Collection, Linen Hall Library, Belfast, P4787.

8 'Civil Rights: Retrospect and Reflection', Address at Corrymeela Conference "Northern Ireland – Finding a Way Forward", 8 October 1988 in *Addresses on Peace in Northern Ireland, 1987–1988*.

9 'Conformity and Conscience', 24th Annual Summer School of the Social Study Conference, St Kieran's College, Kilkenny, 4 August 1976 in *Addresses on Peace in Northern Ireland 1976–1983*.

10 'Reconciliation', Down and Connor Diocesan Pilgrimage to Knock, 9 June 1990 in Northern Ireland Political Collection, Linen Hall Library, Belfast, *Addresses on Peace in Northern Ireland, 1989–1990*.

11 *An Phoblacht,* April, May, and June 1970.

12 *An Phoblacht,* April 1970.

13 *An Phoblacht,* May 1970.

14 See for example Paul VI, *Populorum Progressio*, 26 March 1967, §32, http://w2.vatican.va/content/paul-vi/en/encyclicals/documents/hf_p-vi_enc_26031967_populorum.html (accessed 12 August 2019) which states: 'We want to be clearly understood on this point: The present state of affairs must be confronted boldly, and its concomitant injustices must be challenged and overcome. Continuing development calls for bold innovations that will work profound changes. The critical state of affairs must be corrected for the better without delay.'

15 *An Phoblacht,* June 1970.

16 'Ecumenical "Brundermahl"'.

17 'IRA Not Waging a Just War, Says Bishop Daly', *Irish Times,* 1 January 1980.

18 *Catechism*, §2309. The Catholic Church provides a series of criteria by which the use of force is assessed. The conditions set forth for a just war are as follows: The damage inflicted by the aggressor on the nation or the community of nations must be lasting, grave and certain; all other means of putting an end to it must have been shown to be impractical or ineffective; there must be serious prospects of success; and the use of arms must not produce evils and disorders graver than the evil to be eliminated. The power of modern means of destruction weighs very heavily in evaluating this condition, *Catechism*, §§2307–2317, 2309.

    Once these have been achieved, a further set of criteria must be met which is usually classified in terms of *jus ad bellum* and *jus in bello*. The first set of criteria involves: Legitimate authority; Just cause; Last resort; Need for a declaration of war; Reasonable hope of success; Proportionality; and Right intention. The second set of principles entails: Immunity of non-combatants from direct attack; and Proportionality (of specific tactics). See Brian Orend, 'War', in *Stanford Encyclopaedia of Philosophy*, 2005, *http*://plato.stanford.edu/entries/war (accessed 22 August 2019).

19 'A Just War?'
20 'Christianity: Violence or Pacifism?' Mount Oliver Catechetical Centre, Dundalk, 6 March 1974 in *Addresses on Peace in Northern Ireland, 1968–1975.*
21 Although the IRA never outlines what such routes are.
22 Sinn Féin, *The Sinn Féin/SDLP Talks: January – September 1988* (Dublin: Sinn Féin Publicity Department, 1989), Northern Ireland Political Collection, Linen Hall Library, Belfast, P3396.
23 John Paul II, 'Sermon Given at Holy Mass in Drogheda', 29 September 1979, https://w2.vatican.va/content/john-paul-ii/en/homilies/1979/documents/hf_jp-ii_hom_19790929_irlanda-dublino-drogheda.htm (accessed 22 August 2019).
24 Don Buckley, 'Provisionals Reject Pope's Plea for an End to Violence', *Irish Times*, 3 October 1979.
25 John Lanagan SJ, 'Violence and Injustice in Society: Recent Catholic Teaching', *Theological Studies*, 1985, vol. 46, no. 4, pp. 685–699, 689. Also see for example Gustavo Gutiérrez, 'Notes for a Theology of Liberation', *Theological Studies*, 1970 vol. 31, no. 2, pp. 243–261, especially 250.
26 Irish Republican Army, *Handbook for Volunteers of the Irish Republican Army: Notes on Guerilla Warfare* (Eire: Irish Republican Army Headquarters, 1956), p. 4.
27 See John Eagleson and Philip Scharper (eds.), *Puebla and Beyond* (New York: Orbis Books, 1979); *Populorum Progressio*, §§30–31.
28 'Interview with James Downey, Political Correspondent of the *Irish Times*', 16 August 1976 in *Addresses on Peace in Northern Ireland, 1976–1983.*
29 Cahal Daly, 'Christ and the Irish Crisis', *The Furrow*, 1972, vol. 23, no. 7, p. 403. Cf. James Downey, 'The Saturday Interview: Cahal Daly', *Irish Times*, 28 August 1976; Cahal Daly, *The Price of Peace* (Belfast: The Blackstaff Press, 1991), pp. 66–68.
30 Cahal Daly, 'Violence or Non-Violence', *The Furrow*, 1972, vol. 23, no. 2, pp. 95–106, 99. Cf. Cahal Daly, *Peace the Work of Justice: Addresses on the Northern Tragedy, 1973–79* (Dublin: Veritas, 1979), p. 55.
31 Cahal Daly, *Communities Without Consensus: The Northern Tragedy* (Dublin: Irish Messenger Publications, 1984) p. 19.
32 Cahal Daly, 'Violence Destroys the Work of Justice', *The Furrow*, 1980, vol. 31, no. 2, p. 77.
33 Ronald G Musto, *The Catholic Peace Tradition* (New York: Orbis Books, 1986), p. 199.
34 'A Call to Commitment' St Patrick's Eve Service, St Anne's Cathedral, Belfast, 16 March 1987 in *Addresses on Peace in Northern Ireland, 1987–1988.*
35 *Populorum Progressio*, §31.
36 'A Just War?'
37 Daly, 'Violence Destroys the Work of Justice', p. 71.
38 'Nationalists' despair of political progress and social reform by way of the democratic political process is one of the most persistent and persuasive arguments used by the IRA in their endeavour to secure political support for what they call the armed struggle.' *Communities Without Consensus.*
39 'The Lower Falls Road: A Wronged But Forgiving People', St Peter's Pro-Cathedral, 31 March 1985 in *Addresses on Peace in Northern Ireland 1984–1986.*
40 'Peace Is Mightier Than the Bomb', Address for 1979 World Day of Peace', 1 January 1979, *Addresses on Peace in Northern Ireland, 1976–1983.*
41 'Young People in Crisis – The Youth Service Role', Seminar to Youth Committee for Northern Ireland, Cultra, 18 June 1984 in *Addresses on Peace in Northern Ireland, 1984–1986.* See also 'It is surely the greatest indictment of violence that it can be kept going only by using violence against the very people whom it is

purporting to be liberating. The liberation which those very people are demanding for themselves at this time is liberation from violence, not liberation by violence.' 'Justice Through Peace'.

42 Speaking of the aftermath of the Civil War in Southern Ireland (June 1922–May 1923), he argues that 'our total resources were exhausted for many years in repairing the physical destruction. It was decades before we were able to make any significant economic or social progress. People who extol violence in the present situation would do well to consider how closely set we could now be to an almost identical pattern of division, polarization, recrimination, social stagnation, and economic regression over the next quarter or half century. The welfare of both our countries is at stake.' 'Sermon for Fifth World Day of Peace'.

43 'Building Peace Day After Day', World Day of Peace Address, 1 January 1987 in *Addresses on Peace in Northern Ireland, 1987–1988*.

44 'Peace Is Mightier Than the Bomb'.

45 'It is further necessary, and it is a Christian duty, that everyone should contribute, according to his or her capacity, to the work of reform. Reform is the name for peaceful revolution, which is ultimately the true and Christian form of revolution and which is a condition for justice.' 'Building Peace Day After Day', cf. *Mater et Magistra* and *Populorum Progressio*, §32.

46 Cahal Daly, *Violence in Ireland and the Christian Conscience* (Dublin: Veritas, 1973), p. 42.

47 'Christian Patriotism in Ireland Now', Armagh Catholic Teachers' Guild, 20 May 1972 in *Addresses on Peace in Northern Ireland 1968–1975*.

48 'Reconciliation: The Path to Peace', Address to Mark the World Day of Peace, 1 January 1975, *Addresses on Peace in Northern Ireland, 1968–1975*.

49 Bob Rowthan and Naomi Wayne, *Northern Ireland: The Political Economy of Conflict* (Cambridge: Polity Press, 1988), p. 90.

50 'Peace Is Mightier Than the Bomb'.

51 *Gaudium et Spes*, §16.

52 'Statement Re: Murder of Private John Randall', 29 June 1993 in *Addresses on Peace in Northern Ireland, 1993–1996*.

53 'Northern Ireland: From Impasse to Initiative', Address at Conference on "Action for Justice: The Christian Vision" – Commission for International Justice and Peace – St Mary's College, London, 1 September 1979 in *Addresses on Peace in Northern Ireland 1976–1983*.

54 *Gaudium et Spes*, §19, translation taken from *Catechism*, §27.

55 *Catechism*, §31.

56 *Gaudium et Spes*, §27.

57 Deut 5:17. Some translations list this commandment as 'you shall not murder'; however, in the Catholic tradition, it has remained as 'you shall not kill,' thereby extending the parameters of debate surrounding the perpetrators of violence. For a full discussion of this, see Wilma Ann Bailey, *You Shall Not Kill or You Shall Not Murder? The Assault on a Biblical Text* (Collegeville, MN: The Liturgical Press, 2005).

58 'Statement Re: Murder of Private John Randall'.

59 'Northern Ireland: From Impasse to Initiative'.

60 'Power for Peace', Sermon for Peace Day in St Mel's Cathedral, 1 January 1976 in *Address on Peace in Northern Ireland, 1976–1983*.

61 Daly, *Peace: The Work of Justice*, p. 94.

62 'Violence in the North' St Patrick's Home, Carrick on Shannon, 15 March 1971 in *Addresses on Peace in Northern Ireland, 1968–1975*.

63 'Conformity and Conscience'.

64 Daly, *Peace: The Work of Justice*, pp. 91–96.

65 According to Purcell et al, 'moral injury refers to a lasting sense of guilt, shame, and disillusionment that arises from participating in acts that violate or undermine one's deeply held moral beliefs of sense of justice.' Natalie Purcell, Kristine Burkman, Jessica Keysen, Philip Fucella and Shira Maguen, 'Healing from Moral Injury: A Qualitative Evaluation of the *Impact of Killing* Treatment for Combat Veterans', *Journal of Aggression, Maltreatment and Trauma*, published online 18 April 2018, p. 2. www.tandfonline.com/doi/abs/10.1080/10926771.2 018.1463582 (accessed 22 August 2019).
66 For an analysis of the prevalence of Post Traumatic Stress Disorder in Northern Ireland, see Finola Ferry, Brendan Bunting, Samuel Murphy, Siobhan O'Neill, Dan Stein, and Karestan Koenan, 'Traumatic Events and their relative PTSD burden in Northern Ireland: A consideration of the impact of the "Troubles"', *Social Psychiatry and Psychiatric Epidemiology*, 2014, vol. 49, no. 3, pp. 435–446. See also Corinne Puntill, 'Booze and Anguish Haunt Northern Ireland's Retired Terrorists: Some Regret Not Putting Ballots First', *Global Post*, 15 July 2015, www.pri.org/stories/2015-07-15/booze-and-anguish-haunt-northern-irelands-retired-terrorists-some-regret-not (accessed 22 August 2019).
67 'Power for Peace'.
68 'Power for Peace'.
69 'Conformity and Conscience'.
70 Cahal Daly and Eric Gallagher, *Violence in Ireland: A Report to the Churches* (Belfast: Christian Journals, 1976), p. 49.
71 'Power for Peace'.
72 Jean Vanier, *Encountering the Other* (Dublin: Veritas, 2005), p. 11.
73 1 Jn 4:18–20.
74 Francis, *Lumen Fidei*, 29 June 2013, http://w2.vatican.va/content/francesco/en/encyclicals/documents/papa-francesco_20130629_enciclica-lumen-fidei.html (accessed 23 August 2019).
75 For examples of this, see David Hamilton, *A Cause Worth Living For: My Journey Out of Terrorism* (Godlaming: Highland Books, 2008); Courtney McGrail, 'Paramilitary Provo Turned Pious Parishioner', *Irish Catholic*, 27 April 2017, www.irishcatholic.com/paramilitary-provo-turned-pious-parishioner/ (accessed 23 August 2019); Jamie Wreford, 'God Can Forgive Anyone – Even Murderers – as Former Terrorist and UVF Member Bobby Mathieson Found Out', *New Life Publishing*, 24 May 2014, www.newlifepublishing.co.uk/latest-articles/dir-art/god-can-forgive-anyone/ (accessed 23 August 2019).
76 'A Time for Conversion', Lenten Message, Lent 1987 in *Addresses on Peace in Northern Ireland 1987–1988*.
77 Until 28 March 1972 when Direct Rule was introduced, Northern Ireland was governed from Stormont by a Unionist administration. Daly spends little time considering this administration's record and instead focuses his attention upon the British administrations that governed the region for 26 years until the Good Friday Agreement was reached in 1998. From 1968–1998, power changed hands between the Labour and Conservative parties four times. It is therefore more correct to speak of British governments rather than the British government. The administrations in power were 1966–1970: Labour; 1970–1974: Conservative; 1974–1979: Labour; 1979–1997: Conservative; and 1997–2010: Labour. The Northern Irish policies of each of these administrations is 'best understood as having both strategic continuity and the capacity for tactical adjustment; a focus on the latter can blind one to the importance of the former.' Michael Cunningham, *British Government Policy in Northern Ireland 1969–2000*, 2nd Edition (Manchester: Manchester University Press, 2001), p. 243.

78 Whilst Margaret Thatcher claimed to be a person of faith, it was under her leadership that 'Britain finally became unhinged from its Christian moorings as consumerism became the central source of values and social responsibility.' Eliza Filby, *God and Mrs Thatcher: The Battle for Britain's Soul* (London: Backbite Publishing, 2015), pp. 343–344.

79 Ramsbotham et al define this term as 'peacekeeping and war limitation (geographical constraint, mitigation and alleviation of intensity, and termination at the earliest opportunity).' Oliver Ramsbotham, Tom Woodhouse and Hugh Miall, *Contemporary Conflict Resolution*, 4th Edition (Cambridge: Polity Press, 2016), p. 34.

80 Ramsbotham et al define this as 'a generic term to cover the whole gamut of positive conflict handling. Here, we understand it in a more limited way to be the settlement and containment of violent conflict.' *Contemporary Conflict Resolution*, p. 34.

81 'In December 1971, Reginald Maudling, then British Home Secretary, declared that the situation in Northern Ireland at that time amounted to 'an acceptable level of violence.' Later, Unionist politicians in particular claimed that this term effectively became the security policy of successive British governments who were prepared to countenance paramilitary activity so long as it remained within what it judged to be 'manageable proportions.' CAIN Web Service, 'A Glossary of Terms Related to the Conflict', http://cain.ulst.ac.uk/othelem/glossary.htm (accessed 23 August 2019).

82 'West Belfast – Time for a New Deal', St Luke's Church, Twinbrook, Belfast, 24 April 1988 in *Addresses on Peace in Northern Ireland, 1987–1988*.

83 'West Belfast – Time for a New Deal'.

84 Feargal Cochrane, 'Any Takers? The Isolation of Northern Ireland', *Political Studies*, 1994, vol. 42, no. 3, pp. 378–395, 378–379.

85 '"What a Bloody Awful Country!" The Tory Story of Ireland', *Irish Independent*, 18 February 2018.

86 The Community Relations Act (Northern Ireland) 1969 uses exactly the same language as the Race Relations Act 1968, with the substitution of the word 'religion' for 'race'. HMSO, Community Relations Act (Northern Ireland) 1969, http://cain.ulst.ac.uk/hmso/cra1969.htm (accessed 23 August 2019) and HMSO, Race Relations Act 1968, www.legislation.gov.uk/ukpga/1968/71/enacted (accessed 23 August 2019).

87 Alison McIntyre, 'The Doctrine of Double Effect', *The Stanford Encyclopaedia of Philosophy*, https://plato.stanford.edu/archives/win2014/entries/double-effect/ (accessed 23 August 2019).

88 Michael Walzer, *Just and Unjust Wars: A Moral Argument with Historical Illustrations* (New York: Basic Books, 1977), p. 153.

89 Walzer, *Just and Unjust Wars*, p. 156. Emphasis added.

90 'Ecumenical Brudermahl'. Recent academic research has proven Daly correct in his conclusion, Gary Lafree, Laura Dugan and Raven Korte, 'The Impact of British Counter-Terror Strategies on Political Violence in Northern Ireland', *Criminology*, 2009, vol. 47, no. 1, pp. 17–45.

91 The British Army in its report on Operation Banner (14 August 1969–31 July 2007), the name given to its activities in Northern Ireland, divided the conflict into three phases: August 1969–Summer 1971 was largely characterised by widespread public disorder; Summer 1971 until the mid-1970s is best described as classic insurgency; and the end of the insurgency merged into the phase characterised by the use of terror tactics. This ended with exceptions, with the final ceasefire declared by the paramilitaries in 1996. Prepared under the direction of the Chief of the General Staff, *Operation Banner: An Analysis of Military Operations in Northern Ireland*, July 2006, www.vilaweb.cat/media/attach/vwedts/docs/op_banner_analysis_released.pdf (accessed 23 August 2019).

92 Introduced by the Stormont government with the backing of Ted Heath in August 1971, Martin J McCleery, *Operation Demetrius and Its Aftermath: A New History of the Use of Internment Without Trial in Northern Ireland 1971–1975* (Oxford: Oxford University Press, 2015).

93 Torture in Northern Ireland consisted of the use of the so-called Five Techniques: wall-standing, hooding, subjection to noise, deprivation of food and deprivation of sleep, which according to the 1978 ruling by the European Court of Human Rights constituted inhumane and degrading treatment but fell short of torture. See Samantha Newbury, *Interrogation, Intelligence, and Security: The Origins and Effects of Controversial British Techniques* (Oxford: Oxford University Press, 2015), pp. 62–131.

94 Letter from AW Stephens, Head of DS10 to VHS Benham, Northern Ireland Office, 16 November 1973, FCO 87/248, National Archives, Kew, cited in Andrew Sanders, 'Operation Motorman (1972) and the Search for a Coherent British Counter-insurgency Strategy in Northern Ireland', *Small Wars and Insurgencies*, 2013, vol. 24, no. 3, 465–492, 477.

95 'Statement on the Sunningdale Agreement', 10 December 1973 in *Addresses on Peace in Northern Ireland, 1968–1975*.

96 'The Politics of Peace', Address at Longford on World Day of Peace, 1 January 1978, Northern Ireland Political Collection, Linen Hall Library, Belfast, *Addresses on Peace in Northern Ireland, 1976–1983*.

97 'The Politics of Peace'.

98 'Law and Mercy'.

99 'Violence often erupts in the vacuum left for it by politicians.' Reconciliation: The Path to Peace'.

100 'Northern Ireland: From Impasse to Initiative'.

101 'Northern Ireland: From Impasse to Initiative'.

102 'Ecumenical Brudermahl'.

103 See 'Sermon at the Funeral Mass for Derry Victims', St Mel's Cathedral, 2 February 1972 in *Addresses on Peace in Northern Ireland, 1968–1975*.

104 'Ecumenical Brudermahl'.

105 In the aftermath of an IRA bombing in May 1992, in which a 19-year-old paratrooper lost both of his legs, the behaviour of the Parachute Regiment led to rioting, with the brigadier in the area eventually being relieved of his command. A number of officials, politicians, and prominent nationalists expressed concern about the suitability of the 3rd Battalion, Parachute Regiment (3 Para) for deployment to Northern Ireland. Sam McBride, 'Declassified Files: Official's Private Alarm at Paratroopers' Role in 1992 Coalisland Riots', *Newsletter*, 27 August 2017, www.newsletter.co.uk/news/declassified-files-official-s-private-alarm-at-paratroopers-role-in-1992-coalisland-riots-1–8124200 (accessed 23 August 2019). Such behaviour and attitudes were fairly normal as Nicky Curtis recalled of the Falls road curfew of 1970: 'I know full well that a lot of the lads were taking the opportunity to vent their anger over things already done. Heads were being cracked and houses trashed from top to bottom . . . something more than houses and Provo guns had been destroyed that weekend.' Cited in Sanders, 'Operation Motorman (1972) and the search for a coherent British counter-insurgency strategy in Northern Ireland', p. 469.

106 'Current Issues in Northern Ireland', 5 June 1992 in *Addresses on Peace in Northern Ireland, 1991–1992*.

107 'A Call to Commitment'.

108 'The Politics of Peace'.

109 'Centenary Celebrations of St Paul's Parish', 20 September 1987 in *Addresses on Peace in Northern Ireland, 1987–1988*.

Conclusion

The challenge facing the Catholic Church in Northern Ireland from the 1960s onwards was significant. At a universal level, the Church was trying to understand what the new spirit of *aggiornamento*, ushered in by Vatican II, meant in terms of praxis and relationships – a process which led to fractures that are still very much in evidence today. Such changes affected the island of Ireland in a number of ways. First, the Second Vatican Council transformed the nature of the church-state relationship, ultimately leading to rapid secularisation and uncovering decades of sexual and physical abuse within church institutions.[1] Second, the missionary nature of the church altered, with a renewed focus on the Gospel leading to more diverse forms of evangelisation which focused upon social justice and the agency of the laity as well as spiritual transformation. In Northern Ireland, the Catholic Church was simultaneously plunged into a conflict that was seen by many beyond the region as religious in character, with the bishops being expected to act as de facto spokesmen for 'their community'. For 30 years, Northern Ireland became a place where the Gospel and Catholic social teachings of social justice, peace, nonviolence, reconciliation, and forgiveness were tested to their very limits daily.

The aim of this book was to try and understand how the Catholic Church in Northern Ireland reacted to these challenges. It was not seeking to assess the efficacy or impact of these responses but instead trying to determine what the behaviour of the Church would look like if explored through an ecclesiological rather than political lens. It aimed to understand how the Church spoke in the public square, how it used the Gospel and the Magisterium (most notably Catholic social teaching) to shape its response to the conflict, and to determine if a Catholic public theology emerged during the period from 1968–1998. Whilst it does not deny that the behaviour of some Catholic clerics could be read as political, the presentation of an ecclesiological exploration aims to add more nuance to our understandings of the Catholic Church's reactions to the conflict.

To achieve the overarching aims of this research, it was evident that the Church leadership could not be seen as a unified body speaking with one voice. First, in a situation such as Northern Ireland, leadership can emerge from any quarter with a number of secular or diocesan priests as well as members of religious orders acting as spokespersons for sections of the Catholic community.[2] Second, because of the structure of the Catholic Church, the bishops did not create a unified response to the conflict in the manner, for example, of the US bishops' condemnation of nuclear weapons in 1983.[3] Whilst this is regrettable, it is not surprising as each bishop is completely autonomous within his own diocese. Thus, to comprehend the ecclesiological response to the conflict, the work of individual clerics and their role in the public square have to be studied. The work of Cardinal Cahal Daly, who acted as a peritus at the Second Vatican Council and who was a bishop from 1967 until the ceasefires in 1996, provides an excellent case study for such an endeavour. Daly preached a gospel of justice and peace to a frequently hostile public square in Northern Ireland. In addition to condemning violence, his main contribution was the provision of an ethical roadmap for justice and peace. His work focused upon the whole person, emphasising the need for social as well as spiritual salvation. He sought to focus people's attention upon the intersection of the cross where one's relationship with God meets one's relationship with neighbour, contextualising all of his teaching for Northern Ireland.

What did the Peaceable Kingdom mean to Daly?

Daly understood that the Gospel and Catholic social teaching needed to be placed within the context in which they were being used. Catholics, indeed all Christians, in Northern Ireland could not just be presented with a gospel verse telling them to love their neighbour. They had to be supported and guided towards the best means of achieving this within their local communities and society as a whole. Therefore, all of his writings and sermons were based upon the Gospel and Catholic social teaching, empirical analysis, and dialogue (and I will come to the importance of his methods shortly). Daly used these elements as a means of contextualising the teachings of the Church, thereby enabling the lived Christianity that was so important to his faith and teaching to flourish within communities. It was through such lived Christianity that the Peaceable Kingdom could become a reality. As the preceding chapters have shown, the result of this was a Catholic public theology or roadmap for justice and peace for the people of Northern Ireland which fundamentally sought to eradicate the structural violence that had given rise to the conflict in the first place.

Nothing escaped Daly's attention in his desire to realise the Peaceable Kingdom. His approach to justice and peace in Northern Ireland can be found in two well-known passages from the New Testament. The first from the Gospel of John tells us that Christ came 'that they may have life, and have it abundantly.'[4] Whilst the second from the Letter of James states,

'For just as the body without the spirit is dead, so faith without works is also dead.'[5] At the heart of Daly's vision for the Peaceable Kingdom lay the human flourishing defined by Jesus in John 10:10. But the steps necessary to allow a person to reach their full potential were not individual ones. Rather the promise of John 10:10 could only be achieved through the efforts of the community and society, and within the context described by James. The first pillar of the Peaceable Kingdom, therefore, was an understanding that individual spirituality and social justice were intimately entwined. Individual salvation and the realisation of God's Kingdom on earth, which Daly argued were the two goals of a Christian life, could only be achieved if both were in place and both were being equally attended to. This is a significant theme in his writings. It can be seen emerging in each of the areas covered in this book. He is most directive, however, in his writings on the Church as a contrast society, imploring that people develop their relationship with God into one of freedom which will allow them to flourish spiritually and give them the strength, inspiration, and capacity needed to work for social justice and peace. Thus, the Peaceable Kingdom can only emerge if people pay attention to both strengthening their relationships with God and ensuring that their relationships with others are based upon the teaching to love our neighbour.

Such focus was further developed by Daly in his writings on social and economic justice, political justice, and the impact of direct violence on the people of Northern Ireland. Here, the importance of contextualisation becomes evident. And, it is here that the specific roadmap for justice and peace for Northern Ireland emerges. Through his methodology of reflection upon the Gospel and Catholic social teaching, empirical analysis of the issue under consideration, and dialogue with those most closely involved, Daly demonstrated how to develop the alternative vision of society that was so crucial for the Peaceable Kingdom. Three examples can be used to illustrate this. First, instead of saying that businesses should invest more in deprived areas of Northern Ireland so as to create jobs, he placed his teachings on this within the framework of the Catholic social teaching concept of the 'social mortgage,' showing how such practices were fundamental to the Christian faith. Second, whilst he taught that the political structures in Northern Ireland were unjust, he explained why this was so and suggested alternatives that would create the conditions for human flourishing. Third, when condemning paramilitary and state violence, instead of providing a blanket condemnation, in its place he offered granular detail regarding the damage that this violence was doing to communities, and the moral injury to both victims and perpetrators that was resulting. In all of this can be seen the ultimate aim of Daly's Peaceable Kingdom: the creation of a society in which both structural and direct violence had been eradicated and in which the conditions, specific to that community, necessary to human flourishing were present and were being actively supported.

Daly's legacy for the Catholic Church

Daly left a meaningful legacy to the Church in Northern Ireland and to the Catholic Church as a whole. The leadership of the Catholic Church in Northern Ireland had not been prepared for the task that faced it when the conflict erupted in the late 1960s. It initially sought to act as a spokesperson for the Catholic community, a role which was rapidly taken over by politicians such as Gerry Fitt and John Hume. Being superseded in this manner was fortuitous, as despite past behaviours, it was not the place of the Catholic leadership to speak for or negotiate with the community on matters relating to the nature of the state. This did not signal a loss of authority. Rather, it enabled the Church to enact the leadership mandated to it by Christ and renewed at the Second Vatican Council, namely the missionary activity of preaching the Gospel and teaching that justice and peace should be the foundation stones of every society. What people expected the Catholic Church to do (and this ranges from supporting the violence to ex-communicating terrorists) and what it actually could and was able and wanted to do, were therefore two very different things.

Through his writings on justice and peace, Daly redefined the nature and mission of the Church in Northern Ireland. He was not alone in this but his position as a bishop and later cardinal, and the volume of his work, makes his contribution important. He achieved this through two methods: first, his entire ministry was embedded in the teachings of the Second Vatican Council. All of his interventions in the situation in Northern Ireland were placed within the appropriate frameworks of the Council's teachings and centred upon the need for human flourishing. There was little hint of the triumphalism or sense of entitlement that had characterised earlier Church interventions in matters relating to society. Instead, a more holistic approach to mission can be seen. Through this, everyone – the laity, clergy, and religious – were expected to take responsibility for the transformation of society and in doing so, develop their individual spirituality. Daly taught that faithfulness to the Gospel and the teachings of the Church had to come first and had to infuse every aspect of a person's life. In doing so, he firmly orientated the Church in Northern Ireland towards the world and offered answers to the most pressing questions and issues facing society. His second method, therefore, was to put Christ and the Gospel first. Everything that he did relating to the conflict in Northern Ireland was filtered through the threefold method of Gospel, empirical analysis, and dialogue, resulting in a Catholic public theology for Northern Ireland. This was how the Catholic Church's presence in the public square was and should be vocalised within the region. By deploying such methods, Daly provided an alternative vision of the society towards which people could work. Such teaching has the potential to empower the laity by providing them with the agency necessary to use their expertise to transform society in the region, eradicating structural violence and creating the conditions necessary for human flourishing.

By using such methods, Daly was clearly stating that the Catholic Church in Northern Ireland was not a political entity or a spokesperson for the Catholic community. Rather it was a representative of the teachings of the Gospel and the love of God. Whilst it was not always successful in doing this, it is important to understand that this is how the Catholic Church viewed itself post Vatican II.

Other national Catholic churches[6] too have much to learn from Daly's example as they struggle with secularisation and in particular what this means for their role in society. This has led for the most part to a retreat from the public square just at a time when national and global events mean that the gospel message of justice and peace, and the compassion that flows from it, are most needed. For instance, whilst Pope Francis has been consistently vocal on ecological issues and the climate emergency, the Catholic hierarchy (along with their Anglican counterparts) were notably absent from the debates surrounding the recent Extinction Rebellion protests in London in October 2019.[7] But the example set by Daly shows that the church must voice the message of the Gospel and Catholic social teaching around any issues leading to injustice. Whilst the leadership offered should always be spiritual, such a spirituality extends beyond individual salvation into social justice and the reordering of society along the lines presented to us by Jesus. In this, the Church as an institution needs to be a sign of the Peaceable Kingdom, or a contrast community. In practice, this means that its members need to be held to account for actions that are counter to the Gospel and Catholic social teachings, no matter how distasteful the discussion of such activities are. Furthermore, everyone in the Church is responsible for the establishment of the Peaceable Kingdom, and the laity needs to be supported and energised to exercise their agency within the Church and society. However, none of this can be achieved in an ad hoc manner. This is where the method of envisaging an alternative possible future leading to the Peaceable Kingdom used by Daly is so important. Through it, he provides a strategic and thoughtful manner in which to identify and approach the issues blocking the eradication of structural violence and human flourishing. This is an ongoing task which is vital to the mission of the Church.

The purpose and nature of Catholic social teaching is often difficult for people to comprehend. It does not provide a ready-made handbook for action; rather it is a set of guidelines which need to be approached in a spirit of prayerful endeavour. Daly showed the importance of such contextualisation for Northern Ireland and for any society suffering from structural violence. Whilst the underlying message of his work remains the same – that is, structural violence needs to be eradicated to enable the establishment of the Peaceable Kingdom to emerge – the context has changed. The political and social landscape of Northern Ireland has changed considerably since Daly retired in 1996. Devolved government is in place, two parties previously seen as hardliners are in government, the United Kingdom has left the European Union, and migration to the region has added the spectre of racism to the social problems facing the region. Other problems highlighted by Daly, such as unemployment and deprivation, remain. Structural rather than direct violence is now the main concern preventing the establishment of the Peaceable Kingdom. Northern Ireland therefore needs a new, or updated, Catholic public theology which will take these issues into account and provide a roadmap for justice and peace.

Notes

1 This book has not covered the abuse scandal in the Catholic Church in Northern Ireland as it has been dealt with in a thoughtful and coherent manner elsewhere. For such an analysis of clerical child abuse in Northern Ireland and Daly's role in dealing with the perpetrators, see Margaret M Scull, *The Catholic Church and the Northern Ireland Troubles, 1968–1998* (Oxford: Oxford University Press, 2019), pp. 180–186.
2 For example, the multiple publications and endeavours of Denis Faul and Raymond Murray; the work of Bishop Edward Daly chronicled in *A Troubled See: Memoirs of a Catholic Bishop* (Dublin: Four Courts Press, 2011); the thought-provoking interventions of Brian Lennon SJ; the life of Fr Gerry Reynolds, see Gladys Ganiel, *Unity Pilgrim: the Life of Fr Gerry Reynolds CSsR* (Dublin: Redemptorist Communications, 2019); and the life of Fr Alec Reid, see Martin McKeeven CSsR, *One Man, One God: the Peace Ministry of Fr Alec Reid* (Dublin: Redemptorist Communications, 2017).
3 United States Conference of Bishops, *The Challenge of Peace: God's Promise and Our Responses*, 3 May 1983, www.usccb.org/upload/challenge-peace-gods-promise-our-response-1983.pdf (accessed 26 February 2020).
4 Jn 10:10.
5 Jas 2:26. This verse is best read within the context of verses 14–26.
6 By national Catholic churches I mean Catholic churches within defined geographical regions, such as England and Wales, France, and Canada.
7 Daly was concerned with environmental issues and in his retirement wrote *The Minding of Planet Earth* (Dublin: Veritas, 2004).

Bibliography

Andersen, Karen, 'Ireland in the Twenty-First Century: Secularization or Religious Vitality?', in Detlet Pollack, Olaf Müller, and Gert Pickell (eds.), *The Social Significance of Religion in the Enlarged Europe: Secularization, Individualization and Pillarization* (Abingdon: Routledge, 2012), pp. 51–76.

An Phoblacht.

Appleby, R Scott, 'From State to Civil Society and Back Again: The Catholic Church as a Transnational Actor, 1965–2005', in Abigail Green and Vincent Viaene (eds.), *Religious Internationals in the Modern World: Globalization and Faith Communities Since 1750* (New York, NY: Palgrave, 2012), pp. 319–342.

Archbishop of Canterbury's Commission on Urban Priority Areas, *Faith in the City: A Call for Action by Church and Nation* (London: Church House Publishing, 1985).

Ashley, J Matthew, 'Contemplation in the Action of Justice: Ignacio Ellacuría and Ignatian Spirituality', in Kevin F Burke and Robert Lassalle-Klein (eds.), *Love that Produces Hope, the Thought of Ignacio Ellacuría* (Collegeville, MN: Liturgical Press, 2006), pp. 144–168.

Bailey, Kenneth E, *Jesus Through Middle Eastern Eyes, Cultural Studies in the Gospels* (London: SPCK, 2008).

Bailey, Wilma Ann, *You Shall Not Kill or You Shall Not Murder? The Assault on a Biblical Text* (Collegeville, MN: The Liturgical Press, 2005).

Balasuriya, Tissa, 'Benedict XVI's *Deus Caritas Est* and Social Action', in Philomena Cullen, Bernard Hoose, and Gerard Mannion (eds.), *Catholic Social Justice: Theological and Practical Explorations* (London: T & T Clark, 2007), pp. 41–62.

Benedict XVI, *Jesus of Nazareth*, trans. Adrian J Walker (London: Bloomsbury, 2007).

Benestad, J Brian, *Church, State and Society: An Introduction to Catholic Social Doctrine* (Washington, DC: The Catholic University of America Press, 2011).

Berrigan, Daniel, 'Daniel Berrigan on Contemporary Developments in American Spirituality', *Tikkin*, September–October 1998, vol. 13, no. 5.

Bevans, Stephen B and Roger P Schroder, *Prophetic Dialogue: Reflections on Christian Mission Today* (New York: Orbis, 2011).

Bew, Paul, Peter Gibbon, and Henry Paterson, *Northern Ireland: 1921–2001: Political Power and Social Classes* (New York: Serif Press: 2002).

Blackman, Tim, Eileen Evason, Martin Melaugh, and Roberta Woods, *Housing and Health in West Belfast: A Case Study of Divis Flats and the Twinbrook Estate*

(Belfast: Divis Joint Development Committee, 1987), Northern Ireland Political Collection, Linen Hall Library, Belfast, P7768.

Boff, Leonardo, *Virtues for Another Possible World* (Eugene, ON: Wifp and Stock, 2011).

Bonhoeffer, Dietrich, *Discipleship*, trans. Barbara Green and Reinhard Krauss, Dietrich Bonhoeffer Works, vol. 4 (Minneapolis: Fortress Press, 2003).

Booth, Philip (ed.), *Catholic Social Teaching and the Market Economy* (London: Institute of Economic Affairs, 2007).

Boulding, Elise, *Cultures of Peace: The Hidden Side of History* (Syracuse: Syracuse University Press, 2000).

Brewer, John D, 'Sectarianism and Racism, and their Parallels and Differences', *Ethnic and Racial Studies*, 1992, vol. 15, no. 3, pp. 352–364.

Brewer, John D and Gareth Higgins, *Anti-Catholicism in Northern Ireland, 1600–1998: The Mote and the Beam* (London: Macmillan, 1998).

Brinton, Roland H, *Christian Attitudes toward War and Peace* (New York: Abingdon Press, 1960).

Brown, Callum G, *The Death of Christian Britain: Understanding Secularisation 1800–2000* (Abingdon: Routledge, 2009).

Bruce, Steve (ed.), *Religion and Modernisation: Sociologists and Historians Debate the Secularisation Thesis* (Oxford: Clarendon Press, 1992).

Buckley, Don, 'Provisionals Reject Pope's Plea for an End to Violence', *Irish Times*, 3 October 1979.

Burke, Kevin (ed.), *Pedro Arrupe: Selected Writings* (New York: Orbis, 2005).

Byrne, Seán and Neal Carter, 'Social Cubism- Six Social Forces of Ethnoterritorial Politics in Northern Ireland and Quebec', *Peace and Conflict Studies*, 1996, vol. 3, no. 2, article 5, http://nsuworks.nova.edu/pcs/vol3/iss2/5/ (accessed 22 August 2019).

CAIN Web Service, 'A Glossary of Terms Related to the Conflict', http://cain.ulst.ac.uk/othelem/glossary.htm (accessed 23 August 2019).

Callaghan, James, *A House Divided The Dilemma of Northern Ireland* (London: William Collins & Sons, 1973).

Callaghan, James, *Time and Chance* (London: Politico's Publishing Ltd, 1987).

Calo, Zachary R, 'Catholic Social Thought and Human Rights', *American Journal of Economics and Sociology*, 2015, vol. 74, no. 1, pp. 93–112, 95–103.

Carville, Gary, 'Ireland and Vatican II: Aspects of Episcopal Engagement with and Receipt of a Church Council, 1959–1977', PhD Thesis, Dublin City University, 2018.

Casanova, Jose, *Public Religions in the Modern World* (Chicago: Chicago University Press, 1994).

Charles SJ, Rodger, *Christian Social Witness and Teaching: The Catholic Tradition from Genesis to Centesimus Annus*, vol. 1 (Leominster: Gracewing, 1998).

Chenu, Marie-Dominique, *La "doctrine social" de l'Église comme idéologie* (Paris: Cerf, 1979).

Chief of the General Staff, *Operation Banner: An Analysis of Military Operations in Northern Ireland*, July 2006, www.vilaweb.cat/media/attach/vwedts/docs/op_banner_analysis_released.pdf (accessed 23 August 2019).

Cochrane, Feargal, 'Any Takers? The Isolation of Northern Ireland', *Political Studies*, 1994, vol. 42, no. 3, pp. 378–395, 378–379.

Cochrane, Feargal, *Northern Ireland, The Reluctant Peace* (New Haven, CT: Yale University Press, 2013).

Congar, Yves, *Lay People in the Church: A Study for a Theology of the Laity* (Westminster: Newman Press, 1957).

Congregation for the Doctrine of the Faith, *A Doctrinal Note on Some Questions Regarding the Participation of Catholics in Public Life*, 24 November 2002, www.vatican.va/roman_curia/congregations/cfaith/documents/rc_con_cfaith_doc_20021124_politica_en.html (accessed 22 August 2019).

Crossan, John Dominic, *Jesus A Revolutionary Biography* (New York: Harper One, 1994).

Cunningham, Michael, *British Government Policy in Northern Ireland 1969–2000*, 2nd Edition (Manchester: Manchester University Press, 2001).

Curtice, John and Tony Gallagher, 'The Northern Ireland Dimension', in R Jowell, S Witherspoon, and L Brook (eds.), *British Social Attitudes: The 7th Report* (Aldershot: Gower, 1990), pp. 183–216.

Curtis, Jennifer, ' "Community" and the Re-Making of 1970s Belfast', *Ethnos*, 2008, vol. 73, no. 3, pp. 399–426.

Cusimano Love, Maryann, 'What Kind of Peace Do We Seek? Emerging Norms of Peacebuilding in Key Political Institutions', in Robert J Schreiter, R Scott Appleby, and Gerard F Powers (eds.), *Peacebuilding Catholic Theology, Ethics, and Praxis* (New York: Orbis, 2010), pp. 56–91.

Cusimano Love, Maryann, 'Just Peace and Just War', *Expositions*, 2018, vol. 12, no. 1, pp. 60–71.

Daly, Cahal, *Addresses on Peace in Northern Ireland, 1968–1975*, vol. 1, Northern Ireland Political Collection, Linen Hall Library, Belfast, P13578.

Daly, Cahal, *Addresses on Peace in Northern Ireland, 1976–1983*, vol. 2, Northern Ireland Political Collection, Linen Hall Library, Belfast, P13579.

Daly, Cahal, *Addresses on Peace in Northern Ireland, 1984–1986*, vol. 3, Northern Ireland Political Collection, Linen Hall Library, Belfast, P13580.

Daly, Cahal, *Addresses on Peace in Northern Ireland, 1987–1988*, vol. 4, Northern Ireland Political Collection, Linen Hall Library, Belfast, P13581.

Daly, Cahal, *Addresses on Peace in Northern Ireland, 1989–1990*, vol. 5, Northern Ireland Political Collection, Linen Hall Library, Belfast, P13582.

Daly, Cahal, *Addresses on Peace in Northern Ireland, 1991–1992*, vol. 6, Northern Ireland Political Collection, Linen Hall Library, Belfast, P13583.

Daly, Cahal, *Addresses on Peace in Northern Ireland, 1993–1996*, vol. 7, Northern Ireland Political Collection, Linen Hall Library, Belfast, P13584.

Daly, Cahal, *Addresses on Peace in Northern Ireland, 1997–2001*, vol. 8, Northern Ireland Political Collection, Linen Hall Library, Belfast, P13585.

Daly, Cahal, *Coming Back Home: Pastoral Letter from Bishop Cahal B Daly to his People in Down and Connor, Lent 1983*, Northern Ireland Political Collection, Linen Hall Library, Belfast, P2125.

Daly, Cahal, *We Believe* (Dublin: Catholic Truth Society, 1969).

Daly, Cahal, *A Law of Love* (Hoddesdon: Crux Publications, 1971).

Daly, Cahal, *Christian Authority and Christian Responsibility* (Hoddesdon: Crux Publications, 1971).

Daly, Cahal, 'Christ and the Irish Crisis', *The Furrow*, 1972, vol. 23, no. 7, pp. 399–404, 399.

Daly, Cahal, 'Prayer in the Modern World', *Review for Religious*, 1972, vol. 31, no. 6, pp. 901–914.

Daly, Cahal, 'Violence or Non-Violence', *The Furrow*, 1972, vol. 23, no. 2, pp. 95–106.

Daly, Cahal, *Violence in Ireland and the Christian Conscience* (Dublin: Veritas, 1973).

Daly, Cahal, 'Ecumenism in Ireland Now: Problems and Hopes', *Irish Theological Quarterly*, 1978, vol. 45, no. 1, pp. 3–27.

Daly, Cahal, *Peace the Work of Justice: Addresses on the Northern Tragedy, 1973– 79* (Dublin: Veritas, 1979).

Daly, Cahal, 'Violence Destroys the Work of Justice', *The Furrow*, 1980, vol. 31, no. 2, pp. 71–87.

Daly, Cahal, *Mass and the World of Work* (Dublin: Irish Messenger Publications, 1981).

Daly, Cahal, 'Installation of Bishop Cahal B Daly in the See of Down and Connor', Address before the Final Blessing, 17 October 1982, Northern Ireland Political Collection, Linen Hall Library, Belfast, PH2184.

Daly, Cahal, *Dialogue for Peace* (Dublin: Irish Messenger Publications, 1983).

Daly, Cahal, *Communities without Consensus: The Northern Tragedy* (Dublin: Irish Messenger Publications, 1984).

Daly, Cahal, 'Letter to Jim Prior, Secretary of State for Northern Ireland', 24 July 1984, Public Record Office of Northern Ireland, Belfast, NIO/12/530a.

Daly, Cahal, 'Witnessing the Struggle: Struggling to Witness, Lecture Given under the Auspices of the Irish School of Ecumenics in Heythrop College, London', 24 November 1984, Northern Ireland Political Collection, Linen Hall Library, Belfast, P10469.

Daly, Cahal, 'Justice and Law: The Birmingham Six and the Stalker-Sampson Report', *The Furrow*, 1988, vol. 39, no. 3, pp. 165–171.

Daly, Cahal, *Steps on my Pilgrim Journey: Memories and Reflections* (Dublin: Veritas, 1988).

Daly, Cahal, 'Gospel Values in a Situation of Conflict: Northern Ireland', Parliamentary Wives' Christian Group, London, 14 March 1990, Northern Ireland Political Collection, Linen Hall Library, Belfast, P7647.

Daly, Cahal, *The Price of Peace* (Belfast: The Blackstaff Press, 1991).

Daly, Cahal, 'Living with Difference: How Much Consensus?', Seminar under Auspices of Harriet Brierley Mears Foundation, Fontbonne Academy, Milton, MA, USA, 13 February 1993, Northern Ireland Political Collection, Linen Hall Library, Belfast, P13584.

Daly, Cahal, *Peace Now is the Time* (Dublin: Veritas, 1993).

Daly, Cahal, *Tertullian the Puritan and his Influence* (Dublin: Four Courts Press, 1993).

Daly, Cahal, *The Minding of Planet Earth* (Dublin: Veritas, 2004).

Daly, Cahal and Eric Gallagher, *Violence in Ireland: A Report to the Churches* (Belfast: Christian Journals, 1976).

Daly, Edward, *A Troubled See: Memoirs of a Catholic Bishop* (Dublin: Four Courts Press, 2011).

Dauenhauer, Bernard P, *Paul Ricoeur: The Promise and Risk of Politics* (Lanham, MD: Rowman and Littlefield, 1998).

Dear, John, *Daniel Berrigan SJ Essential Writings* (Maryknoll, NY: Orbis Books, 2009).

DeYoung, Elizabeth, 'The New Lodge and the "New Belfast"?: A Case for Community-Led Development', Report Prepared for Aston Community Trust, July 2016.

DeYoung, Elizabeth, 'Girwood Barracks: Power, Politics and Planning in the Post-Ceasefire City', PhD Thesis, University of Liverpool, 2018.

Divis, Flats, *The Dreadful Enclosure* (Belfast: Art and Research Exchange, 1985), Northern Ireland Political Collection, Linen Hall Library, Belfast, P2484.

Divis Study Group, *Balconies, Brits and Bin Lids: An Oral History of Divis Flats* (Belfast: Divis Study Group, 1998), Northern Ireland Political Collection, Linen Hall Library, Belfast, P9137.

Dixon, Paul, 'Paths to Peace in Northern Ireland (II): The Peace Processes 1973–74 and 1994–1996', *Democratization*, 1997, vol. 3, no. 4, pp. 1–25.

Dorr, Donal, *Spirituality and Justice* (Maryknoll, NY: Orbis Books, 1985).

Dorr, Donal, *Option for the Poor and for the Earth: From Leo XIII to Pope Francis* (Maryknoll, NY: Orbis, 2016).

Douglass, James W, *The Non-Violent Cross: A Theology of Revolution and Peace* (London: Macmillan, 1968).

Duffy, Angela, *Informers in 20th Century Ireland* (Jefferson, NC: McFarland, 2018).

Eagleson, John and Philip Scharper (eds.), *Puebla and Beyond* (New York: Orbis Books, 1979).

Elliott, Marianne, *The Catholics of Ulster, A History* (London: Penguin, 2000).

Elliott, Marianne, *When God Took Sides: Religion and Identity in Ireland* (Oxford: Oxford University Press, 2009).

Ellsberg, Robert (ed.), *Dorothy Day, Selected Writings* (Maryknoll, NY: Orbis, 2005).

Ferry, Finola, Brendan Bunting, Samuel Murphy, Siobhan O'Neill, Dan Stein, and Karestan Koenan, 'Traumatic Events and their Relative PTSD Burden in Northern Ireland: A Consideration of the Impact of the "Troubles"', *Social Psychiatry and Psychiatric Epidemiology*, 2014, vol. 49, no. 3, pp. 435–446.

Filby, Eliza, *God and Mrs Thatcher: The Battle for Britain's Soul* (London: Backbite Publishing, 2015).

Francis, *Lumen Fidei*, 29 June 2013, http://w2.vatican.va/content/francesco/en/encyclicals/documents/papa-francesco_20130629_enciclica-lumen-fidei.html (accessed 23 August 2019).

Francis, *Evangelii Gaudium*, 24 November 2013, http://w2.vatican.va/content/francesco/en/apost_exhortations/documents/papa-francesco_esortazione-ap_20131124_evangelii-gaudium.html (accessed 13 August 2019).

Fullenbach, John, *The Kingdom of God: The Message of Jesus Today* (Eugene, OR: Wifp and Stock, 1995).

Fulton, John, *The Tragedy of Belief: Division, Politics and Religion in Ireland* (Oxford: Clarendon, 1991).

Gaillardetz, Richard R and Catherine E Clifford, *Keys to the Council: Unlocking the Teaching of Vatican II* (Collegeville: Liturgical Press, 2012).

Gallagher, Anthony M, 'Employment, Unemployment and Religion in Northern Ireland', Majority Minority Review 2, https://cain.ulster.ac.uk/csc/reports/mm210.htm (accessed 21 August 2019).

Gallagher, Anthony M, *Majority Minority Review 2: Employment, Unemployment and Religion in Northern Ireland* (Coleraine: Centre for the Study of Conflict,

University of Ulster, 1991, http://cain.ulst.ac.uk/csc/reports/majmin2.htm#contents (accessed 21 August 2019).

Galtung, Johan, 'Violence, Peace, and Peace Research', *Journal of Peace Research*, 1969, vol. 6, no. 3, pp. 167–191.

Galtung, Johan, 'Cultural Violence', *Journal of Peace Research*, 1990, vol. 27, no. 3, pp. 291–305.

Ganiel, Gladys, *Unity Pilgrim: The Life of Fr Gerry Reynolds CSsR* (Dublin: Redemptorist Communications, 2019).

Graham, Elaine, *Between a Rock and a Hard Place: Public Theology in a Post-Secular Age* (London: SCM, 2013).

Grassi, Joseph A, *Informing the Future: Social Justice in the New Testament* (New York: Paulist Press, 1989).

Greeley, Andrew, *No Bigger than Necessary* (New York: Meridian Books, 1977).

Greeley, Andrew, *The Catholic Imagination* (Los Angeles: University of California Press, 2001).

Groody, Daniel G (ed.), *Gustavo Gutiérrez Spiritual Writings* (Maryknoll, NY: Orbis, 2011).

Gutierrez, Gustavo, 'Notes for a Theology of Liberation', *Theological Studies*, 1970 vol. 31, no. 2, pp. 243–261.

Gutiérrez, Gustavo, *The Theology of Liberation: History, Politics, Salvation*, trans. Sister Cardidad Inda and John Eagleson (London: SCM, 1974).

Gutiérrez, Gustavo, *The Power of the Poor in History*, trans. Robert R Barr (London: SCM, 1979).

Gutiérrez, Gustavo, 'The Option for the Poor Arises from Faith in Christ', *Theological Studies*, 2009, vol. 70, pp. 317–326.

Haight, Roger S J, 'Praxis', in Judith A Dwyer (ed.), *The New Dictionary of Catholic Social Thought* (Collegeville: Liturgical Press, 1994), pp. 776–777.

Haines, Joe, *The Politics of Power* (London, Jonathan Cape Ltd, 1977).

Hamilton, David, *A Cause Worth Living For: My Journey Out of Terrorism* (Godalming: Highland Books, 2008).

Hanson, Eric O, *The Catholic Church in World Politics* (Princeton: Princeton University Press, 1987).

Hanson, Sharon, 'The Secularisation Thesis: Talking at Cross Purposes', *Journal of Contemporary Religion*, 1992, vol. 12, no. 2, pp. 159–179.

Hasan, Rumy, 'Riots and Urban Unrest in Britain in the 1980s and 1990s: A Critique of Dominant Explanations', in Michael Lavalette and Gerry Mooney (eds.), *Class Struggle and Social Welfare* (London: Routledge, 2000), pp. 173–198.

Hauerwas, Stanley, *The Peaceable Kingdom: A Primer in Christian Ethics* (South Bend, IN: University of Notre Dame Press, 1983).

Head, Wilson A, 'Community Development in Post-Industrial Society', in Dan A Chekki (ed.), *Community Development* (New Delhi: Vikas Publishing, 1979), pp. 101–115.

Hehir, J Bryan, 'The Just-War Ethic and Catholic Theology: Dynamics of Change and Continuity', in Thomas A Shannon (ed.), *War or Peace? The Search for New Answers* (New York: Orbis, 1980), pp. 15–39.

Hehir, J Bryan, 'Religious Activism for Human Rights: A Christian Case Study', in John Witte and Johan van der Vyver (eds.), *Religious Human Rights in Global Perspective*, vol. 1 (Leiden: Brill, 1996), pp. 97–120.

Hennessy, Kate, *Dorothy Day: The World will be Saved by Beauty. An Intimate Portrait of My Grandmother* (New York: Scribner, 2017).

Hillesum, Etty, *An Interrupted Life: The Diaries and Letters of Etty Hillesum 1941–43*, trans. Arnold J Pomerans (London: Persephone Books, 1999).

Himes, Kenneth R, 'Pacifism and the Just War Tradition in Roman Catholic Social Teaching', in John A Coleman (ed.), *One Hundred Years of Catholic Social Thought: Celebration and Challenge* (New York: Orbis, 1991), pp. 329–344.

Himes, Kenneth R (ed.), Lisa Sowle Cahill, Charles E Curran, David Hollenbach, and Thomas Shannon (associate eds.), *Modern Catholic Social Teaching: Commentaries and Interpretations* (Washington, DC: Georgetown University Press, 2005).

Himes, Kenneth R, *Christianity and the Political Order: Conflict, Cooptation, and Cooperation* (New York: Orbis, 2013).

HMSO, Race Relations Act, 1968, www.legislation.gov.uk/ukpga/1968/71/enacted (accessed 23 August 2019).

HMSO, Community Relations Act (Northern Ireland), 1969, http://cain.ulst.ac.uk/hmso/cra1969.htm (accessed 23 August 2019).

HMSO, The Future of Northern Ireland, 1972, http://cain.ulst.ac.uk/hmso/nio1972.htm (accessed 22 August 2019).

HMSO, Northern Ireland Constitutional Proposals, March 1973, https://cain.ulster.ac.uk/hmso/cmd5259.htm (accessed 22 August 2019).

HMSO, The Sunningdale Agreement, 9 December 1973, http://cain.ulst.ac.uk/events/sunningdale/agreement.htm (accessed 22 August 2019).

HMSO, Fair Employment Act (Northern Ireland), 1976, http://cain.ulst.ac.uk/hmso/fea1976.htm (accessed 21 August 2019).

Hollenbach, David, 'Common Good', in Judith A Dwyer (ed.), *The New Dictionary of Catholic Social Thought* (Collegeville: Liturgical Press, 1994), pp. 192–197.

Hollenbach, David, 'Pacem in Terris and Human Rights', *Journal of Catholic Social Thought*, 2013, vol. 10, no. 1, pp. 5–15.

Holy See, *Catechism of the Catholic Church*, 1994, www.vatican.va/archive/ENG0015/_INDEX.HTM (accessed 21 August 2019).

Holy See, *The Compendium of the Social Doctrine of the Church*, 2004, www.vatican.va/roman_curia/pontifical_councils/justpeace/documents/rc_pc_justpeace_doc_20060526_compendio-dott-soc_en.html (accessed 13 August 2019).

Hoppe, Thomas, 'Human Rights', in Judith A Dwyer (ed.), *The New Dictionary of Catholic Social Thought* (Collegeville: Liturgical Press, 1994), pp. 454–470.

Irish Catholic Bishops' Conference, *The Work of Justice*, September 1977, shortened version available at www.catholicbishops.ie/wp-content/uploads/images/docs/pastoral%20letter%20-%20the%20work%20of%20justice.pdf (accessed 21 August 2019).

Irish Catholic Bishops' Conference, *Justice, Love and Peace: Pastoral Letters of the Irish Bishops, 1969–1979* (Dublin: Veritas, 1979).

Irish Independent

Irish Republican Army, *Handbook for Volunteers of the Irish Republican Army: Notes on Guerilla Warfare* (Eire: Irish Republican Army Headquarters, 1956).

Irish Stationery Office, *Bunreacht Na hÉireann – Constitution of Ireland* (Dublin: Irish Stationery Office, 1942).

Irish Stationery Office, *Bunreacht Na hÉireann – Constitution of Ireland* (Dublin: Irish Stationery Office, 2015), www.irishstatutebook.ie/eli/1972/ca/5/enacted/en/html (accessed 22 August 2019).

Irish Times.

John XXIII, *Mater et Magistra*, 15 May 1961, http://w2.vatican.va/content/john-xxiii/en/encyclicals/documents/hf_j-xxiii_enc_15051961_mater.html (accessed 13 August 2019).

John XXIII, *Pacem in Terris*, 11 April 1963, http://w2.vatican.va/content/john-xxiii/en/encyclicals/documents/hf_j-xxiii_enc_11041963_pacem.html (accessed 21 August 2019).

John Paul II, 'Sermon given at Holy Mass in Drogheda', 29 September 1979, https://w2.vatican.va/content/john-paul-ii/en/homilies/1979/documents/hf_jp-ii_hom_19790929_irlanda-dublino-drogheda.htm (accessed 22 August 2019).

John Paul II, *Laborem Exercens*, 14 September 1981, http://w2.vatican.va/content/john-paul-ii/en/encyclicals/documents/hf_jp-ii_enc_14091981_laborem-exercens.html (accessed 21 August 2019).

John Paul II, *Salvifici Doloris*, 11 February 1984, http://w2.vatican.va/content/john-paul-ii/en/apost_letters/1984/documents/hf_jp-ii_apl_11021984_salvifici-doloris.html (accessed 21 August 2019).

John Paul II, 'Development and Solidarity Two Keys to Peace', World Day of Peace Message 1987, 8 December 1986, http://w2.vatican.va/content/john-paul-ii/en/messages/peace/documents/hf_jp-ii_mes_19861208_xx-world-day-for-peace.html (accessed 22 August 2019).

John Paul II, *Sollicitudo Rei Socialis*, 30 December 1987, http://w2.vatican.va/content/john-paul-ii/en/encyclicals/documents/hf_jp-ii_enc_30121987_sollicitudo-rei-socialis.html (accessed 13 August 2019).

John Paul II, *Centesimus Annus*, 1 May 1991, trans. Donders, www.cctwincities.org/wp-content/uploads/2015/10/Centesimus-Annus-The-Hundredth-Year.pdf (accessed 13 August 2019).

John Paul II, 'The Family Creates the Peace of the Human Family', World Day of Peace Message 1994, 8 December 1993, https://w2.vatican.va/content/john-paul-ii/en/messages/peace/documents/hf_jp-ii_mes_08121993_xxvii-world-day-for-peace.html (accessed 22 August 2019).

John Paul II, 'Address of His Holiness Pope John Paul II to the Diplomatic Corps', 13 January 2003, http://w2.vatican.va/content/john-paul-ii/en/speeches/2003/january/documents/hf_jp-ii_spe_20030113_diplomatic-corps.html (accessed 22 August 2019).

Jørgensen, Knud, 'Mission as a Ministry of Reconciliation: Hope in a Fragile World', *Transformation*, 2014, vol. 31, no. 4, pp. 264–272.

José Inocencio Alas, *Land, Liberation, and Death Squads: A Priest's Story, Suchitoto, El Salvador, 1968–1977*, trans. Robin Fazio and Emily Wade Hill (Eugene, OR: Resource Publications, 2017).

Ladd, George E, *The Gospel of the Kingdom* (Grand Rapids, MI: Eerdmans Publishing Co, 1959).

Lafree, Gary, Laura Dugan, and Raven Korte, 'The Impact of British Counter-Terror Strategies on Political Violence in Northern Ireland', *Criminology*, 2009, vol. 47, no. 1, pp. 17–45.

Lamb, Matthew L, 'Solidarity', in Dwyer (ed.), *The New Dictionary of Catholic Social Thought*, pp. 908–912.

Lanagan SJ, John, 'Violence and Injustice in Society: Recent Catholic Teaching', *Theological Studies*, 1985, vol. 46, no. 4, pp. 685–699.

Lassalle-Klein, Robert, 'Jesus of Galilee and the Crucified People: The Contextual Christology of Jon Sobrino and Ignacio Ellacuria', *Theological Studies*, 2009, vol. 70, pp. 347–376.

Layman's Daily Missal, Prayer Book and Ritual (London: Burns and Oates, 1966).

Lederach, John Paul, *The Moral Imagination: The Art and Soul of Building Peace* (Oxford: Oxford University Press, 2005).

Lennon S J, Brian, *After the Ceasefires: Catholics and the Future of Northern Ireland* (Dublin: Columba, 1995).

Leo XIII, *Rerum Novarum*, 15 May 1891, http://w2.vatican.va/content/leo-xiii/en/encyclicals/documents/hf_l-xiii_enc_15051891_rerum-novarum.html (accessed 13 August 2019).

Levine, Daniel H, *Religion and Politics in Latin America: The Catholic Church in Venezuela and Columbia* (Princeton: Princeton University Press, 1981).

Lewis, C S, *The Four Loves* (London: Geoffrey Bles, 1960).

Liechty, Joseph, 'The Nature of Sectarianism Today', in Trevor Williams and Alan Falconer (eds.), *Sectarianism, Papers of the 1994 Corrymeela Ecumenical Conference* (Dublin: Dominican Publications, 1995), pp. 9–29.

Liechty, Joseph and Cecelia Clegg, *Moving Beyond Sectarianism: Religion, Conflict, and Reconciliation in Northern Ireland* (Dublin: The Columba Press, 2001).

Lohfink, Gerhard, *Jesus and Community: The Social Dimension of Christian Faith*, trans. John P Galvin (Philadelphia: Fortress Press, 1984).

Lucchetti Bingemer, Maria Clara, 'The Journey of Etty Hillesum from Eros to Agape', in K A D Smelik (ed.), *The Ethics and Religious Philosophy of Etty Hillesum: Proceedings of the Etty Hillesum Conference at Ghent University, Jan 2014* (Leiden, Boston: Brill, 2017), pp. 68–89.

Macnee, Columbanus, 'An Open Letter to Bishop Cahal Daly', *Fortnight*, March 1984, pp. 2–3.

Malcolm, Teresa, 'Cardinal Calls for Prisoner Transfer', *National Catholic Reporter*, 26 April 1996.

Martin, David and Rebecca Catto, 'The Religious and The Secular', in Linda Woodhead and Rebecca Catto (eds.), *Religion and Change in Modern Britain* (Abingdon: Routledge, 2012), pp. 373–390.

Martin, James, *Jesus A Pilgrimage* (New York: Harper, 2014).

Maslow, Abraham, *Motivation and Personality* (New York: Harper and Brothers, 1954).

McAfee Brown, Robert, *The Ecumenical Revolution: An Interpretation of the Catholic-Protestant Dialogue* (London: Burns and Oates, 1967).

McAfee Brown, Robert, *Gustavo Gutiérrez- An Introduction to Liberation Theology* (Maryknoll, NY: Orbis, 1990).

McBride, Sam, 'Declassified Files: Official's Private Alarm at Paratroopers' Role in 1992 Coalisland Riots', *Newsletter*, 27 August 2017, www.newsletter.co.uk/news/declassified-files-official-s-private-alarm-at-paratroopers-role-in-1992-coalisland-riots-1-8124200 (accessed 23 August 2019).

McCann, Dennis P, 'Signs of the Times', in Judith A Dwyer (ed.), *The New Dictionary of Catholic Social Thought* (Collegeville: Liturgical Press, 1994), pp. 881–883.

McCleery, Martin J, *Operation Demetrius and its Aftermath: A New History of the Internment without Trial in Northern Ireland 1971–1975* (Oxford: Oxford University Press, 2015).

McElroy, Gerald, *The Church and the Northern Irish Crisis, 1968–86* (Dublin: Gill and Macmillan, 1994).

McGrail, Courtney, 'Paramilitary Provo Turned Pious Parishioner', *Irish Catholic*, 27 April 2017, www.irishcatholic.com/paramilitary-provo-turned-pious-parish ioner/ (accessed 23 August 2019).

McIntyre, Alison, 'The Doctrine of Double Effect', *The Stanford Encyclopaedia of Philosophy*, https://plato.stanford.edu/archives/win2014/entries/double-effect/ (accessed 23 August 2019).

McKeeven CSSR, Martin, *One Man, One God, The Peace Ministry of Fr Alec Reid* (Dublin: Redemptorist Communications, 2017).

McManus, Seán, *The MacBride Principles*, University of Minnesota Human Rights Library, December 1997, http://hrlibrary.umn.edu/links/macbride.html#principles (accessed 21 August 2019).

McNamara, Kevin, Meeting with Rt Hon Kevin McNamara MP, RE: The MacBride Principles, 6 February 2002. Dr Kevin McNamara Private Papers.

McNamara, Kevin, Account of conversation with Cardinal Daly, 7 February 2002, Dr Kevin McNamara, Private Papers.

McNamara, Kevin, Interview with Cardinal Cahal Daly, 7 February 2002, Dr Kevin McNamara Private Papers.

McNamara, Kevin, *The MacBride Principles: Irish America Strikes Back* (Liverpool: Liverpool University Press, 2009).

Murray OP, Paul, *Aquinas at Prayer: The Bible, Mysticism and Poetry* (London: Bloomsbury, 2013).

Murtagh, Brendan, 'New Spaces and Old in "Post-Conflict" Belfast', Divided Cities/ Contested States Working Papers, no. 5, p. 4, www.conflictincities.org/PDFs/ WorkingPaper5_10.9.08.pdf (accessed 21 August 2019).

Musto, Ronald G, *The Catholic Peace Tradition* (New York: Orbis Books, 1986).

Nava, Alexander, *The Mystical and Prophetic Thought of Simone Weil and Gustavo Gutiérrez: Reflections on the Mystery and Hiddenness of God* (New York: State University of New York Press, 2001).

Neely, Brent, 'Jesus at the well (John 4: 4–42): Our approach to the "other"', *Theology*, 2018, vol. 121, no. 5, pp. 332–340.

Neill, William J V, Diana S Fitzsimons, and Brendan Murtagh, *Reimagining the Pariah City: Urban Development in Belfast and Detroit* (London: Avebury, 1995).

Nelson, Sarah, 'Protestant "Ideology" Considered: The case of "discrimination"', in Ivor Crewe (ed.), *The Politics of Race* (London: Croom Helm, 1975), pp. 155–187.

Neuhaus, Richard John, *The Catholic Moment: The Paradox of the Church in the Postmodern World* (San Francisco, CA: Harper and Row, 1987).

Neumann, Peter R, *Britain's Long War: British Strategy in the Northern Ireland Conflict, 1969–1998* (London: Palgrave Macmillan, 2003).

Newbury, Samantha, *Interrogation, Intelligence, and Security: The Origins and Effects of Controversial British Techniques* (Oxford: Oxford University Press, 2015).

Nolan OP, Albert, *Jesus Before Christianity* (Maryknoll, NY: Orbis Books, 1992).

Nygren, Anders, *Agape and Eros*, trans. Philip S Watson (London: SPCK, 1953).

O'Boyle, Edward J, 'Blessed John Paul II on Social Mortgage: Origins, Questions, and Norms', *Logos: A Journal of Catholic Thought and Culture*, 2014, vol. 17, no. 2, pp. 119–135.

O'Collins SJ, Gerald, *Living Vatican II: The 21st Council for the 21st Century* (New York: Paulist Press, 2006).

O'Connor, Fionnuala, *In Search of a State: Catholics in Northern Ireland* (Belfast: Blackstaff, 1995).

O'Hagan, Dara, 'Allies or Antagonists? Irish Catholicism and Irish Republicanism During the 1980s', Unpublished PhD, Queen's University, Belfast, 1998.

O'Malley, John W, *What Happened at Vatican II* (Cambridge, MA: Harvard University Press, 2008).

Orend, Brian, 'War', in *Stanford Encyclopaedia of Philosophy*, 2005, http://plato. stanford.edu/entries/war (accessed 22 August 2019).

Oxfam International, *An Economy for the 99%: It's Time to Build a Human Economy that Benefits Everyone, not Just the Privileged Few*, January 2017, www.oxfam.org/sites/www.oxfam.org/files/file_attachments/bp-economy-for-99-percent-160117-en.pdf (accessed 21 August 2019).

Palanque, J R, *Saint Ambroise et L'empire Romain* (Paris: de Boccard, 1933).

Paul VI, *Opening Speech to the Second Session of the Vatican Council*, trans. Ana Elvia Carrasco Bustillos, 29 September 1963, https://w2.vatican.va/content/paul-vi/it/speeches/1963/documents/hf_p-vi_spe_19630929_concilio-vaticano-ii.html (accessed 19 December 2016).

Paul VI, *Ecclesiam Suam*, 6 August 1964, §42, http://w2.vatican.va/content/paul-vi/en/encyclicals/documents/hf_p-vi_enc_06081964_ecclesiam.html (accessed 13 August 2019).

Paul VI, *Lumen Gentium*, 21 November 1964, www.vatican.va/archive/hist_coun cils/ii_vatican_council/documents/vat-ii_const_19641121_lumen-gentium_ en.html (accessed 21 August 2019).

Paul VI, *Ad Gentes, On the Mission of the Church*, 7 December 1965, www.vatican. va/archive/hist_councils/ii_vatican_council/documents/vat-ii_decree_19651207_ ad-gentes_en.html (accessed 21 August 2019).

Paul VI, *Dignitatis Humanae*, 7 December 1965, www.vatican.va/archive/hist_coun cils/ii_vatican_council/documents/vat-ii_decl_19651207_dignitatis-humanae_ en.html (accessed 21 August 2019).

Paul VI, *Populorum Progressio*, 26 March 1967, http://w2.vatican.va/content/paul-vi/en/encyclicals/documents/hf_p-vi_enc_26031967_populorum.html (accessed 12 August 2019).

Paul VI, *Octogesima Adveniens*, 14 May 1971, http://w2.vatican.va/content/paul-vi/en/apost_letters/documents/hf_p-vi_apl_19710514_octogesima-adveniens.html (accessed 13 August 2019).

Paul VI, 'If You Want Peace, Work for Justice', World Day for Peace Message for 1972, 8 December 1971, http://w2.vatican.va/content/paul-vi/en/messages/ peace/documents/hf_p-vi_mes_19711208_v-world-day-for-peace.html (accessed 13 August 2019).

Paul VI, *Evangelii Nuntiandi*, 8 December 1975, http://w2.vatican.va/content/paul-vi/en/apost_exhortations/documents/hf_p-vi_exh_19751208_evangelii-nuntiandi. html (accessed 13 August 2019).

Perreau-Saussine, Emile, *Catholicism and Democracy: An Essay in the History of Political Thought*, trans. Richard Rex (Princeton: Princeton University Press, 2001).

Pius XI, *Ubi Arcano Dei Consilio*, 23 December 1922, http://w2.vatican.va/content/ pius-xi/en/encyclicals/documents/hf_p-xi_enc_23121922_ubi-arcano-dei-consilio. html (accessed 13 August 2019).

Pius XI, *Quadragesimo Anno*, 15 May 1931, http://w2.vatican.va/content/pius-xi/en/encyclicals/documents/hf_p-xi_enc_19310515_quadragesimo-anno.html (accessed 21 August 2019).

Pius XI, *Divini Redemptoris*, 19 March 1937, https://w2.vatican.va/content/pius-xi/en/encyclicals/documents/hf_p-xi_enc_19370319_divini-redemptoris.html (accessed 21 August 2019).

Pius XII, *Radio Message Given to the World*, 23 December 1948, https://archive.org/details/1948christmasmespius (accessed 13 August 2019).

Power, Maria, Interview with Cardinal Cahal Daly, Belfast, 3 February 2000.

Power, Maria, *From Ecumenism to Community Relations: Inter-Church Relationships in Northern Ireland 1980–2005* (Dublin: Irish Academic Press, 2007).

Power, Maria, 'Getting to Know the Other: Inter-church Groups in Belfast and the Peace Process', in Marianne Elliott (ed.), *The Long Road to Peace in Northern Ireland*, 2nd Edition (Liverpool: Liverpool University Press, 2007), pp. 192–206.

Power, Maria, 'Of Some Symbolic Importance but not Much Else: The Irish Inter-church Meeting and Ecumenical Dialogue in Northern Ireland since 1980', *Journal of Ecumenical Studies*, 2008, vol. 43, no. 1, pp. 111–123.

Power, Maria, 'Building Peace in Northern Ireland', in Maria Power (ed.), *Building Peace in Northern Ireland* (Liverpool: Liverpool University Press, 2011), pp. 1–17.

Power, Maria, Interview with Kenneth Bloomfield, Belfast, 23 June 2011.

Power, Maria, 'Providing a Prophetic Voice? Church Leaders and Faith-Based Peacebuilding in Northern Ireland', in Maria Power (ed.), *Building Peace in Northern Ireland* (Liverpool: Liverpool University Press, 2011), pp. 73–92.

Power, Maria, 'Cahal Brendan Daly (1917–2009)', in *Oxford Dictionary of National Biography*, Oxford University Press, January 2013, www.oxforddnb.com.liverpool.idm.oclc.org/view/article/101596 (accessed 13 August 2019).

Power, Maria, 'A Serious Moral Question to be Properly Understood: The Catholic Church and Human Rights in the 1980s', in Tim White (ed.), *Northern Ireland and International Relations* (Manchester: Manchester University Press, 2017), pp. 131–143.

Power, Maria, 'Alternative Possible Futures: Unearthing a Catholic Public Theology for Northern Ireland', in Christopher R Baker and Elaine Graham (eds.), *Theology for Changing Times: John Atherton and the Future of Public Theology* (London: SCM, 2018), pp. 158–174.

Power, Maria and Christopher Hrynkow, 'Transforming the Centre: Popes on Inter-Religious Dialogue as a Path to Multi-Track Peacebuilding', *International Journal for Peace Studies*, 2018, vol. 23, no. 2, pp. 33–47.

Power, Maria and Christopher Hrynkow, 'Qualified Advocacy for JustPeace: The Pope's World Day of Peace Messages (1968–2020) in Historical and Ethical Perspective', *Peace and Change: A Journal of Peace History*, 2020, vol. 45, no 3

Powers, Gerard, 'From an Ethics of War to an Ethics of Peacebuilding', in Heinz Gehard Justenhoven and William A Barbieri (eds.), *From Just War to Modern Peace Ethics* (Berlin: De Gruyter Press, 2012), pp. 275–312.

Puntill, Corinne, 'Booze and Anguish Haunt Northern Ireland's Retired Terrorists: Some Regret not Putting Ballots First', *Global Post*, 15 July 2015, www.pri.org/stories/2015-07-15/booze-and-anguish-haunt-northern-irelands-retired-terrorists-some-regret-not (accessed 22 August 2019).

Purcell, Natalie, Kristine Burkman, Jessica Keysen, Philip Fucella and Shira Maguen, 'Healing from Moral Injury: A Qualitative Evaluation of the *Impact of Killing* Treatment for Combat Veterans', *Journal of Aggression, Maltreatment and*

Trauma, published online 18 April 2018, p. 2. www.tandfonline.com/doi/abs/10. 1080/10926771.2018.1463582 (accessed 22 August 2019).

Radcliffe OP, Timothy, *Why go to Church? The Drama of the Eucharist* (London: Bloomsbury, 2008).

Radcliffe OP, Timothy, *What is the Point in Being a Christian?* (London: Bloomsbury, 2013).

Rafferty SJ, Oliver P, *Catholicism in Ulster, 1603–1983, An Interpretive History* (London: C Hurst and Co, 1994).

Rafferty SJ, Oliver P, *Violence, Politics and Catholicism in Ireland* (Dublin: Four Courts Press, 2016).

Ramsbotham, Oliver, Tom Woodhouse, and Hugh Miall, *Contemporary Conflict Resolution*, 4th Edition (Cambridge: Polity Press, 2016).

Ratzinger, Cardinal Joseph, *Libertatis Conscientia*, 22 March 1986, www.vatican. va/roman_curia/congregations/cfaith/documents/rc_con_cfaith_doc_19860322_ freedom-liberation_en.html (accessed 21 August 2019).

Rogers, Richard, *A Place for All People: Life, Architecture and the Fair Society* (Edinburgh: Canongate, 2017).

Rolston, Bill, 'Reformism and Sectarianism', in John Darby (ed.), *Northern Ireland: The Background to the Conflict* (Belfast: Blackstaff, 1983), pp. 198–199.

Rommen, Henri, *The State in Catholic Social Teaching* (St Louis: Herder, 1945).

Rose, Richard, *Governing without Consensus* (London: Faber and Faber, 1971).

Rosland, Sissel, 'Narratives of Legitimacy: Political Discourse in the Early Phase of the Troubles in Northern Ireland', *Peace and Conflict Studies*, 2008, vol. 15, no. 1, article 2, https://nsuworks.nova.edu/pcs/vol15/iss1/2/ (accessed 22 August 2019).

Rowthan, Bob and Naomi Wayne, *Northern Ireland: The Political Economy of Conflict* (Cambridge: Polity Press, 1988).

Roy, Megan Deirdre, 'Divis Flats: The Social and Political Implications of a Modern Housing Project in Belfast, Northern Ireland, 1968–1998', *Iowa Historical Journal*, 2007, vol. 1, no. 1, pp. 1–44.

Russell, Raymond T, 'Fair Employment in Northern Ireland: The Decades of Change (1990–2010)', Northern Ireland Assembly Research and Information Service Research Paper, 10 August 2012, www.niassembly.gov.uk/globalassets/docu ments/raise/publications/2012/general/12112.pdf (accessed 21 August 2019).

Sandal, Nukhet, *Religious Leaders and Conflict Transformation: Northern Ireland and Beyond* (Cambridge: Cambridge University Press, 2017).

Sanders, Andrew, 'Operation Motorman (1972) and the Search for a Coherent British Counter-Insurgency Strategy in Northern Ireland', *Small Wars and Insurgencies*, 2013, vol. 24, no. 3, pp. 465–492.

Scull, Margaret M, 'Religion from Rome, Politics from Home?: The Catholic Church and the Northern Irish Troubles, 1968–94', PhD Thesis, University of London, 2017.

Scull, Margaret M, *The Catholic Church and the Northern Ireland Troubles, 1968–1998* (Oxford: Oxford University Press, 2019).

Second Vatican Council, *Unitatis Redintegratio*, 21 November 1964, www.vatican. va/archive/hist_councils/ii_vatican_council/documents/vat-ii_decree_19641121_ unitatis-redintegratio_en.html (accessed 13 August 2019).

Second Vatican Council, *Christus Dominus*, 30 October 1965, www.vatican.va/ archive/hist_councils/ii_vatican_council/documents/vat-ii_decree_19651028_ christus-dominus_en.html (accessed 13 August 2019).

Second Vatican Council, *Gaudium et Spes*, 7 December 1965, www.vatican.va/archive/hist_councils/ii_vatican_council/documents/vat-ii_const_19651207_gaudium-et-spes_en.html (accessed 13 August 2019).

Second Vatican Council, *Lumen Gentium*, 21 November 1968, www.vatican.va/archive/hist_councils/ii_vatican_council/documents/vat-ii_const_19641121_lumen-gentium_en.html (accessed 13 August 2019).

Sharp, Gene, *From Dictatorship to Democracy* (London: Serpent's Tail, 2012).

Sinn Féin Education Department, *The Sinn Féin/SDLP Talks: January – September 1988* (Dublin: Sinn Féin Publicity Department, 1989), Northern Ireland Political Collection, Linen Hall Library, Belfast, P3396.

Sinn Féin Education Department, *Freedom* (Dublin: Sinn Féin Education Department, 1991), Northern Ireland Political Collection, Linen Hall Library, Belfast, P4787.

Somerville, Peter, 'Conservative Housing Policy', in Hugh M Bochel (ed.), *The Conservative Party and Social Policy* (Bristol, Policy Press, 2011).

Sowle Cahill, Lisa, *Love your Enemies: Discipleship, Pacifism, and Just War Theory* (Minneapolis: Fortress Press, 1994).

Sowle Cahill, Lisa, *Blessed are the Peacemakers: Pacifism, Just War and Peacebuilding* (Minneapolis, MN: Fortress Press, 2019).

Sowle Cahill, Lisa, 'Just War, Pacifism, Just Peace and Peacebuilding', *Theological Studies*, 2019, vol. 80, no. 1, pp. 169–185.

Spitzer SJ, Robert, *God So Loved the World: Clues to our Transcendent Destiny from the Revelation of Jesus* (San Francisco: Ignatius Press, 2016).

St Ignatius of Loyola, *Personal Writings Reminiscences, Spiritual Diary, Select Letters Including the Text of The Spiritual Exercises*, trans. Joseph A Munitiz and Philip Endean (London: Penguin, 2004).

Swartley, Willard M, *Covenant of Peace: The Missing Peace in New Testament Theology and Ethics* (Grand Rapids, MI: William B Eerdmans Publishing Company, 2006).

Teague, Paul, *Northern Ireland: The Political Economy of Peace*, The Senator George J Mitchell Institute for Global Peace, Security and Justice Working Paper Series, IGPSJ WP 01-16, October 2016, www.qub.ac.uk/Research/GRI/mitchell-institute/FileStore/Filetoupload,727473,en.pdf (accessed 21 August 2019).

Torrance, Alan J, 'Forgiveness and Christian Character: Reconciliation, Exemplarism and the Shape of Moral Theology', *Studies in Christian Ethics*, 2017, vol. 30, no. 3, pp. 293–313.

Tracy, David, *The Analogical Imagination* (New York: Crossroads, 1982).

Troeltsch, Ernst, *The Social Teaching of the Christian Churches*, 2 vols (New York: Harper and Row, 1960).

Ulster Unionist Party, *Peace Order and Good Government* (1973), Northern Ireland Political Collection, Linen Hall Library, Belfast, P1218.

United Nations, *Universal Declaration of Human Rights*, 10 December 1948, www.un.org/en/documents/udhr/ (accessed 21 August 2019).

United States Conference of Bishops, *The Challenge of Peace: God's Promise and Our Responses*, 3 May 1983, www.usccb.org/upload/challenge-peace-gods-promise-our-response-1983.pdf (accessed 26 February 2020).

United States Institute of Peace, Glossary, www.usip.org/glossary/mutually-hurting-stalemate (accessed 5 November 2017).

United States National Conference of Catholic Bishops, 'The Challenge of Peace: God's Promise and Our Response. A Pastoral Letter on War and Peace', 3 May 1983, §70, www.usccb.org/upload/challenge-peace-gods-promise-our-response-1983.pdf (accessed 22 August 2019).

Vallier, Ivan, *Catholicism, Social Control, and Modernization in Latin America* (Englewood Cliffs: Prentice Hall, 1970).

Vanier, Jean, *Encountering the Other* (Dublin: Veritas, 2005).

Verstvaeten, Johan, 'Towards Interpreting the Signs of the Times, Conversation with the World, and Inclusion of the Poor: Three Challenges for Catholic Social Teaching', *International Journal of Public Theology*, 2011, vol. 5, pp. 314–330.

Viviano, Benedict, *The Kingdom of God in History* (Wilmington, DL: Michael Glazier, 1988).

Volf, Miroslav, *A Public Faith, How Followers of Christ Should Serve the Common Good* (Grand Rapids, MI: Brazos Press, 2011).

Walzer, Michael, *Just and Unjust Wars: A Moral Argument with Historical Illustrations* (New York: Basic Books, 1977).

Watt, Paul, ' "It's Not for Us" Regeneration, the 2012 Olympics, and the Gentrification of East London', *City: Analysis of Urban Trends, Culture, Theory, Policy and Action*, 2013, vol. 17, no. 1, pp. 99–119.

Weil, Simone, *Waiting for God* (New York: Harper Modern Classics, 1951).

Whyte, John H, *Church and State in Modern Ireland 1923–1979*, 2nd Edition (Dublin: Gill and Macmillan, 1980).

Williams, Rowan, *Being Christian* (London: SPCK, 2014).

Williams, Rowan, 'Transforming Words, Transforming Relations', "Making all things new?" Evangelii Gaudium and Ecumenical Mission, St John's College, University of Cambridge, 29 June-1 July 2015, http://evangeliigaudium.co.uk (accessed 1 January 2017).

Wreford, Jamie, 'God can Forgive Anyone – Even Murderers- as Former Terrorist and UVF Member Bobby Mathieson Found Out', *New Life Publishing*, 24 May 2014, www.newlifepublishing.co.uk/latest-articles/dir-art/god-can-forgive-anyone/ (accessed 23 August 2019).

Wright, N T, *Jesus and the Victory of God* (London: SPCK, 2012).

Young, Michael and Peter Wilmott, *Family and Kinship in East London* (London: Penguin, 1957).

Zimmerman, R, 'The Etho-Poietic of the Parable of the Good Samaritan (LK 10:25–37). The Ethics of Seeing in a Culture Looking the Other Way', *Verbum et Ecclesia*, 2008, vol. 29, no. 1, pp. 269–292.

Index